TORCHLIGHT PARADE

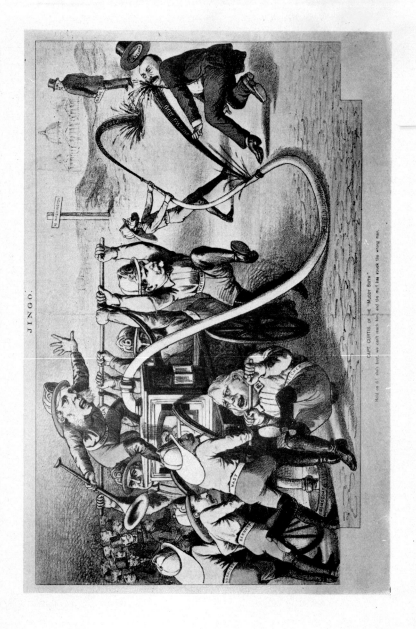

JINGO.

CAPT. CURTIS, OF THE "MUDDY SIXTH"

Hold on if I don't hurt, we can't reach him, and the mud has struck the wrong man.

TORCHLIGHT PARADE

Our Presidential Pageant

BY

SHERWIN LAWRENCE COOK

MINTON, BALCH & COMPANY
NEW YORK　：　：　：　1929

COPYRIGHT, 1929,

BY

SHERWIN LAWRENCE COOK

Printed in the United States of America by
J. J. LITTLE AND IVES COMPANY, NEW YORK

TO
GERTRUDE BAYLEY
In recognition of long and unfailing friendship

"And he gave it for his opinion, that whoever could make two ears of corn or two blades of grass to grow upon a spot of ground where only one grew before, would deserve better of mankind, and do more essential service to his country, than the whole race of politicians put together."

—SWIFT

PREFACE

Occasionally in the old days, in lieu of a preface, there was to be found an "Author's Apology." In this particular case it is incumbent upon the Author to offer, if not an apology for this book, at least an explanation of its title. The reader will find here next to no actual reference to torchlight parades, although some of the elders in Roxbury will smile in recollection of a certain demonstration in 1896, when a young man just of voting age, resplendent in "Prince Albert," borrowed silk hat and red cotton sash, was swept up the main streets ahead of the McKinley legions by an enthusiastic mount, which insisted that he should have been the Chief Marshal instead of one of the local respectables riding in seemliness and order. With his first duty to his borrowed head covering, he clung to it with one hand and did his best with the other to rein in his rented Bucephalus, his short stirrups causing his unconscious heel to beat a tattoo on the ribs of the offending steed, ever urging him to greater celerity; a veritable John Gilpin in the cause of sound money. Even now, more than thirty years afterward, it is not one of my happiest recollections.

But the swing, the noise, the enthusiasm of torchlight parades—all emotional rather than mental—do typify in some degree the spirit of our presidential campaigns and in this respect the title does indicate what I have tried to express.

Doctor Johnson, in one of his Idler essays, has told us that, when two books are brought together, some ambitious writer will make another out of them. Although I have consulted more than the number included in the estimate of that literary leviathan, I must, of course, plead guilty to having built half of this book on mere records, some dry, many fascinating, all with human nature to be discovered between the lines. But although records have been useful, every campaign since that of 1880, of which I have a clouded memory, has touched me with its excitement, its argument, its spectacle. In fact, my parents used to relate that a few months after the election of 1876, I astonished a crowded street car, when passing a flag, by crying out, apparently apropos of nothing, "Hurrah for Hayes and Wheeler." The teacher in the grammar school was quite right in telling my mother that I clearly showed that I was brought up in a political atmosphere. For the first dozen years of my life the major conversational topic at table between my father and my uncles was politics. Something of the glamor of these campaigns from the days of Garfield to those of Hoover does, I think, abide with me. I have had my experience in most elections, local and national. I have served (in its more respectable day, I am feign to claim) in the Boston city government. I have been a doomed party nominee for Congress, in the Taft-Roosevelt year. I have been on the stump to a greater or less extent in every election but one from 1896 to 1924 inclusive. I have, I think, learned something about my subject at first hand from these experiences, something of enthusiasm, something of disillusion. But it has not been very much after all. Nobody can learn the motivation of politics with a scientific certainty, as we all have been made to realize by the success of Calvin Coolidge, who is the antithesis of what a successful politician ought to be, judging by the measurements which before his advent had been universally accepted. Still, however little I have learned from the rough and tumble of political warfare, the tang of it still remains, and I hope some of it has got into this book.

I have no doubt that the guns of political battleships may be turned upon my dory. But if it should be sunk by the ten-inch guns of accepted opinion of fact, I shall still tread water and stick to my beliefs concerning the characters of whom I have written, for they are made up from all the circumstances and set in what I conceive to be the atmosphere of the scene.

I make no claim that this book is entirely impartial and absolutely fair. If it were it might lose in warmth what it would gain in dignity. No man who has been in these struggles, even as the most inconspicuous of privates or non-commissioned officers, could write of them without prejudice. All I can claim, and this I do claim, is that I have not been unaware of my prejudices and have honestly tried to be fair.

I am glad to have given my expression to my belief in the validity of Hayes's title. For many years I believed that two exceedingly great men strove for the presidency, and that while both were honest in their belief in their election, Tilden should have been seated. Then I began to study the question, and more and more the validity of Hayes's title impressed itself upon me. I was forced to the conclusion that Mr. Rhodes and most of our historians have been too much swayed by sympathy for the loser. After my study I found Professor Paul Leland Haworth's book, "The Hayes-Tilden Disputed Election," and I urge any reader who wants to go into the matter a little further to peruse this remarkable piece of research and argumentation. It seems to me that the contested election was the outcome of Reconstruction. Since emancipation the Republican party has been no real friend of the Negro. Lincoln recommended that those Negroes who had fought for the Union, and the very intelligent, should be enfranchised. Sumner, Stevens, and the radicals then in control, pitchforked the whole of a newly liberated and infant race into the entire responsibility of local government. They focused on the Negro's defenseless head a seemingly unquenchable animosity for which they and not he were to blame. At the election of 1876 the Southern whites tried to do what they have done successfully since. The laws then stood the strain and the popular abrogation of them was not successful in Tilden's day. Pos-

terity has long since decided that the premature act of the
radicals was bad judgment; some day it will decide that the
action of the Republican party in leaving the Negro to his own
destruction in the crisis it had itself created, was a crime. The
party started something it could not finish under any circumstances, but it left everything at loose ends and walked away.
It has made platform gestures for the Negro's vote, but in
reality it has passed by on the other side.

It is curious also, in consideration of the character of Hayes
and Tilden, how Hayes grows and how Tilden shrinks. John
Bigelow's superman has disappeared from historical writing
to-day. Denis Tilden Lynch and M. R. Werner in their stories
of Tammany Hall, neither of them sympathetic to that organization, tend to reveal Tilden in the newer colors.

The other chapters need no especial explanation, nor would
the one on the contested election but for my admission that I
am not unconscious of my prejudices and my feeling that in
this case it was study and not prejudice which reversed my
position and made me file a dissenting brief in spite of such
historical authorities as Rhodes, Oberholtzer and the rest.

I would gladly have had six months in which to have contemplated at leisure the campaign of 1928, but that was of
course impossible. I wrote that chapter before the official records of the conventions were published, and my figures are
those of the press at this time. Not all the official state returns
had been officially promulgated and I eked them out with the
reliable figures of the Associated Press. I wonder if my desire
to be fair to Smith has not made me a little neglectful of
Hoover, for whom I voted with a conviction, still unshaken,
that he is the greatest man my party has nominated since
Abraham Lincoln.

The months I have spent on this book have given me two
strong convictions. First, that the nominating convention, for

which I offer no substitute, least of all direct nominations, is, with all its silly hurly-burly and its absence of anything like deliberativeness, a pretty poor method for parties to use as a medium for presenting candidates to the country. Second, that the English system of using election machinery to determine a single issue is far better than ours in fixing on a man, when a multiplication of issues precludes a clear mandate on anything. What issue did our last election determine? None whatever!

It is with more than the conventional sense of obligation that I make acknowledgment for many courtesies to Mr. Charles Knowles Bolton, Librarian of the Boston Athenaeum, and to all his assistants, most particularly Miss Gregory, Miss Bradford and Miss Gardner; I have received much courtesy and kindness from the authorities at the New York Public Library, especially in the American History department, and from Mr. Frank Weitenkampf of the print room. Mr. Julius H. Tuttle, Librarian of the Massachusetts Historical Society, and Mr. Matthews of the Boston Public Library have been generous of their time and knowledge in the matter of illustrations. Mr. David W. Bailey of the Harvard publications has been wise and generous in criticism and advice, both general and technical. There is a new chapter here in the place of one he found "dull and uninspiring."

Among the many friends I have bored with my exuberance I must thank Juliana and Jacques Bubsee, in whose North Carolina home at Jugtown all of this book was discussed and some of it written; Gertrude and James W. Knight, who endured after-dinner readings of many of these chapters; my cousins, Ann and Winthrop Nay, whom I afflicted in the same way; and especially John Hunter Sedgwick, who kept me "on the job" when I would otherwise have given up. Mrs. M. E. Hodgdon, the joint secretary of the writers who frequent the Boston Athenaeum, has never failed me in delivery of manuscript on time, not the commonest of stenographic virtues, as all literary workers know.

SHERWIN LAWRENCE COOK.

Roxbury, Massachusetts
January 15, 1929.

CONTENTS

CONTENTS

ILLUSTRATIONS

TORCHLIGHT PARADE

CHAPTER ONE

A FEUD AMONG THE FEDERALISTS

MR. ADAMS of Massachusetts was leaving town. With coach and four he was posting through the streets of Washington—forlorn, unfinished, ill-paved, unbeautiful Washington. It was early in the morning of a certain March day in the first year of the nineteenth century. Dreary enough as the slight beginnings of a capital undoubtedly were, they must have looked still drearier to this stout, elderly gentleman who was taking his leave abruptly and without formality. Splashing through the unpaved, muddy, deep-rutted streets, he passed the little groups of houses then, for the most part, quite unlovely. Truly Washington, the American capital, was a bugbear to the foreign legations exiled from livelier purlieus and the elegancies of sophisticated courts. But dreary and crude as the town was, the leave-taking was by no means a happy one for this doughty little man, fleeing the sight of the triumphs of his opponents, before his dignities were stripped from him. Perhaps he turned and looked back for a moment at the small unfinished capitol, so sightly on its hilltop. If he did we can be sure he did not heave a sigh. No, if he gave way to any noise, he grunted.

Few men who have left so high a fame as John Adams have played in harder luck. He was a good sturdy egotist, and everything seemed to conspire to wound his self pride. In New York, twelve years before, at the only inauguration at which the Vice President shared no honors with his chief, he had seen a military man who had reached his commanding

3

position in war largely through Adams's efforts, which he later repented, made President amid such plaudits that the sound lawyer and tested civic servant, who had been in office for two months already, was quite forgotten—and he thought that he should not be forgotten. And eight years after that in Philadelphia he stood in the chief place. This was his day! Alas! he witnessed a tremendous to-do over the retiring chief which left him quite neglected. Again he found himself playing second fiddle. True, the military hero was Washington, the absolute flower of American greatness above all his fellows. But Adams had never seen that greatness. To him the dull dignity was visible but hardly more, which perhaps is the best sign of the deficiencies of Mr. Adams of Massachusetts.

And now he had been expected to play another subordinate part at another inauguration. In effect he was to walk meekly at the chariot wheels of that fellow Jefferson, who with the help of that arch traitor Hamilton, had elbowed him out of office. Well, he would not do it. Hence he was galloping out of town, up into Maryland, with the little Massachusetts town of Braintree as his final destination. Anyhow, he had physicked those Republicans at the end. That man Marshall of Virginia was a strong character and a convinced Federalist. He had made him Chief Justice and the term was for life. Let the radical Mr. Jefferson put that in his pipe and smoke it. Still, even that had pleased many whom he did not enjoy pleasing, for, after all, much as he resented Jefferson's taking his place, he had found that a man's foes are of his own household. "Of his own household, his own household, household, household, household." Did not the hoof beats of the horses keep time as the embittered old statesman let the words ring in his brain? And what a pity! The party of eminence and dignity went out of power because of the feud between the two men who, after Washington, were the chieftains of this party, one, as Henry Cabot Lodge, who seems to have understood them both, admirably puts it, the leader *de jure*, the other, the leader *de facto*.

It had lasted a long time, this feud. Although Hamilton had flung out of Washington's military family during the Revolution, he probably resented the stupid and mean intrigue of those subordinate generals of Washington who sought to supplant him with Gates. The alert West Indian must have had a contempt for the politicians (the predecessors of those who plagued Abraham Lincoln with a "committee on the conduct of the war") who sympathized with the movement, and among those was John Adams.

So when after a good deal of effort the former colonies had managed to pull themselves together under a constitution and the choice of a President must be made, Hamilton, who, having been the chief force, through his "Federalist" papers, in getting the constitution adopted by the states, just as Madison had been the greatest force in the convention which drew it, began to cast his eye over the horizon and not in Adams's direction. Of course Hamilton was a Federalist. These stalwart conservatives, far more by force of character and governing ability than by any real popularity, were the ruling party. Without them there had been no constitution. Washington was, by conviction and by association, a Federalist, although he did his honest best not to be partizan and to conceal his predilection. This first test of the elective provisions of the constitution was sure to eventuate in Washington's election as President. Even so restless a spirit as Jefferson agreed in this and even said that although in his opinion the provisions of the Constitution really meant a life tenure of the President, there would be no need to amend it by limiting the term while Washington held the office.

The vice-presidency was in question. There was no man in the Federalist party who undisputedly stood second to Washington. Hamilton was brilliant and able, in spite of his petty talents for wire-pulling. His brilliance and assiduity had made him without question the most vital political force in the party. He was not old enough to be eligible for either office, although having been in the country at the time of the adoption of the Constitution, his West Indian birth did not bar him as is often supposed. But even if he could have had the place, he would have been uncomfortable in the vice-presidency. He intended his rôle should be that of a Warwick.

The geographical question was conspicuous even in the first election. Virginia was to furnish the President; let the North have the Vice President. Massachusetts then was the leading northern commonwealth, and a Massachusetts man would "balance the ticket." There was Hancock, whose bold hand was such a challenge on the Declaration of Independence. He would have made an excellent Vice President, for he was ornamental, had plenty of money and liked to cut a dash. There was Knox, the sturdy and loyal old bookseller who became so useful an officer in the Revolution, a man whom Washington deeply respected and whom he would gladly have welcomed. But though good words were said of both these men, the fact remained that the chief statesman of Massachusetts was John Adams, a sound lawyer, a strong constitutionalist and a stubborn patriot. As public opinion drifted to him, Hamilton must have made a wry face. Since Adams had not been entirely friendly to Washington in the mid-Revolutionary days, the chief was discreetly approached and offered no objection.

So public opinion, without any formal nomination, put the Federalist party behind Washington and Adams. That the Federalist electors would all vote for this pair seemed inevitable until Hamilton began to be active. The faulty provisions of the Constitution as it was adopted did not provide for separate ballots for President and Vice President. If there was a majority, the highest vote on the single ballot elected the President, and the next, also providing it was a majority,

By the United States in Congress

assembled,

SEPTEMBER 13, 1788.

WHEREAS the Convention assembled in Philadelphia, pursuant to the Resolution of Congress of the 21st February, 1787, did, on the 17th of September in the same year, report to the United States in Congress assembled, a Constitution for the People of the United States; whereupon Congress, on the 28th of the same September, did resolve unanimously, " That the said report, with the Resolutions and Letter accompanying the same, be transmitted to the several Legislatures, in order to be submitted to a Convention of Delegates chosen in each State by the people thereof, in conformity to the Resolves of the Convention made and provided in that case:" And whereas the Constitution so reported by the Convention, and by Congress transmitted to the several Legislatures, has been ratified in the manner therein declared to be sufficient for the establishment of the same, and such Ratifications duly authenticated have been received by Congress, and are filed in the Office of the Secretary---therefore,

RESOLVED, That the first Wednesday in January next, be the day for appointing Electors in the several States, which before the said day shall have ratified the said Constitution; that the first Wednesday in February next, be the day for the Electors to assemble in their respective States, and vote for a President; and that the first Wednesday in March next, be the time, and the present Seat of Congress the place for commencing Proceedings under the said Constitution.

Call for the First Election

elected the Vice President. In the event of a tie, the House of Representatives must decide between them, and, if a majority was lacking, the House was to make choice from the first five.

Now if all the party votes (and none other) were cast for both candidates, there would be a tie and Washington would be put to the humiliation of seeking election from Congress. Hamilton was the most influential man with Washington then living. He did not propose that any tie should occur. Now Hamilton was almost the only sensible man who believed such a contingency possible. Even then there were the beginnings of two parties, the Federalists and the opposition, to be known as Republicans and later as Democrats, destined to be the one indestructible party of our national history. There would be electors representing both of these parties, with the Federalists in probable majority. Both these factions would unite on Washington, there was no doubt of that. No anti-Federalist would vote for Adams. But Hamilton, seemingly greatly disturbed over this possibility, began a campaign to prevent Adams being an equal candidate with Washington.

There was just one man in the country who believed that these were equal candidacies; that was John Adams himself. Yes, Mr. Adams took himself very seriously indeed. And although he had a right to think well of himself, there is no doubt that he overdid it.

Hamilton began the active opposition to Adams which was to bear such bitter fruit by writing to his friends all over the country, urging a movement, ostensibly, perhaps honestly, in Washington's interest, which would keep a number of votes away from Adams. He succeeded perhaps better than he intended, although it seems fairly sure, from his subsequent acts, that he secretly desired to clip the wings of this coming Vice President and to injure his future prospects.

Adams was an Adams; he had all the bigness and littleness

of that famous family. Absolutely pure, intellectual and industrious, he may honestly be called great. But he was vain, sensitive and irritable. There was absolutely no danger of his being tied with the General. The electoral college gave Washington sixty-nine votes, which were all that were cast, while Adams received less than half that number. If Adams had got the entire Federalist support he would not have limped into office and, whether the motive was high or personal, the fact that the sensitive but honest and patriotic Adams was so flouted was attributable to Alexander Hamilton and to him only.

At the next election there was no friction in the predominant party. Washington was the choice of the country, as he had been before, receiving all the votes, while all the Federalist votes were cast for Adams.

Four years later, however, the old feeling burst out with new energy. In that memorable statement which set a precedent that has never yet been broken, Washington declined to serve longer. Hamilton had proved a constructive statesman of a high order, but he had little personal popularity and was not considered, perhaps to his disappointment. Outside of Adams, John Jay was the most available man. But Jay had just returned from England where he had negotiated an unpopular treaty and Adams was thought to be the stronger. A conference of Federalist members of Congress recommended him to the country. This was the first formal nomination that is recorded in the history of the Presidency. Thomas Pinckney, a man of considerable parts and useful public service but in no wise comparable to Adams, Hamilton or Jay, was at the same time nominated for Vice President. The fact that he was a South Carolinian was potent in his selection.

Once more Hamilton showed his hand. This time it was the vice-presidency that he was solicitous about. He liked Pinckney as much as he disliked Adams. He knew that the seed he had sowed eight years before might blossom now; that some electors might cut Pinckney for the sake of making Adams sure of the presidency rather than let his respectable running mate be tied with him and so send both to the uncertainties of the House. So now Hamilton, instead of suggesting that the vice-presidential candidate be cut, urged that he be loyally supported. He now urged that the New Englanders show unquestioning loyalty to Pinckney and that they let the Massachusetts candidate take his chances that the electors at the South would show equal loyalty. It was known that there was a strong likelihood that this would not happen, and Hamilton—though his biographers credit the sincerity of his motives—did not conceal the fact that he would at least view such a result with equanimity. This caused a schism that had the exactly opposite effect of what Hamilton intended and probably was what cost Pinckney the vice-presidency. The Northern electors were suspicious of the Southern, and, believing that Hamilton intended bringing Pinckney in over Adams, they acted accordingly, and knowing the Northern feeling, a similar demonstration was made in Pinckney's favor in the South.

Adams won, but poor Pinckney fell by the wayside. Adams received 71 votes and became President. Jefferson had 68 and became Vice President, and Pinckney received 59. If the Federalist vote in South Carolina, which was deliberately given to the Anti-Federalist Jefferson, had been cast for Adams, and the votes in New England that were wasted upon minor Federalists in anticipatory reprisal, had been cast for Pinckney—Adams would have led the poll with 79, Pinckney would have had nearly the same amount, and Jefferson would have been third. This is approximately what the figures would have been had not Hamilton intervened.

Party discipline had not then become established firmly. The electoral system was still to a degree separated from partizan dictation and the electors did not consider that their votes could have no relation to their desires or be virtually delivered in advance. This result would not have been possible after the elector practically ceased to be a free agent.

Hamilton was a greater man than all this makes him appear and the responsible modern biographers of Adams and himself now join in putting the best construction possible upon his acts, but at best they must be considered as reflecting on his political wisdom, and if it was his primary intention to ruin Adams at least it is certain that in such an event Hamilton would have had no regrets. It was but natural that Adams should only see that Hamilton, when Adams was a candidate for Vice President, had striven to keep the election from being thrown into the House and, when he was the presidential nominee, had endeavored to do just that if nothing worse. This was not the best kind of knowledge for a sensitive, autocratic and outspoken old man to possess at the outset of his administration, but it had been borne in upon Adams pretty strongly. Thus bad began while worse remained behind.

Then along came the French war scare and Washington was called back to the Army. Adams, as President, was the constitutional Commander-in-Chief. But in effect he relinquished that. If Washington came in he was to have the naming of his subordinates, Adams acting as Washington wished. When Hamilton was made the senior Major General, the crusty President found it a bitter pill to swallow. Washington was inclined to let Hamilton have a controlling influence in these preliminaries. Adams was right so far as military proprieties went, perhaps so far as military wisdom was concerned. Knox and Pinckney, the other generals, were older soldiers and Hamilton had not proved himself a better. When Adams yielded he did so ungraciously and in the best Adams manner. He wanted to appoint a brilliant young lawyer of New York with some military experience named Aaron

Burr to the position of Brigadier General but Hamilton, and therefore Washington, would have none of him; therefore the appointment was not made. Adams believed his failure to do this was the cause of Burr's political antagonism and, of course, blamed Hamilton.

Adams had in his cabinet three men, legacies from Washington's administration, Wolcott, Pickering and McHenry. They were all Hamilton henchmen and secretly disloyal to their chief. As election approached, the opposition in Adams's cabinet, amounting almost to treachery, became unmistakable, and two of the Hamiltonians—McHenry and Pickering—were dismissed. Hamilton's wrath now reached the boiling point. From the dismissed ministers and—what was worse—from Oliver Wolcott, still Adams's Secretary of the Treasury, he obtained the facts about the administration with which he decided to attack it. He wrote a bitter and denunciatory letter for private distribution, keeping his regularity by a lame and impotent closing paragraph in which he declared his intention to vote for the nominee he had spent his time in denouncing as unfit. How far this letter would have gone and whether or not Hamilton would have overcome his spleen and suppressed it, no one can tell, for Aaron Burr, the vice-presidential nominee of the Republican party, obtained a copy from the printing office, probably by subterranean methods, and all secrecy was at an end. The election was lost. The Republican candidates received 73 votes apiece. Adams had 65 and Charles C. Pinckney, his running mate, 64. A change of 5 votes would have changed the result and Hamilton's own state cast 12.

It is said that Dryden found English literature brick and left it marble. Almost as much might be said of the Federalist party. It certainly found this government in chaos and left it strong and united. Autocratic and narrow, it was certain ultimately to go down before the onward march of popular suffrage; but that it fell as it did was tragic and pitiful, and was due to the stubborn blindness of one of its greatest statesmen and the mad resentment of another.

But the difficulties of the election were not yet over. From the returns in the possession of the public Jefferson and Burr were tied. The impasse which Hamilton had feared in 1789 had come in 1801. The country understood which office each man had been elected to fill but the House of Representatives must make the formal designation. If Jefferson and Burr were tied in the electoral count the House must break the tie. If there happened to be any reason for throwing out the returns of any Republican state, all four candidates would be eligible before that tribunal. Then Adams and Pinckney would be elected if the Federalists were wise or, if the hatred of Adams was sufficient, Pinckney would be made President and as Adams would have refused the lower place, Jefferson or Burr would be the Vice President. But no one expected such a contingency, though we shall see how clearly it came to arise.

Aaron Burr, destined to be the scapegoat of his historical day, was a man of manners, polish and magnetism, but he represented a lower type of politics than Jefferson, who himself was shrewd, clever and not above a bit of demagoguery now and then. Burr is supposed to have set about undermining his chief. His biographers deny it. But it has always been the fashion to pour obloquy on Burr. Without Burr's association with Tammany, Jefferson would never have been a possibility. New York City decided the state and New York State the nation. Whatever Burr's attitude there was no doubt about the attitude of some of the Federalist congressmen. Here was a chance to strike a blow at Jefferson, their dearest foe, and sow dissension in the party. Burr's chances before the House seemed excellent and he did not publicly repudiate them. Here Hamilton's patriotism and honor asserted itself. He had quite as great a hatred for Jefferson as for Adams and one much better founded. He was then on outwardly friendly terms with Burr. He knew, however, whom the people had meant to elect and he knew, with all his trickiness, that Jefferson was a greater statesman and a safer man than Burr. He threw the whole weight of his influence with the Federal members for Jefferson, an influence destined finally to settle the issue.

This was the situation when Congress assembled on February 11, 1801, for the electoral count. Jefferson was Vice President. As the presiding officer of the Senate he must receive the votes from the tellers and announce them. Here seems to have occurred the first informality in registering votes in the history of American elections, an informality which but for Jefferson's being in a position to look out for himself, would very possibly have cost him the great office he sought. According to Matthew Davis, biographer of Burr, the "Aurora" of February 16 contains reference to "some informality in the votes of Georgia." The same authority tells us that Senator Wells of Connecticut was the teller who opened the envelope of Georgia and found that the return of the votes "was not authenticated by the signatures of the electors, or any of them, either on the outside or the inside of the envelope, or in any other manner." It merely contained a statement that four votes had been cast for Jefferson and Burr.

He consulted the other tellers and on their advice handed the envelope to Jefferson, stating to him that the vote was informal, expecting him to refer it to the joint convention. Jefferson, seldom bold, was courageous enough in that instance. He declared, without any other statement, that Georgia had cast four votes for Thomas Jefferson and four votes for Aaron Burr, thereby keeping the road open. Had he done otherwise he would probably have lost the presidency.

As the result of the tie the choice between Jefferson and

Burr went to the House. Here the battle was bitter. The vote was by states. At first Jefferson had eight, Burr six and the votes of Maryland and Vermont were equally divided. Thirty-five times from February 11 to February 17 was this result repeated. Then many Federalists declined to vote. Hamilton's efforts had had their effect and the alignment changed in Jefferson's favor. He received the votes of the two states which had been divided. Two others, Delaware and South Carolina, now divided and Burr received four, all from New England. Jefferson had won, thanks to Burr and Tammany and perhaps to his own shrewd, quick thinking on the day of the electoral count.

Jefferson's simplicity became the watchword on the day of Inauguration, as, angry and embittered, Adams made his way back to Braintree. Time heals many wounds. Adams lived to see his son in his seat, but not long enough to see him leave it even as he had himself. It may be that in those quiet autumn years the Continental Congress and the Declaration of Independence, which Jefferson had drawn for the committte of which they both were members, loomed larger in his memory than later contention. These old rivals became reconciled and exchanged friendly and cordial letters, though they never again met. There is something infinitely appealing in the kindly words that passed between them in this mellow twilight. When Adams lay on his deathbed on the birthday of the nation he had helped to make, his last words were: "Thomas Jefferson still survives," and yet by one of the strangest coincidences in history, his great antagonist had bowed to the last enemy only a few hours before on the same day. Did they face the unknown together?

The chapter cannot close without a reference to Hamilton. Burr's ambition again asserted itself. In less than four years he sought the governorship of New York. He had worn out his welcome as a Democrat. Jefferson now hated him and

Burr was now playing for Federalist support. Hamilton again thwarted him and divided the Federalists, and the Democrat was elected. As Mr. Lodge says of Hamilton: "Over and over again he had described Burr in language which, as he was well aware, implied in that day a readiness to answer for it in the field." To this accounting Burr held him. Burr prepared for the meeting by pistol practice; Hamilton, by setting his affairs in order. They met on a beautiful summer morning at Weehawken. Burr, untouched, went forth to dissipation, intrigue and a wounded name. The death of Alexander Hamilton on the shores of the Hudson River is the last episode of a chapter in the history of American partizan contention unrivaled in animosity and bitterness.

CHAPTER TWO

FRONTIERSMAN AGAINST PURITAN

WITH Jefferson safely ensconced in the White House, presidential elections lose interest as contests for nearly a quarter of a century. Before the next election the constitution was changed, so that the electors voted separately for President and Vice President. An impasse like that of 1800 could not happen again. Jefferson's re-election was easily accomplished.

Then came the days of Madison and Monroe and the "era of good feeling," in which occurred the re-election of Monroe with no opposing candidate. But when the campaign of 1824 came around the "era of good feeling" was seen to have been but a calm before a storm, a storm which marked a struggle of great excitement, which carried with it seeds of bitterness which were to last a generation. The Federalists were dead and the Whig party had not yet come upon the scene. All the candidates represented the same party. This was a legitimate outcome of the "era of good feeling" and certainly made bad feeling enough for a generation. That a contest of persons and not of issues is the least noble that can be waged had been proved times without number, and this was no exception. Every President since Washington's Vice President had succeeded him had served as Secretary of State. Madison and Monroe had served their predecessors in that capacity and the premiership of the cabinet had come to be considered the logical stepping stone to the post of Chief Magistrate. This position was held with dignity and great ability by John

Quincy Adams. In the cabinet Mr. Adams had a rival in Mr. Crawford, the Secretary of the Treasury, a man of respectable parts, who was strong with the old line Democrats of the South. So far as the old régime had a "machine" it was with Crawford. The Speaker of the House had been till recently Henry Clay, magnetic, brilliant, at the height of his powers at forty-seven. Clay's conduct as speaker had raised the office to one of the greatest importance and high dignity in the government and it was one from which the occupant might aspire to the presidency, regardless of precedent. Calhoun and DeWitt Clinton were also in a receptive frame of mind and had influential support, but they were soon crowded out. Suddenly among these promising candidates there came another, much to the discomfort and disgust of the leading statesmen of the time, irrespective of their choice among the others. This was Andrew Jackson, the hero of New Orleans, a man untrained and unaccustomed to statecraft, despite the fact that he had just been elected to the Senate from Tennessee, where he sat uninfluential and almost unnoticed. But Jackson, who was not at first considered seriously, appealed strongly to the popular imagination, and in a friend from Tennessee, Major William B. Lewis, he had a campaign manager who was a new development in politics, now familiar enough, alas. Clever, unscrupulous, audacious, capable of great finesse and the now too familiar art of uniting the power of the unthinking and impressionable, like those of his ilk who have succeeded him, he knew how to "deliver the goods," and yet a mass meeting in Louisville declaring for Jackson issued an address which declared Jackson to be no office-seeker nor a party man and said that if elected he would owe it to no congressional caucus, nor any legislative cabal and that he would have no hungry office seekers to reward. In the light of subsequent history, this was indeed a remarkable proclamation.

Andrew Jackson himself was one of the most interesting figures a democracy has ever produced. Among all our statesmen—if indeed he can be so called—no man so elemental in motives, philosophy or temperament ever reached so high an elevation. A boy in the days of the Revolution, he was a soldier at fourteen. His education was somewhat defective but he was admitted to the practice of law in days when the laxness of the restrictions was extreme. He even sat on the bench in high courts of primitive days in Tennessee, but he was primarily a man of action. He had commanded the American troops in the spectacular battle of New Orleans, the battle that, however, was fruitless because the peace treaty had been signed at Ghent before it occurred. Modern means of communication would have made it impossible. The brief campaign had been most creditable to Jackson's energy and military judgment, and also to the fighting spirit of his little army, made up of untrained men. Jackson had prosecuted the Seminole War and summarily executed certain soldiers and civilians. He was gentle to women, guileless among those he trusted, a tremendous hater, choleric and excitable.

He is to-day one of the two historic idols of the Democratic party. It is perhaps worth while to inquire what that other historic idol—Thomas Jefferson—thought of him. Despite the fact that he himself had not been unwilling to play to the gallery, within limits, he said concerning Jackson and his aspirations: "He is one of the most unfit men I know for the place. He has very little respect for laws or constitutions, and is, in fact, an able military chief. His passions are terrible. He has been much tried since I knew him, but he is a dangerous man."

This opinion is to be found quoted and practically endorsed in "A History of the American People," by Woodrow Wilson, a Democrat of some importance. In the same work Mr. Wilson says that Jackson stood for the abandonment of "the leadership of trained and trusted men" and had set to work to "set aside every tradition of national politics."

But there was one tradition which ought to have been set aside. The members of the government, the Cabinet, the Senate and the House, even before the days of the "era of good feeling" when there were no partizan issues, had developed a pleasant practice of dictating who should be President. The caucus of the Congress and the succession of secretaries had almost made an oligarchy. There was no American king but "King Caucus" it was said. The system was intolerable to the common man. It was intolerable to Jackson. It comprehended, perhaps, "the leadership of trained and trusted men" but that made little difference to the ordinary voter. The divine right to make a mess of things is the most cherished jewel of democracy. And after all it *is a right*. Excellent as was the dynasty of superiority which began with Washington and ended with Quincy Adams, certain as it is that no six successive Presidents since that day have approached their average in ability and patriotism, they did not belong to the people. It was government *for* the people, in some respects rather better than we have had since then. But it was in no wise *of* the people. Our "masters and pastors" may be excellent men but we want to have a finger in this pie even if we muddle things a little. We may be patient under nominations made by conventions which except in theory are as far from us as possible. We may accept minority rule through plurality choice, in easily manipulated direct nominations. We may reject that most sensible of all governmental panaceas, proportionate voting. But there always is a pretense that we have something to do with it all. And in many cases we do. Tom Reed laid the nomination of Blaine and the subsequent defeat of his party not to the wicked politicians but to the popular desire which controlled the delegates. In what Jackson fought against, however, the people mattered not at all in any primary choice. They might take their choice of two or more gentlemen who, however much they differed in policy, were the same sort, all members of this club. The sturdy, irascible Jackson was just the man to believe this condition of affairs a scandal. No wonder that the peppery and vigorous "Old Hickory" seemed quite beyond consideration to the gentlemen who controlled things and that they were greatly affronted by his assumption that he *could* be voted for. It was quite against the order of things. Had this sensible but headstrong old soldier no sense of propriety? Apparently not. His friends capitalized his picturesqueness as well as his undoubted courage both physical and moral, and his explosiveness, sometimes irresponsible, endeared him to those from whom his managers sought votes.

Clay, who had better balance, was hardly less picturesque. He had been elected to the Senate from Kentucky before he had reached the legal age, but no voice had been raised to object to his taking his seat. With his senatorial reputation behind him, he was elected to the lower branch of Congress and his extraordinary popularity is attested by his election to the speakership as a new member. Eloquent, dashing, with the faults and virtues of the time, an inveterate gambler, but long headed, patriotic and statesmanlike, "Harry of the West" was a popular idol. Adams was the cold, austere, inflexible personification of the New England conscience, the type of Puritan who, for a principle, would go in glorified but impersonal isolation to stake or block. Admired for his intellect, trusted for his honesty, he was without such friends as Clay and Jackson had grappled to themselves with hooks of steel.

Struggles in the past had all been between the older types. Even Burr had had pretensions to statesmanship, and although Jackson sat, inconspicuously, in the Senate, he did not seem to be a formidable candidate. It could not be that this peppery son of Tennessee would be dangerous. The people were electing a President, not a military dictator. Burr had failed in his attempts. Why worry? The leaders had no conception of the strength behind Jackson. The susceptibility of the people to the blandishments of popular campaigning had never been tested. The campaign was enthusiastically contested, but in the view of the capital the result seemed to lie between the three statesmen, Adams, Crawford and Clay. But the unexpected happened; Lewis "knew the game", as we would say to-day. He should have; so far as the United States goes, he invented it.

Despite the public rebellion against "King Caucus" known of all men and against the formal objections by several states, the friends of Crawford, led by Martin Van Buren, soon to become an out and out Jacksonian, forced the holding of a caucus, which, being attended by only sixty-six members, discredited itself. Of course it named Crawford.

But a caucus of this kind had no great effect and the campaign went vigorously on. Crawford's weakness was apparent. Jackson came forward by strides. He epitomized then and ever after what the common man was fighting for.

When the electoral vote was determined, it was found that Jackson led the poll. He was far, however, from the one hundred and thirty-one votes necessary for a majority, having received ninety-nine, or fifteen more than Adams. Crawford got forty-one, and Clay, to his bitter disappointment, was last with thirty-seven. Jackson had carried Pennsylvania and New Jersey, most of the South, and the young West, except Ohio. Outside of a few scattering votes in the South and one in Illinois, Adams's strength lay in the practical unanimity of New York and New England. Clay had Ohio, Missouri, his own Kentucky and four from New York. Crawford had his own state of Georgia, Virginia, and eight scattering.

The election was thrown into the House for the second time. The strongest candidate before the Representatives would have been Clay, but he was barred, as the choice was to be made from the three highest. There is little doubt that had he received but three electoral votes which were among the scattering given Mr. Crawford, who had, as Mr. Schurz aptly says, merely that "temporary sort of greatness which appears in history as the reputation of a reputation", Henry Clay would have been the sixth President of the United States. He was still the foremost and strongest man in Congress. His influence among his colleagues in the House was undiminished and it was the House that was to elect the President. The crown could not be his to wear; it was his to bestow and to withhold. Crawford had represented more nearly the things for which Clay had stood, but, although he afterwards recovered, he was then a paralytic, and Clay gave him no consideration. Jackson began sedulously to cultivate the President maker, despite the fact that up to that time he had displayed an open personal hostility to him. Their mutual friends wined and dined them and Jackson on one occasion insisted on taking Clay home in his carriage. Adams, on the other hand, as was to be expected of one of his family, held rigidly aloof; he could not have courted any man's favor, even if he would. Clay had no predilection for Adams, and had opposed many of the policies for which, as Monroe's Secretary of State, Adams had stood. He had also strongly opposed Jackson when he was under criticism for his conduct in the Seminole War. He had been with Adams and Monroe, however, on the question that has since been known as the Monroe doctrine.

Clay was a trained statesman and so was Adams. Jackson had had no considerable training and it seemed to those who observed him that what he had had been wasted. Clay had spoken very decidedly, if inferentially, against Jackson in a speech deprecating the manufacture of "political heroes" which he had made in the House. Despite the fact that Jackson's friends made overtures to Clay with the chief place in the incoming administration as a bait, Clay remained imperturbable. Lewis and Senator Eaton of Tennessee, who later became the husband of the redoubtable Peggy O'Neal, of whom we shall say something later, were small men and they could not believe that under the circumstances Clay could be against them without a *quid pro quo*. And although they had not been above such a thing themselves, they meant to make so much of this imaginary circumstance as either to coerce Clay or to make capital for Jackson four years later. They could not succeed in the former purpose, but in the latter they were disgracefully successful. Before the vote was taken in the House, a newspaper article appeared charging a corrupt bargain by which Clay was to throw the election to Adams, in return for which Adams was to make Clay Secretary of State. This was said to be on the authority of an anonymous member of the House. Clay was bitterly indignant and in his heat not only published a denial but intimated that, if the unknown member would reveal himself, shots would be exchanged. The opposition immediately trotted out one Kremer, a foolish member of no standing, who was so ridiculous in the eyes of his colleagues that a duel between him and Clay would have been absurd. Clay in the House moved an investigation of the charges and said that it was the only notice he could take of an attack coming from such a source. Kremer with bravado said that he would prove his statements and that he would be at the disposal of the committee. An investigation was the last thing that Lewis and Eaton wanted and subsequently in a letter, of which Eaton was probably the author, Kremer made a high and mighty argument about the powers of the House and freedom of speech, and declined to appear. On the same day that Kremer's letter was placed before the House, Adams was elected President.

How far did the votes of the delegations in the House of Representatives represent the voters in the final decision? In Congress each state cast a single vote determined by the majority of the members from that state. Maryland had given Jackson seven electoral votes representing, according to Stanwood's authoritative table, the choice of 14,323 inviduals and had given Adams only three, but these three represented a little over a hundred more voters than did Jackson's seven. Crawford here got a single vote in the electoral college representing a popular endorsement of about three thousand. In the Congressional runoff Jackson got the votes of three members and Adams five and so Adams carried the state, not altogether an unfair result.

North Carolina however nullified its popular and electoral choice. It gave Jackson its electoral vote by a majority of about 5000 over Crawford. But in Congress ten of its members voted for Crawford, one for Adams, two for Jackson.

Let us see what Clay did for his candidate. Illinois was a Jackson state. It had only a single congressman, a Clay man who registered his vote and that of his state for Adams. This single vote was of as much importance as the twenty-five Jackson votes in Pennsylvania. Clay was influential in Louisiana, another Jackson state which now registered for Adams by two votes out of the three it possessed. Then Kentucky, Missouri, and Ohio, the three Clay states, went to Adams at their leader's behest, and there you are.

Adams had in the House thirteen states, Jackson seven, and Crawford four. Jackson lost four states which he had carried on the electoral vote. Add these to his total and subtract from Adams the three of these which went for him and Jackson would have been elected eleven to ten. But giving Adams Maryland, to which he seems to have had at least as legitimate a right as Jackson, the total would have been exactly reversed. This ought to have been the result. The vote of the congressmen in North Carolina, Louisiana and Illinois cannot be considered a triumph of representative government.

Adams then offered the Secretaryship of State to Clay. In this Adams did what in all the circumstances was the natural and fitting thing to do, and he was not the man to be turned from what seemed to him a matter of public policy by the lusty cries of a pack of blatherskites. Clay deliberated a few days and then accepted. It is probable that he felt more concern than did Adams over the effect of the appointment on public opinion, but he saw that failure to accept would be pointed to as a cowardly hesitancy to accept the fruits of a bargain with perhaps as much effect as anything which could come as a consequence of grasping the nettle. In the words of the ablest of the grandsons of Adams, to be found in his Life of John Randolph, Clay "caused Mr. Adams's election and like the man of honor and courage he was he stood by the President he had made."

That there was no basis of fact for the charges is now susceptible of definite proof. Clay had told various persons, including Benton, that he should vote for Adams before he had any interview with Adams himself, the date of which interview is fixed by that diary, now published, which Adams kept with such great particularity. The vials of wrath were nevertheless poured on the two high-minded statesmen. Randolph, who never lacked gall, denounced the association in a famous phrase, as "the coalition of Blifil and Black George, —the combination, unheard of till now, of the Puritan with the Blackleg." Jackson, who was always credulous and unreasoning when touched personally, believed the charge implicitly. With his violent temper and his vigorous talent for hatred, he could never be reasoned out of a belief, however ill-founded, and this was one that he nursed faithfully. To those around him, hungry for the power which would come to them from one who they knew would "take care of his friends", there was no desire to cross him in what to them was his profitable delusion. Clay made a statement at some length which was to thinking men a complete vindication. It was so termed in letters sent him by John Marshall, Judge Story and Daniel Webster, all really great lawyers. An able argument might as well have been used to stay a spring freshet. For four years the men bent on making Jackson President fed the public with this story in all forms. No canard in the history of politics was longer or more tenaciously believed.

Adams's administration, like that of his father, was able, honest, valuable to the country, but with no element of human appeal. Jackson, though intending to contest again, was inclined to take the result good-naturedly, but his cordiality to Adams at a reception where they met was so frigidly received as to anger the old soldier and make him the more ready to believe the bargain canard. Adams made no effort for re-election and did not even attempt to prevent office holders, whose intuitions taught them to face the rising sun, from assisting Jackson in his aspirations. The anti-Jackson party was bereft of their candidate's assistance and they waded quite as deeply in the mire as did their opponents. Jackson idolized his wife. There had been some informality in their marriage, coming out of a misunderstanding of statutes, and on this his opponents ghoulishly seized, a wicked and inexcusable thing. His military executions were harped on and broadsides decorated with black borders and somber coffins were widely distributed. A Democratic editor in New Hampshire is said to have offset this by a bantering charge that Jackson's greatest crime had not been given, that he ruthlessly killed some hundreds of British tourists intent on visiting the city of New Orleans.

A BRIEF ACCOUNT OF THE

EXECUTION

OF THE SIX MILITIA MEN.

Nothing could stop the impetus of Old Hickory. He rode into office on his personal popularity and the bribery and corruption canard. Political psychology was understood by Lewis and Eaton and they knew that if they took no notice of disproof but kept up a constant reiteration of a lie it would become as useful as if it were true. Their great stock in trade was this lie. When it swept Jackson into office it had served its purpose, but it lived for many years.

This lie embittered Clay's entire career and if it did not trouble Adams so much it was because of his utter contempt and aloofness. It brought Jackson to the height of his power and gave him the opportunity to reward his friends and punish his foes, the two greatest pleasures he had in life. But it did not stay the career of Henry Clay or that of John Quincy Adams, for the one—though he never attained the Presidency—was to be the foremost of Whig statesmen, while the other, with a highly distinguished career behind him, was to become superlatively great on the floor of Congress, fighting single-handed and alone—the Old Man Eloquent, who was to die, practically in his tracks, murmuring, "This is the last of earth. I am content."

As for Jackson, he continued to be the idol of his party until his death in 1845. It is a singular fact, however, that, although he was always Tennessee's favorite son and especial hero, that state, after the General left office and returned to the Hermitage, never supported any presidential candidate with whom Jackson was allied, nor even its own citizen, James K. Polk, but was always carried for the Whig ticket through the efforts of Hugh L. White and John Bell, much to the disgruntlement of Old Hickory. There never was a political ointment, no matter how fragrant, but had its fly, and it was in the Tennessee campaigns of his later years that Jackson found his.

CHAPTER THREE

TIPPECANOE AND TYLER TOO

THERE was much rejoicing when Jackson was inaugurated. The crush of the populace was tremendous and the enthusiasm unbounded. The erect white-haired figure of Old Hickory had picturesqueness and dignity. Although he headed the first movement to utilize the unrestrained voter for personal politics, he did not look the part of the demagogue. For eight years he was a notable figure and no matter how many of his policies may have been suggested by others, it was his own dominant force that maintained them. We are not concerned with his administration in our pursuit of the drama of the presidency, except as it developed the figures that combated in that vividly remembered struggle, the campaign of 1840.

John C. Calhoun had been Vice President with Adams and had been re-elected. His allegiance was to the Democracy and it was at first expected that he would be Jackson's successor. Jackson, however, was not only honest but he had that egotism in his honesty that made him believe that no one could be equally honest who was not in personal agreement with him. Little by little Jackson began to hear that Calhoun had expressed his disapproval of certain of his military acts and policies and he gradually withdrew his friendship. Then came the nullification threat and Jackson's famous toast to the Union in Calhoun's presence.

All this was further accentuated by a social tempest which raged around Jackson's cabinet. Major Eaton, who, with Lewis, had done four years of wire pulling for his chief, was rewarded with the Secretaryship of War. In Washington in those days a favorite tavern had been that kept by one O'Neal. Its popularity had been greatly enhanced by the dash, sparkle and impudence of his pretty daughter Peggy. She was a lady of easy manners and made herself exceedingly popular with the masculine habitués, one of whom had been Eaton. She married a naval officer of unimportant rank and is supposed to have led him a very lively dance. Her name was coupled with Eaton's at this time and when the husband blew his brains out she married him. All this made a scandal which no previous President would have tolerated in his official family, but Jackson had suffered by the charges arising from his own marriage with Mrs. Robards, whose divorce was not perfect at the time of the ceremony, and he became an eager partizan of pretty Peggy, whom he had been made to believe a very ill-used woman. He insisted on the recognition of Mrs. Eaton in Washington society. The wife of the Vice President refused to give this recognition. So did the wives of the cabinet members. There was rebellion even in the White House. Jackson's own sister would have nothing to do with Mrs. Eaton and was summarily packed off to Tennessee. The cabinet officials told Jackson in reply to his remonstrances that this was no political affair and that they never interfered with their wives' choice of friends. This finally led to a reconstruction of the cabinet and certain offending officers lost office to keep self-respect. Jackson sent Eaton to Spain as minister and Mrs. Eaton was accepted there, but when she returned home she was mixed up as a go-between in an unsuccessful effort at graft in which she conveyed a message from a contractor to the wife of Postmaster-General Kendall, assuring her if the Postmaster-General allowed certain claims she would be presented with a carriage and pair. That was the end of Pretty Peggy, who, if her hardfaced portraits are to be trusted, had very little real prettiness after all.

The Secretary of State was Martin Van Buren of New York. "Little Van", as he was affectionately called by his friends, had been a poor boy and had risen to high position by honesty and ability. He was a clear thinker and an effective speaker. He was an elegant figure and had marked social qualities. So completely was he the gentleman that there can be no doubt that, had he been married, he would have taken the same attitude in this tempest in a teapot as did his cabinet colleagues. But he was a widower and his attitude toward Mrs. Eaton for that reason could be very different from that of the others. He was polite and deferential to all women and made no exception of Peggy.

If Martin Van Buren had not been a widower he might never have been President of the United States. As it was, he won Jackson's heart and although, when the cabinet crisis came about, it was deemed discreet that he retire with the rest, it was to England as minister. On Jackson's re-election, he returned to America as Vice President and as the predestined successor to Old Hickory.

To say that the Eaton affair was the only thing that gave Van Buren this eminence would be unfair to an able statesman and an admirable gentleman, but few non-political events have such far-reaching results as did this. It certainly was of great injury to Calhoun, and it was probably this personal, social opposition to the old chieftain's wishes which tinged his memory of the nullification days when Jackson in his old age voiced his regret at not having "hanged John C. Calhoun."

At the end of Jackson's second term, the party which came in partly as a protest against the presidential succession of the old régime went before the country with an heir apparent. Van Buren had no difficulty in being elected, but once he entered upon his duties he found that he was an heir indeed. Jackson had sowed the wind for Van Buren to reap the whirlwind. A dozen things militated against the President, all inherited from his predecessor. Finally, a financial panic began in 1837 and, although confidence was to some degree restored, and Democrats generally elected in 1839—when in Whig Massachusetts the Van Buren candidate for Governor was successful by a majority of a single vote—it broke out again and the chances for Van Buren's election seemed slim.

The Whigs nominated General William Henry Harrison, the hero of Tippecanoe. John Tyler of Virginia was nominated for Vice President. This last was one of those expedient nominations, a sheer bid for votes, Tyler being a distinguished anti-Van Buren Democrat, and its sequel was what might have been expected. Now the party which had first used a military chief to supersede a tried civic servant, found the shoe pinching its own foot. Van Buren's Vice President was Richard M. Johnson, "Dick" as he used to be called. He had been an Indian fighter, a colonel and was reputed to have slain Tecumseh in single combat. He was to add the "military touch" to the Democratic ticket. But Johnson was a frank and honest man and when he visited New York during the summer and was hailed as the real hero of Tippecanoe and Fort Meigs, he refused to be made ridiculous and referred to his gallant commander, General Harrison.

The diary of Philip Hone, that militant Whig who at one time was Mayor of New York, gives a remarkable picture of the days in which he lived. The author's pictures of Van Buren at this time are significant. Hone was a Harrisonian but he was opposing Van Buren only on political grounds and from a sense of duty. Van Buren was a dignified and affable gentleman and treated his opponents as gentlemen and often as friends. On his inauguration Hone recorded: "He will be a party President but he is too much of a gentleman to be governed by a rabble who surrounded his predecessor and administered to his bad passions." Hone could see only this side of Jackson. "As a man, a gentleman, and a friend, I have a great respect for Mr. Van Buren." As the day recedes this verdict of Hone's becomes more and more that of the American people.

Early in the campaign the drift was distinctly toward Harrison, but campaigns do not always end as they begin and the Democrats were not entirely without hope. But, alas! It fell to a Democratic editor to perpetrate the Burchardism of his time. He suggested that Harrison was an uncouth frontiersman who would be better contented with his lot if left in his log cabin with plenty of hard cider. Now Harrison was not an entirely uneducated man. He knew something of the classics and ancient history. While it was said, no doubt apochryphally, that Jackson's only speech in Latin consisted of unrelated phrases, "E Pluribus Unum, In Hoc Signo Vinces, Sine Qua Non," the story is authentically related that Webster, after revising Harrison's inaugural, had told his wife that he had been obliged to kill off a fabulous number of Roman pro-consuls.

It was true that Harrison had lived simply and without pretense. If the editor in question had learned nothing from Eaton and Lewis, the Whig managers had. They made the attack react. The Log Cabin became the symbol of the campaign. It was a symbol to conjure with. It was good Old Hero stuff. It stirred the popular imagination. At every Whig celebration a log cabin was made a feature. Log cabins were mounted on wheels and drawn through the streets by teams of white horses, surrounded by enthusiasts singing campaign songs about "Tippecanoe and Tyler too", and proclaiming, "Van Van is a used up man." There was one song which I have heard sung in a quavering voice by one who as a young man participated in the campaign, which included this, the only verse now remembered:

32

> "We'll put him into the Capitol
> We know a capital way,
> We'll sing a Harrison song by night
> And fight his foes by day."

All this was made more potent in the light of contrast. This leader of the Democrats, this successor of the rough and almost primitive Jackson, dared to have breeding, tact and taste. While Harrison was not so uncouth as his partizans sought to make him seem for the delectation of the commoner, it was easy to compare the candidates to the disadvantage of Van Buren before the "dear peepul". So the Whigs sang:

> "Let Van from his coolers of silver drink wine,
> And lounge on his cushioned settee,
> Our man on his buck-eye bench can recline,
> Content with hard cider is he."

Woodworth's old ballad, then new, "The Old Oaken Bucket" was pressed into service, the refrain of the parody being:

> "The iron-armed soldier, the true-heatred soldier,
> The gallant old soldier of Tippecanoe."

Huge wooden balls decorated with campaign mottoes and cumbersome wit were pushed from town to town, some making long pilgrimages. I suppose they were re-painted now and then. "Hail to the Chief" furnished a song for these adventures:

> "Hail to the ball which in grandeur advances,
> Long life to the yeomen who urge it along;
> The abuse of our hero his worth but enhances
> Then welcome his triumphs with shouts and with song."

The Whigs fought with the impetus which comes from a vision of victory and the Democrats, well entrenched, stub-

bornly held their ground. But even in New York, Little Van's
own state, the Harrison enthusiasm was unbounded. On the
anniversary of the battle of Fort Meigs in which Harrison
had borne his part, a celebration was held. There was not one
procession alone, but processions in all the wards; flambeaux,
log cabins and all the campaign devices were abundant. The
parades converged at Niblo's Garden where the speeches were
made and the enthusiasm was unbounded.

In Baltimore there was a ratifying convention which
brought 30,000 Whigs together. The procession was a long
one. Every state was represented. The log cabin was the dominant feature, state after state having brought their own.
There were also the now familiar balls rolled by citizens typi-
fying the momentum of the Whig cause. Clay and Webster
were both there and made addresses but even then it was the
carnival spirit which ruled the day. But on that day the Harri-
sonians did not have it all their own way. The procession was
assaulted and one of the paraders, a Baltimore carpenter
named McLaughlin, was killed. The body of another parader
wearing a Harrison badge was found in a basin.

New York City had a great log cabin which could, and
often did, hold great congregations of citizens. In Dayton,
Ohio, a hundred thousand citizens held an open air meeting
and covered ten acres. Boston Common was the rendezvous
for the chief New England celebration. A procession of more
than thirty thousand formed there. There were several thousand horsemen at its head and forty carriages containing
Revolutionary veterans. Delegations nearly all had floats.
Lynn, a shoe-making center, presented a huge boot. New Bed-
ford sent a genuine whale boat mounted on wheels, fully
equipped and manned by six old masters of whale ships. The
ever present cabin and the rolling ball were not neglected.
After parading through the city and circling Faneuil Hall,
it crossed over into Charlestown and up to the summit of

Bunker Hill, where Webster presided at a giant ratification meeting.

At last on October 5 came the anniversary of another military victory of Harrison's, the battle of the Thames. The campaign was nearly at its apex and all over the country the Whigs made it a gala day. Parades, banquets, rallies were held by the hundred. After this day and with the news from the states voting in October which indicated a substantial Whig victory, the Democrats tried to turn the tide by charges of fraud in the Pennsylvania election. It was alleged that a man and presumably many had been hired to go from New York and vote in Philadelphia and many prominent New York Whigs, notably Governor Seward, were implicated. But all this came to nothing. It was ignored and generally disbelieved and was probably untrue.

Although Webster and Clay and the brilliant Tom Corwin of Ohio were constantly on the stump and made clear, cogent and eloquent arguments, the prevailing meeting was a carnival in which the traditional hard cider libation was not forgotten. Although the Van Buren men tried to bring the campaign to the level of seemly argument, even as had the Adams men twelve years before, they found they might just as well have argued with a tidal wave. Harrison went in with a handsome endorsement. And yet the entrenched Democracy had stood up well under the strain. Although Van Buren received only sixty electoral votes, the popular votes showed him less than a hundred and fifty thousand behind in a total of two million four hundred thousand, and left the Democracy ready to fight again another day.

One likes to think of Van Buren as Hone saw him in the White House when he, an opponent fresh from the hustings, called upon him before the inauguration to pay his personal respects. "He received me alone in his study, in the kindest and most gracious manner; talked a little about the late political contest, professed an undiminished friendship for me, notwithstanding my opposition, which, he said he had been gratified to learn, had been unaccompanied by the use of any expression of personal disrespect. He is fat and jolly, with the same self-satisfied smile on his countenance. A stranger would be greatly at a loss to discover anything to indicate that he was a defeated candidate for the high office which he is about to vacate." When early in February Harrison arrived in town with much noisy acclaim and parade, Van Buren showed him gracious attention, returned his call, fixing an inauguration custom, and had him to dinner at the White House. He is one of our Presidents who knew the profession of gentleman in every phase.

The Whigs were in transports of joy, but never was a victory more short-lived. Within a month after the inauguration their idol was dead and John Tyler became the first Vice President to succeed to the presidency by virtue of his office, to break with the party that had elected him, to insure the election of Polk, and to go down in history as the president of the peace conference in 1861 and the only ex-President to give allegiance to the Southern Confederacy.

CHAPTER FOUR

TWO FRUITLESS QUESTS

THE presidency is a tantalizing Will o' the Wisp. Its pursuit has tortured many a man, and its attainment has been accomplished by some who had no expectation of securing the prize. A few men pre-eminent in their day have sat in the chair but not many. After those earliest years when the electoral possibilities implicit in mass psychology had not been discovered, it is hard to pick out a President who at the time of his election was the greatest man of his party. Lincoln when renominated was, of course, not only his party's but his country's pre-eminent figure. In a sense Grant may have been. With Lincoln in his grave, Grant was the chief figure of his time, but he was a pathetic figure in the White House, a simple soldier surrounded by false friends. Cleveland goes down in history as the greatest man in his party in his day, but his background at the time of his first election was meager compared with that of Bayard. Roosevelt will be remembered as the dominant man in his party during only his term of service. Wilson would "bear like the Turk no brother near the throne" and, however grudgingly obedience was yielded to him, we must admit that he ruled his party. Since Jackson these five have been the only predominant party leaders to attain the chief magistracy of the republic and, with the exception of Grant and possibly Cleveland, they were not the great men in their parties at the time they reached the goal. Seward overshadowed the early Lincoln. Roosevelt got in by the back door. Wilson was one of several nearly equal contenders, and was nominated, under the peculiar rules of his party convention, only after another candidate had received a majority of the votes. Bryan was then the first man in the Democratic party.

Availability is the invariable acid test of candidates. To that and that alone did the distinguished collection of comparative mediocrities who have attained the presidency owe their preferment. Not that availability has always compelled the nomination of men of slight talents. Distinguished and able statesmen have, by its exactions, been chosen from among candidates every bit their equals. Availability absolutely dictated the nomination of Lincoln. On the other hand, it has resolutely barred the door to some giants of our political life. Some of our greatest statesmen have been keenly ambitious for this honor, denied them not only once, as in the case of Seward and Reed, but many times, as in the case of Clay, Webster, and Blaine. The efforts of Blaine will be described in the story of a later day. The futile striving of the earlier giants, whose ardent desire to be President disturbed even their dreams, must now claim our attention.

From the time that they reached national prominence until they disappeared almost simultaneously from public life, three men were the dominant figures in national legislation: Clay, Webster, and Calhoun. Each ardently wished to be President. To Calhoun, because his theories and principles were the theories and principles of the minority, we have done slight justice. He was a statesman of high character and pure life, with no touch of the demagogue about him. It early became evident, however, that if the Southern point of view was to be represented in the presidency it would usually be by Northern men. In the time when contemplated nullification was agitated, Jackson's quick antagonism put Calhoun in a precarious position politically and, though he was always in a receptive mood, he soon ceased to strive. Not so with his great rivals. Neither Clay nor Webster ever gave up hope of attaining the coveted prize and this desire fretted them like the shirt of Nessus. Three times was Clay nominated, only to be defeated by Adams, Jackson, and Polk. He was a candidate in two conventions of the Whig party in 1840 and 1848,—only to be put aside for untrained men to whom the party owed not a tithe of the debt it owed to its great statesman; and the untrained men were both elected. Clay's bitter comment that he was always run when sure of defeat and denied the nomination when election was fairly probable, a comment made at the time of Harrison's nomination, was true to the end of his life.

Clay's first battle has already been described. When, eight years afterward, the "Old Hero" made his canvass for his second term, "Harry of the West" made his next unavailing canvass. It would have been impossible to defeat the new Democracy. The newly awakened power was not to be stilled and the vote of one illiterate could offset that of the best trained and deepest thinking man alive. There was another element which brought confusion: the new Anti-Masonic party, composed of men who feared that political power was exerted through secret conclave, and who sought to curb it. William Wirt, Attorney General in the Adams cabinet, was made the candidate of the party. Clay was opposed to any proscriptive political policy. The politicians hoped to get Wirt out of the fight after Clay should be nominated by the Whigs, as he was sure to be. Both men were types of old statesmanship; they had worked together; they were warm friends. Wirt would gladly have yielded. At last it was found to be certain that Clay could not get the Anti-Masonic nomination in any case, and Wirt stayed in. It is hard to see how, even without this contingency, Clay could have had any reasonable hopes; and, although there was a feeble attempt to coalesce in New York, this new party might well have discouraged any man. Yet hope springs eternal in the human breast, especially when the presidency is concerned. No man is so easily self-hypnotized as a politician in the midst of a battle, and before the end of the campaign Clay and Webster were writing each other congratulatory letters on the prospects.

But Jackson never doubted the result. He said to his friend Hill, the New Hampshire editor, "Isaac, it'll be a walk. If our fellows didn't raise a finger from now on the thing would be just as well as done. In fact, Isaac, it's done now."

Jackson's "fellows," however, continued to raise more than fingers, in fact they raised Cain. There was no diminution of their shouts nor of their "bribery and corruption" cry. Jackson swept the country off its feet and left the conservatives dazed at the magnitude of Clay's defeat. Jackson's popular majority was nearly 125,000, a magnificent one in those days. Of electoral votes he received 219 against Clay's 40 and Wirt's 7.

Four years afterwards, when the "heir apparent" was forging to the front, Clay bided his time, but in 1840 he was again a candidate. He was the undoubted choice of the convention, but the leaders, including Thurlow Weed, were on the lookout for a "hero." In the semi-obscurity of the office of clerk of the Federal Court in Cincinnati was William Henry Harrison. He was trotted out and after a brief campaign, he was jockeyed into the nomination by an adoption of the unit rule. Clay's friends, who could have controlled the convention, were aghast when they saw what unwittingly they had done, but it was too late. The nomination had been made and Clay, with ample reason to be disgruntled, exclaimed, "My friends are not worth the powder and shot it would take to kill them. If there were two Henry Clays, one of them would make the other President of the United States." Clay stood by the nomination of Harrison and worked hard and enthusiastically for the ticket. When the victory was won, however, he held aloof and refused to accept the Secretaryship of State under the man in whose name he had been defeated.

Clay's defeat by Polk was unlooked for and was almost a

stunning blow, not only to him but to his friends. The story of his battle with the Tennessean is rather a pitiful one. Clay was easily nominated, and it seemed as if the coveted honor was finally to be his. But his ambition thwarted itself. Tyler was endeavoring to bring about the annexation of Texas by negotiations with that somewhat shadowy republic. Clay wrote a statesmanlike letter upon the question, taking the highest moral ground. If he had been willing to stand upon that letter it might have elected him. But he found it unpopular in certain circles in the South and in two other letters he strove to "explain" it. His explanations, logically considered, did not qualify his position and so did not suit those they were intended to placate, but they did make certain Whig supporters see that he was endeavoring to temper the wind to the shorn lamb. Clay had "trimmed" in their estimation, and there stood the uncompromising Birney at the head of the Liberty party. New York went for Polk. If it had gone for Clay he would have been elected. Birney got fifteen thousand votes in New York and Polk's plurality was only five thousand. High-tariff Pennsylvania was taken from Clay by Democrats who stole his thunder and made their battle cry "Polk, Dallas, and the Tariff of 1842." This was as if a state in 1892 had cried "Cleveland, Stevenson, and Protection." But Dallas, running for Vice President, was a Pennsylvanian and this battle cry gave their local favorite the votes of the state. As President of the Senate, Dallas repaid the confidence reposed in him by breaking a tie vote and repealing the tariff of 1842 for which his supporters had shouted.

The result of this election came to the country as a surprise, and even the Democrats (according to Schurz) respected the great statesmanship of Clay too much to exult openly over the success of a man so much his inferior.

Still Clay kept on. He was seventy-one years old when the election of 1848 approached. Again he saw the prize in his grasp. But even his greatest friends had no such vision. Clay's defeat in that convention reminds one of the broken Blaine and his last pitiful contest in 1892. American politics had ridden roughshod over them both. Even Crittenden, Clay's admirer and disciple, believed his selection over Taylor impossible. This feeling was so deeply echoed that, for the first time in a convention where Clay was a candidate, Kentucky was substantially divided. When Clay was thus defeated once more by a "military hero" who for forty years had never even voted, his rage and disgust got the better of him. He refused to support Taylor who, according to Clay, had announced his intention to run against the Kentuckian had the latter received the nomination. "Magnanimity," said Clay, "is a noble virtue but it has its limits and the line of demarkation between it and meanness is not always discernible."

Webster's quest was even more ill-fated, for in its wake we see the tragic seventh-of-March speech and Whittier writing "Ichabod" across the forehead of the fallen idol. Webster would have indignantly denied that he made this speech as a bid for Southern support, and he would have believed in the denial; but gnawing ambition was too inextricably blended with his very being not to have affected him, even though he deceived himself about his motives. He ran against Van Buren in 1836 with a local nomination, carrying Massachusetts, while other Whig states chose electors for White, Harrison, and Mangum, hoping to throw the election into the House. Had they succeeded, as they did not, Webster would not have been one of the first three, so he would not have been eligible for election. In 1840 he had desired the nomination but was not formally a candidate. In 1844 he left the field to Clay. Four years later he unsuccessfully contested with Taylor, Clay, and Scott for the Whig nomination. His total vote never reached twenty-five on any ballot, and he was finally left by all but the faithful Massachusetts fourteen. He saw the con-

The Political Funeral of Clay

vention turn to the man whom he had characterized (and appropriately) as an illiterate frontier colonel.

Still Webster pursued the elusive prize. He never felt surer of attaining his end than at the next election when to the clearer view of his friends, his prospects were darkest. He believed he held the balance of power between Fillmore and Scott, who were evenly balanced, and that with his thirty-two votes in the convention one of them eventually would come to him. He held his compact strength fairly well, but instead of coming to Webster some of Fillmore's vote went to Scott, and "Old Fuss and Feathers" was chosen to lead the Whig party in its last contest to inglorious and final defeat.

One of the shrewdest political manipulators of his day was Thurlow Weed. He believed in his party and wanted it to win, therefore his choice of candidates was generally based on the question of availability. Twice he records conversations with Webster in which he (Weed) correctly prophesied the Whig nominees. First his choice was Harrison; eight years later it was Taylor. Webster scoffed at both predictions. Weed suggested each time that Webster modify his candidacy to that for second place. Each time the Massachusetts statesman vehemently refused. Webster was probably more eager for the presidency than any man of his time, not even excepting Clay. He might have had the vice-presidency with either of these two men, both of whom died early in their administrations, to be succeeded by Tyler and Fillmore. In the place of either of these men, except for his imperious pride, Daniel Webster might have stood.

From the Whig convention of 1852, which was held at Baltimore, Webster's friend Harvey,—the admirer who enacted Boswell to the statesman's Johnson,—hastened to Washington as soon as the nomination of Scott had been consummated. Webster met him at the door with an expression of grief. Neither could bear to speak of the result which the telegraph had communicated to the defeated candidate. Rufus Choate, who had been Webster's spokesman, soon arrived. Still no word was uttered about the convention. To Choate it seemed as if some one had died in the house, so sombre and grief laden was the atmosphere. The meal to which they sat down with Mrs. Webster seemed to him like the first meal after the return from the burial of a loved one.

Finally Webster and Choate went into another room and had their talk out. Choate told him who had been faithful and who vacillating. It was one of the saddest conversations in which the great lawyer had ever taken part, and there in a side room in Washington the majestic Massachusetts senator turned away forever from his buried hopes.

Later in the evening this tragic meeting was interrupted by the sound of mirth and rejoicing. Blatant and resounding, a band came down the street. A celebration was on foot, a celebration of the third military nomination by the Whig party, of the third victory of martial glory over competence and statecraft. It was fitting that the blare of brass and the rattle of drums should celebrate so splendid a triumph. With almost brutal enthusiasm the serenaders halted before the house of the majestic senator whose splendor had impressed the nations of the earth. The air was rent with lusty cheers for Scott, "the next President." Webster must perforce come out and show himself, as conquered sovereigns were wont to march at the wheels of Cæsar's chariot. *Vox populi, vox dei!* In spite of the plea that he was not well and had retired, the throng persisted. The tyranny of the populace is never to be denied. His heart was wrung, perhaps broken, but he would not wear it on his sleeve. He would be majestic to the end. He pointedly omitted to mention the name of Scott. He closed his speech as only Daniel Webster could close a speech:

"Of one thing, gentlemen, I can assure you," said he, "that no one amongst you will enjoy a sounder night's sleep than shall I. I shall rise in the morning, God willing, to the performance of my duty with the lark, and though I cannot equal him in sweetness of song, he will not greet the purpling east more joyous and jocund than I."

Soon after, Webster left the capital and Washington saw him no more.

As Clay had refused to support Taylor, so did Webster abandon Scott. He advised his friends to vote for General Pierce, the New Hampshire nonentity nominated by the Democrats. As Mr. Lodge says in his biography of Webster, this was absolutely indefensible. But it was profoundly human. It was the last political act of a breaking giant, deeply wounded, whose disappointment brought about a depression which weakened his power of resistance, even to disease.

Pierce was elected. "Old Hickory," "Old Tippecanoe" and "Old Rough and Ready" had all achieved their ambitions, but the electorate drew the line at "Old Fuss and Feathers." How far Webster's defection encouraged others, it is impossible to say. The Democratic victory was too overwhelming, however, to believe that Webster's support would greatly have changed matters. Massachusetts did not follow Webster and was one of the four states to return Scott electors.

When the election was held Webster was beyond the influence of struggle or of faction. He had seen a New England summer pass with the lapping waters of Massachusetts Bay at his very feet. When the autumn came, at his beautiful home in Marshfield, with the cool breezes of the sea playing around his massive forehead, he died, and it seemed to his friends as if the very gods of Olympus must have gathered closer upon their seats to give him room.

When I think of him, dying, with his great disappointment fresh and poignant, when I think of all he did for his beloved Union, and how external was this failure, when I think of the great reply to Hayne and then of the seventh-of-March speech, I remember Thackeray's essay on a great and gloomy genius and feel like saying of Daniel Webster, as he did of Swift: "So great a man he seems to me, that thinking of him is like thinking of an empire falling."

CHAPTER FIVE

THE MARCH OF FREEDOM

THE romance of American politics can never be written without telling the inspiring story of the party of freedom. Beginning in 1840 with a meagre seven thousand votes, it marched steadily with no backward step until in 1860 it elected its candidate on a platform opposed to the extension of slavery, and, inferentially at least, favoring restriction. It furnishes one of the purest, greatest and most romantic chapters in the history of politics of any nation. Captious critics may point to the differences of name and, to some extent, of personnel in the technical party organization, but the insurgent swell, ever carrying its principles forward as irresistibly as the movement of a rising tide, was the force which was the real and unchanging substance of the Liberty, Free Soil and Republican parties. The Democratic and Whig parties were both anxious not to alienate the votes that defended slavery. Jackson's opinion of abolitionist agitators was vigorous and denunciatory even for him. The Whig attitude was more cautious than outspoken. This party included for a long time, in its membership in the North, men who were unfriendly to slavery; but it also had, even in Boston, its wealthy and satisfied business men who wanted no disturbance of prosperity (largely dependent upon textiles in New England) even in the interests of humanity. This was the famous coterie which, to some extent at least, financed Daniel Webster and finally came to be known as "Cotton Whigs." The Whig organization no more intended to alienate this element than it did to drive

47

away its slave-holding electorate. It elected only two Presidents, and one of these, General Taylor, was a Louisiana slave-holder. There was little in party politics to encourage the straight abolitionist, and many such, like Garrison, held aloof from any participation in the government.

But there enters into the story of abolition one of the most striking and yet least recognized figures in the history of American politics. In 1792 James Gillespie Birney first saw the light in Danville, Kentucky. He came from good Scotch-Irish stock, was born into a slave-holding family, and, when he came to maturity, held slaves himself. He was graduated at Princeton, then the College of New Jersey, and studied law in Philadelphia. On his return to Kentucky he began a political career in the legislature. After a few years he moved to Alabama. There he was county attorney, an Adams candidate for presidential elector in 1828, a member of the legislature, and mayor of Huntsville. A slave owner, he was gentle and humane, thereby resembling the great majority of Southern gentlemen who held slaves. Always upright and cultured, he was in the best sense a man of the world. In mature years, without temporary exaltation, he became a convinced Christian and joined the Presbyterian Church. A logical thinker and an honest man, he could not reconcile slave-holding with these convictions. Slowly and surely he marched along the anti-slavery road. First he embraced the doctrine of colonization, with its purpose of sending negroes to Liberia. He became agent of the American Colonization Society. Then he took another step and became an advocate of gradual and compensated emancipation. He next freed his own slaves under the legal provisions for manumission. Finally the inexorable path of logic led him to absolute emancipation. He had returned to Kentucky by this time and decided to publish an abolition newspaper, *The Philanthropist*. The local opposition was such that he removed to free territory and produced the paper in Cincinnati, where the opposition turned out to be quite as strong. Once his printing press was thrown into the river. On several occasions he faced mobs with cool courage and unruffled calmness. He succeeded in publishing the paper. His courage and ability became known throughout the United States and at last he was called to New York to become the secretary of the National Anti-Slavery Society.

In 1840 the Democrats placed Van Buren on a platform which clearly indicated that the party would resist any attempt at Federal interference with slavery, while it was just as evident that the Whig party would never challenge the Democracy on this doubtful and dangerous issue. Its candidate, "Old Tip," had said that abolitionist schemes were such that only a devil incarnate could look at them with approbation.

There were many voters to whom human liberty was above all other issues, and they did not intend to endorse the decided position of the Democrats or the timid performance of the Whigs. Out of such enthusiasts the Liberty party was formed at Albany, New York, in a small mass convention including delegates from only six states. This little band had courage, intelligence, and integrity. There was no uncertain tone in their platform and when James G. Birney was asked to stand upon it as their candidate he accepted the duty. The movement carried with it no promise of victory, but it was both ideal and practical. Ideal, because it held uncompromisingly for a great principle; practical because the vote was not wasted, there being nothing to hope from either the Democrats or the Whigs. The party received no name at this convention. At the election Birney received only seven thousand votes, from but twelve states. Only in the states of Rhode Island, Delaware, and Arkansas did Van Buren, the major loser of the election, get as few votes as did Birney throughout the whole country, and yet Birney, bearing in mind the words of the English martyr, Latimer, might have said to his followers, "We have this day lighted such a candle in America as please God shall never be put out."

In 1844 Birney again ran. The cause was marching on. Although still hopelessly in the minority, he received nine times as many votes as he had received four years previous. This time he had votes in every free state, whereas before Indiana had not been represented.

Birney was now at the close of his career. Less than a year after this election he was thrown from a horse and suffered in consequence a stroke of nervous paralysis. For twelve years he was an invalid, not always bed-ridden, but without the unhampered use of his organs of speech. In any event it would have remained for others to reap what he had sown. The pioneer fighter, with the early antagonisms of the unsuccessful days upon his shoulders, is never the most available candidate when victory is in sight. So it would have been with him. But in all the list of men who fought the fight of human rights,— philosophers, orators, poets, and statesmen,—there will be found few names as illustrious as that of James Gillespie Birney.

In 1848 the Democrats put forward Lewis Cass, a Northern man with Southern sympathies; the Whigs, the non-voting, "illiterate frontier colonel," who hailed from Louisiana and held slaves. In this contingency another anti-slavery nomination was inevitable, but few in Birney's day would have foreseen the one that was to be made. The party which had generally been known as the slavery party, which had annexed Texas and fought the Mexican War at the behest of the slave interest, had begun to feel the working of the leaven. In some of the Northern states, particularly in New York, there were two Democratic factions, known as the Hunkers and the Barnburners. The first sustained the Polk administration on the Texas issue, the latter opposed it. The leader of the Barnburners was Martin Van Buren, and the man whom Birney had run against in 1840 now succeeded him as the anti-slavery standard bearer, being persuaded to accept the nomination of the convention of what was now known as the Free Soil party. As the vote had increased from seven thousand in 1840 to sixty-two thousand in 1844, so now it increased to two hundred and ninety thousand. Although no electoral votes were cast for Van Buren, yet in three states, including New York, he defeated Cass. This vote, however, was not the normal anti-slavery vote, as was shown at the next election, but was in part the result of a fusion with the Barnburners, who had not previously made common cause with them and never did again.

In 1852 the Free Soil convention met in Pittsburgh and made what would now be called a straightforward "middle of the road nomination." Van Buren and the Barnburners had returned to their Democratic allegiance. John P. Hale of New Hampshire was made the candidate. No better choice could have been made. He had been an anti-slavery Whig and, as a member of Congress, had stood with the aged and militant Adams against the gag rule. To the great honor of New Hampshire, he had been the first anti-slavery senator in the United States and had held the fort alone till the advent of Chase and Seward. He was a hard, clean fighter, pugnacious and yet good-tempered. Many stories have been told of his quick retorts in debate. To the taunt of Cass of Michigan that the gentleman from New Hampshire had earned the sobriquet of "the Granite Goose," he is said to have suggested that the ponderous statesman was merely a Michi-gander. On Toombs' suggesting that Milton had him in mind when he penned the words, "Hail, horrors, hail!" the quick retort was that whoever might have been in Milton's mind there could be no doubt about the mental processes of Dr. Watts when he cried out, "Hark from the Toombs that doleful sound." Hale made a good run, although the total free soil vote was greatly decreased by the defection of the Democratic allies of four years before and fell off one hundred and thirty-five thousand, ninety-five thousand of which was in New York, the Van Buren stronghold. This indicates as clearly as anything can that the loss was not a diminution of the real anti-slavery fighting strength.

Before another election the anti-slavery party took another and its final name. Various communities claim the honor of being the birthplace of the Republican party. Which is deserving the distinction is of slight consequence. For our purposes it is sufficient to know that in 1854 the first Republican National Convention was held in Pittsburgh to formulate party principles and government, and that subsequent to the election of that year there were fifteen Republicans in the Senate and one hundred and eight in the House. When the time for the Presidential election arrived the Whig party as a serious factor had disappeared. The American party, popularly remembered as the "Know Nothings," had absorbed many. Others had gone over to the Democrats, and the rest, probably the major portion, had cast their lot with the hopeful young party with a moral issue that was forging to the front. The Americans put up Millard Fillmore. The Democracy, after a stubborn contest in which Pierce and Douglas had been candidates, nominated James Buchanan, a man of dignity, apparent rectitude, and respectable parts, who had been Secretary of State and Minister to England, whose chief claim to fame was his part in the Ostend Manifesto, which was a declaration that we could and should annex Cuba, a declaration clearly dictated at that time by the exigencies of slavery. The Republicans referred to the manifesto as "the highwayman's plea that might makes right." Although Buchanan was supported generally in the convention by Northern delegates, the *Richmond Enquirer,* the most ardent of slave journals, declared that "he never gave a vote against the interests of slavery and never uttered a word which could pain the most sensitive Southern heart," a statement that held true to the end of his career.

All eyes turned to the Republican convention. There could be no doubt that the new party would debate every inch of ground with the party then in control of the government, and that the Fillmoreans could only hope to influence the result. Seward was the representative Republican in national life and would have received the nomination had he been willing to contest for it, but he held aloof. The two most promising candidates were Mr. Justice McLean of the Supreme Court, who had been known to be in a receptive mood for more than a quarter of a century, and John C. Fremont of California, the young and picturesque explorer who had planted the American flag on the highest peak of the Rockies, who had been courtmartialed for insubordination and then reinstated by authorities fearful of public opinion, and who had married the daughter of Senator Benton under romantic circumstances which were then fresh in the public mind. Dashing figure as Fremont was, there were many leaders, including Abraham Lincoln, who questioned his solidity. But when could a dignified, elderly, and prosaic Judge, with only ability to recommend him, hope to beat an attractive and well-advertised Lochinvar? Fremont won the nomination handily. Then began a campaign of splendid vigor and exaltation. At first the great issue was the struggle between slavery and freedom in Kansas, and it was a potent issue during the whole campaign, but soon it became known that the South would refuse to acquiesce in the election of a candidate committed to the restriction of slavery. It was early understood that a vote for Buchanan or Fillmore was a vote to avoid the issue of secession. Still, all the votes that went beyond the spirit of compromise and stood for an enlightened patriotism were on one side. It was freedom against bondage; humanity against expediency. "Vote as you pray" came into being as a political watchword. Dr. Rhodes, the chief authority upon that period says truly: "No candidate for President ever had his election urged in words that breathe forth purer aspirations, and more sublime and cogent reasons have never been given for political work." Never in the history of this nation, perhaps of any nation, did so many great moral leaders participate in election activities as in the first two campaigns of the Republican party. Washington Irving, the dean of American letters, early came out for Fremont. So did Emerson, Bryant, and Longfellow. N. P. Willis, then at the age of fifty, declared it to be his purpose to cast his "virgin vote" for the "Pathfinder." Whittier did not hesitate to put his splendid talents to out-and-out partizan use, writing such poems as that containing the words:

> "Sound the trumpet strong and high!
> Country and Liberty!
> Freedom and Victory!
> These words shall be our cry,—
> Fremont and Victory!"

George William Curtis in perhaps the finest partizan oration of American letters declared that the American scholar "to-day must know that Freedom always has its Thermopylae, and that his Thermopylae is called Kansas." Pulpit politics are usually of doubtful taste and value, but it was not so in this campaign. Probably more and more effective election sermons were preached in 1856 than in any other presidential campaign before or since. Altogether it was such a campaign as makes the blood dance to read of it. To have led such a one would have been glory for any man. Fremont will always be a figure of happy memory because of that victorious defeat. Defeat it was, but it was one that gave the Democrats cause to ponder. Buchanan's popular plurality was half a million and Fillmore received nearly 900,000 votes, the great bulk of which would never have gone to Buchanan. Even at this,

Buchanan probably could not have been elected except that he made concessions in his speeches to the spirit of Free Kansas, intimations which he afterwards callously repudiated.

But after all "there is a divinity that shapes our ends, rough-hew them how we will." Although Buchanan will go down to history as perhaps our weakest and least admirable President, he was not obliged to confront secession until after the election of his successor. Fremont, who made a most effective candidate, would not have made an able President. His subsequent career proves this without doubt. The South would have seceded in 1856, just as it did in 1860, had he been elected. It would have been a great misfortune for him to have confronted such a problem. He was not the man to declare, as did he who was to come after him: "We will say to the Southern disunionists, 'we *won't* go out of the Union and you *shan't.'* "

The disinclination of Seward to contest the nomination seems another instance of providential good fortune. If the great Whig leader had made as good a contest as did Fremont in 1856, and there is no reason to doubt he would, nothing could have prevented him from being the nominee in 1860, when he would have been elected and at liberty to put into action that suicidal policy of provoking a foreign war to solidify the nation which he urged upon Lincoln. The election of Buchanan was crippling to his own reputation, but it cleared the way for a man fashioned for the crisis and delayed that crisis till he came.

CHAPTER SIX

THE PRELUDE TO THE TEMPEST

FROM the day of Buchanan's election it was perfectly evident that the most critical contest which the Democratic party had ever faced would occur four years later. Every element of influence that the administration could exert was put forth to perpetuate the Southern and slave-holding wing in power. The President in his inaugural made a most extraordinary announcement. In effect he proclaimed, with a complacency that admitted of no possible question as to the trend of the decision, that the Supreme Court would soon hand down its judgment in the Dred Scott case. That such a statement could be made on a judicial matter by the President was theretofore an unheard of thing and ought to have been impossible. Yet the President spoke truth, and the famous decision was immediately enunciated. A phrase, isolated from its context, was seized upon by opponents of the decision; and it was everywhere stated and believed that Chief Justice Taney had declared in the majority opinion, of which he was the author, that a Negro had no rights which a white man was bound to respect. The Chief Justice, in an historical sketch of the status of the Negro in America, had merely stated that this had been the attitude of the eighteenth century. Nevertheless, another passage of the decision declared the Negro "subordinate and inferior . . . subjugated by the dominant race" and, whether emancipated or not, without "rights or privileges but such as those who held the power and the government might choose to grant them." The Republicans had always denied the right to hold slaves in the territories and the decision nullified this contention.

Stephen A. Douglas, the "Little Giant" from Illinois, had led his party in abandoning the Missouri Compromise, leaving the territories to exercise "popular sovereignty"; and now, against his will, the whole administration began to use its utmost powers to bring Kansas into the Union as a slave state, regardless of the wishes of its population. These were heavy-handed methods indeed. Like all such efforts, they weakened rather than strengthened the Democratic party before the people. There was no attempt at that conciliation of a portion of the opposition which, above all things, keeps a party in power.

Douglas saw this and stood against coercion by Buchanan and his followers. Buchanan retaliated by an effort to discountenance Douglas. So pronounced was this effort that much sympathy went to Douglas from the Republican leaders. They forgot the Missouri Compromise repeal. They forgot that he had stood by without interfering when Preston Brooks had beaten Charles Sumner into insensibility. When he came up for re-election to the Senate, men like Greeley were for at least a temporary alliance with him. Not so with the Republicans of his own state. They had a champion ready to enter the lists.

Abraham Lincoln had been a member of Congress in 1845 and, refusing an appointment as Governor of Oregon at the hands of President Taylor, had retired to the practice of law at the end of his service. Douglas and the repeal of the Compromise had aroused him and brought him back to politics. An anti-Nebraska Whig, he had made common cause with the anti-Nebraska Democrats. Quaint, original, shrewd, profound, he was already acknowledged the ablest man of an able group. In spite of those throughout the country who thought an enthusiastic return of Douglas would be the best rebuke to

Buchanan, this group of Illinois Republicans decided to oppose him. With Lincoln as their candidate, they made a determined campaign. Its great feature was the debate between the candidates. In seven places these champions contested from rough-hewn, outdoor platforms. It was the most direct campaign between two men of which American history takes note.

In Freeport Lincoln, against the sober judgment of his friends, insisted on asking Douglas if the people of a territory could "in any lawful way, against the wish of any citizen of the United States, exclude slavery from its limits" under territorial government. Lincoln's friends saw that an adroit answer would help Douglas. What they did not see—and what Lincoln did see—was that an adroit answer which would meet Douglas's immediate purpose, would stand between the "Little Giant" and the South in the presidential election to come. Lincoln shot his bolt, not to further his own ambition, but to divide the Democracy for the benefit of the next Republican presidential candidate, whoever he might be. At that time it was generally expected that Seward would be the nominee. The utterance of the "Freeport question" was an act of unpretentious heroism, coupled with intense political sagacity. It was typical of Lincoln.

In answer to Lincoln's question Douglas replied, "It matters not which way the Supreme Court may decide . . . slavery cannot exist a day or an hour anywhere unless it is supported by local police regulations." This subtle answer saved his popular sovereignty doctrine, but it tremendously angered the South.

In spite of the feeling of Lincoln's friends that tactics like these would lose him the election, he fought on with courage. He lost, but the laurels were all his. He had worsted Douglas in debate, and he had carried the popular majority. Though no ballots were directly cast for Lincoln or Douglas, the vote for the legislators who were to elect the Senator showed a Republican majority, although the division into districts was such that the Democrats chosen gave that party a slight lead. But Lincoln had achieved his purpose. From the day Douglas flouted the Dred Scott decision his party was divided. Douglas himself led one wing in the Senate. At the head of the other stood a brilliant, fearless, sincere champion of states' rights and slavery. Destined to be the best-hated man of his time, Jefferson Davis had character and honest purpose, was kindly by nature, a gentle master to his slaves, quick to take or give offence, but emphatically a gentleman. As the events of the time recede, men see the logic of both views on the constitutional question of the inter-relation of the states, and this generation need have no hatred for a man—like Davis—carried fearlessly along by the consistency of his beliefs.

The most startling event of this time was not to happen at the polls or in legislative halls, but at Harper's Ferry in Western Virginia. In the border fights of Kansas no fighter had borne a more terrible reputation than John Brown. Half ruffian, half hero, he was always a fanatic. His was one of the most remarkably individual characters in the history of mankind: a mixture of ruthlessness and gentleness, with a directness of thinking and action that admitted of no contradiction. He was as austere as the terrible Puritans of Cromwell's Ironsides and so unswerving from his honest convictions that he himself becomes a standard of comparison. The bloody struggles of Kansas, where he had seen the actions of the border ruffians, had inspired him to bitter reprisals. "An eye for an eye and a tooth for a tooth" had been his inspiration in conducting one of the most cold-blooded massacres conceivable at Pottawatomie. "Without shedding of blood there is no remission of sins" was one of his favorite texts.

This man now conceived the idea of gathering a small expedition, collecting arms and ammunition, settling somewhere in the South, and at the proper time summoning the Negroes to join him and sweep the country, recruiting ever new forces, as he advanced, from among the escaping slaves. It is not remarkable that such a wild scheme should have lodged in his embittered brain. What is remarkable is that this man, by his force of character and enthusiasm, should have been able to impress his point of view upon certain kindly and noble men in the North. He received aid and comfort from such men as Gerritt Smith, Thomas Wentworth Higginson, Dr. Samuel Gridley Howe, Theodore Parker, and George L. Stearns. Frank B. Sanborn, always impetuous and then in the fire of youth, seems to have been his closest Northern friend. With money raised by these men, all of whom, excepting Smith, lived in Massachusetts, Brown hired a farm for himself and his followers near Harper's Ferry. One October night a little posse of fourteen whites and five blacks crossed the Potomac under his lead,—expecting, as he had written to Sanborn, "to effect a bitter conquest, even though it be like the last victory of Samson." A few men, armed and determined, can accomplish a great deal before an outraged community recovers from shock. By midnight Brown was the master of the situation. He held Harper's Ferry and controlled the bridge approaching it. He had taken numerous hostages, including a great grand-nephew of George Washington. But his triumph was short-lived. All the following day desultory fighting went on. By a singular irony, the first to fall at the hands of the raiders was a free Negro, the porter of a train which had been halted at the bridge which Brown held. By night militia organizations had reported, citizens having arms had united in military units, and a company of marines under Robert E. Lee arrived to regain the United States Armory and Arsenal which Brown held. The son of Light Horse Harry was to restore to liberty the scion of the Washingtons. Lee's lieutenant was the dashing "Jeb" Stuart.

The small and hopelessly outnumbered band had retired by

that time into an engine house on the armory grounds where they had been besieged all the afternoon. Brown had lost none of his calm courage, but the ferocity which had distinguished him in Kansas was lacking. He treated his hostages well and prevented his followers from shooting at unarmed men. Some historians think Brown had softened in his nature. It rather seems that his elemental sense of crude justice had a rough logic. He had massacred men on the banks of the Pottawatomie in stern reprisal. There he was an avenging angel, self-appointed. Here he was the aggressor and, righteous as he believed his cause to be, his actions had invited all men's hands against him. He was the same Brown as of old, and his bitter logic actuated him as it had in the past. With one son dead and another dying at his side, he felt the wounded man's pulse' with one hand and used his rifle with the other, giving directions as coolly as any general surveying a great battlefield. At last morning came. Lee called on the little garrison to surrender and was refused. Nothing remained but to take the engine house by storm. With a ladder for a battering ram, the doors were burst open and the marines poured into the little building. Brown was cut down by sabres. Of the original party of nineteen only five were taken prisoners. Four had got away and the rest had been killed. The casualties of those opposing Brown were fourteen, only five of which were fatal.

Virginia and the South were in a panic. Abolition had coined its bitter phrases and its zealous condemnation into lead and steel at last. Southern men had done as bad things in Kansas and had been opposed by equal violence, but all that had been on Northern ground. Now violence had set its foot upon Southern soil. Complicated with this was the fear of a servile insurrection, a terrible possibility. These men had come with Northern support. Who could tell how much else had been secretly arranged or where and when another outbreak would come? This time it had failed, but who could say but the next would be better planned? The whole South called for speedy vengeance on the culprits. States are made up of individuals and all history shows that governments do not rise superior to the impulses of their inhabitants. In this time of stress it was not to be expected that Virginia would act with great restraint.

At least Brown received an orderly and formal trial, fairer, as he said, than he had expected. Had his crime been a foul murder, inspired by hatred or greed, committed with no public purpose, he would not have been hurried to his trial in the way he was. Wounded, he was unable to sit in a chair but lay inside the bar on a cot. He pleaded in vain for a delay on the ground that he was too weak to take part in his defense and that he had been made temporarily deaf by the wounds in his head. This delay was denied him and when his counsel, assigned him by the courts, felt it honorably incumbent upon them to retire from the case, because of a lack of confidence the prisoner had expressed in them, the court gave young Hoyt of Massachusetts, just admitted to the Bar, who had appeared just before as volunteer counsel, only a few hours to familiarize himself with the details of the case and with Virginia law and practice, in spite of his plea for necessary time for preparation. None of these things would have been denied an ordinary malefactor. Yet, when all is said, none of these things would have helped Brown. The facts were incontrovertible. Brown was legally guilty of treason, incitement and murder. The old man expected his fate and exulted in it.

The pure flame of fanatical sacrifice burned in him. He said he was worth more to hang than for any other purpose. His vision on the verge of eternity seemed to penetrate the veil of the future. If Virginia's vision had equalled Brown's, her astute leaders would have declared him insane and sent him to an asylum. Only in that way could they have stifled the cries of lovers of liberty and nullified his influence in death.

She missed her opportunity and gave Brown his. And so, without a tremor, he went quietly and happily to the scaffold, knowing that his death was not to be in vain. John Brown was a violent, honest, misguided man. Virginia allowed him to become a martyr.

Abolition in its most radical form had done its best. It had cast a die. But nothing had been accomplished, except stirring the passions of both sides. The next move must be left to the second line of offense. It must be made at the presidential election of 1860 by the political party of freedom. The impulses of the heart must be guided by the intellect. Still, as this time approached, men could not forget the sacrifice of John Brown and they remembered his words to Senator Mason—"I think, my friend, you are guilty of a great wrong against God and humanity." They remembered his calmness and courage. They forgot the bloodiness of his deeds and saw in him a symbol and a saint.

CHAPTER SEVEN

AND THEN THE DELUGE

NEVER was a year fraught with graver possibilities for
a great nation than the year of 1860, as it dawned on
the United States. The air was heavy with portents. The struggle between slavery and abolition was seething in Congress.
All that the Republican or anti-slavery party demanded was
the restriction to the South of its "peculiar institution," but
the unerring instinct of the slavery men told them that this
demand rested on a deeper and more profound feeling. At this
time, when it came to abstract logic, the South had the better
of the argument. The Southern attitude may have been wrong
but, granting the premises, it was logical and consistent. The
North denied these premises and then failed to reach consistency and logic, for she adopted methods of restriction, not
of suppression. There was where the original Abolitionists
took honest issue with the Republicans. But the Republicans
knew that they did not live in a millennium. They knew where
they fell short of their own best impulses. Their great men
had spoken of a "higher law" than man's, had declared that
"a house divided against itself" could not stand, had called
the conflict between freedom and slavery "irrepressible." In
view of these declarations, the Republicans' position now
seems mere temporizing.

Yet the Republican conscience was good. Confronted by
the limitations of public opinion, they attempted all that could
at that time be done. Their practical leaders would not try to
do more and so left the Abolitionists, in glorified isolation,

pointing to the ultimate. Sixty-eight years later the enlightened conscience vindicates the Republican programme.

When the year 1860 came, it witnessed a bitter struggle over the speakership in the House of Representatives. It was finally settled in February by the election of a Republican. The Senate had three leaders. William Henry Seward of New York led the Republicans. The administration Democrats were headed by Jefferson Davis, and Stephen A. Douglas was the spokesman of a small group of Democrats who had not passed under the Caudine forks of the Buchanan administration. His following on the floor of the Senate was small indeed, but not his following in the party in the North. Douglas was an avowed candidate for the presidency. Could he be nominated without a party split and the election confined to the candidates of but two parties, he must carry, however grudgingly, the Southern states and with his Northern strength might be elected. It is clear now that this was the only way in which it would have been possible to defeat the Republican attack.

The Democratic convention met in Charleston, South Carolina, in the heart of the pro-slavery territory, in April, and the moderate delegates saw little of the far-famed Southern hospitality. There were two distinct factions. The Southern delegates were pretty solidly aligned with Davis, not necessarily as a candidate but as a leader. The spirit of the North was strongly with Douglas, but he had the administration against him and it had made some inroads in his strength. Still he had the majority of the delegates. But he did not have a majority of the states, the Buchanan strength having gained a majority of delegates both in California and Oregon. As all committees in national political conventions are composed of a representative from each state, this was an important matter. The committee on permanent organization presented Caleb Cushing of Newburyport, one of Davis's chief Northern supporters, as presiding officer, and unwilling to disturb any possible harmony, the Douglas majority permitted his election. More serious was the question of the platform.

The committee was frankly Douglas and anti-Douglas, with the exception of a Massachusetts delegate, Benjamin Franklin Butler, militia general, lawyer and mill owner, who, although he was instructed for Douglas, "flocked by himself," and on the question of nomination voted thirty-seven times for Jefferson Davis, with whom his relations were later to become somewhat strained. This committee for five days tried to bring in a platform that would be satisfactory to all the delegates. There are times when all the subtleties of statecraft fail, when situations take control of men and compromise is futile. Such a time had arrived and, after a wrangle lasting five days, both factions presented their platforms to the convention, while Butler asked that it merely affirm the resolutions of four years before. The debate was stormy and thrilling. The platform of the Douglas minority of the committee was adopted by the Douglas majority of the convention. Then came what all had feared and none had the greatness to prevent, a bolt. The seed which the awkward Illinois lawyer had planted at Freeport two years before had borne fruit. The great majority of the Southern delegates, who from the start had meant to rule or ruin, withdrew from the convention.

The remaining delegates determined by resolution that two-thirds of the full convention—two hundred and two votes—should be necessary to nominate. Douglas led on every ballot, but his highest vote was only one hundred and fifty-two and a half. Baffled and discouraged, but still hoping that in some way harmony might be reached, the convention adjourned on May 3 to meet in Baltimore on the 18th of the following month.

That this hope was a vain one and that this was realized by many intelligent men is shown by the assembling six days later in Baltimore of the convention of the Constitutional Union party. The men who formed this party, which elected its delegates long before the Charleston split became an accomplished fact, saw clearly that the Democratic party was to be hopelessly divided. They also felt sure, from the rumblings which had been so distinct four years before, that the election of a Republican would be the prelude to secession and civil war. Composed largely of old line Whigs reinforced by some members of the American party who had generally been Whigs in an earlier day, they met for no other purpose than to save the Union. The platform they adopted contained only one resolution and that, with a little more elaboration, refused to recognize any principle beyond—"the Constitution of the country, the Union of the states and the enforcement of the laws." It was a convention of able, patriotic and deeply concerned men. On the second ballot it nominated John Bell of Tennessee for President over the sturdy and picturesque Sam Houston, and then jointed Edward Everett to the ticket. This was sometimes called the Kangaroo ticket, because its chief strength was said to be in the tail. This was unjust to Bell, who had been speaker of the national House and with Hugh L. White had carried on the anti-Democratic leadership in Tennessee and who, despite the strength of Jackson, had not lost the state at a presidential election since he first opposed Old Hickory.

There was nothing lugubrious about the next convention to be held. A Republican victory was in the air when on May 16, in a "wigwam" especially built for it, the National Republican Convention met in Chicago. From all over the country there poured into Chicago enthusiastic members of the young party bent on declaring principles and nominating candidates which would turn the nation's face toward the sun. With them the words of Paul, "Old things have passed away. Behold all things are become new," might have been used for a battle cry.

From Massachusetts came the polished George Ashmun and George S. Boutwell, the ex-governor, who had begun his political life in the Democratic party and who was destined to return to it more than thirty-five years later, on the issue of Imperialism. There was also a thick-set, curly haired man from Hingham, John A. Andrew, destined to become one of a coterie of great war governors. New York sent its greatest political manager, Thurlow Weed, the thin, sharp-featured, clear-headed Evarts, destined to take part in more legal proceedings of national and international importance than any American before or since his day, and George William Curtis, editor and idealist. In the Pennsylvania section sat David Wilmot, famed for the Wilmot proviso. With him came Thaddeus Stevens, lame, frail, of scintillating mind and cynical tongue. Ohio sent the greatest spellbinder of his day, the eloquent and humorous Tom Corwin, and that sturdy old-time abolitionist, the venerable Joshua R. Giddings. As a substitute, on an Oregon credential, with carte blanche to do his worst to Weed and Seward, his old allies, now *persona non grata,* sat Horace Greeley, the great editor who had done so much to make the party. Wisconsin sent the tall, angular Schurz, on the threshold of a remarkable career and even then counted among the party notables. Gideon Welles represented Connecticut. Francis P. Blair, the friend of Jackson, and his two sons were present representing Missouri and Maryland, and were given especial ovations. The state in which the convention was held was represented by an aggressive and remarkable body of men. At the head was David Davis, a vigorous personality, and later himself a presidential aspirant. John M. Palmer, just beginning a career destined to be notable in war and peace, was also a delegate. Attached to this delegation was a young, ardent lawyer with a distinct talent for military organization and discipline, E. E. Ellsworth, within the year to lead the Fire Zouaves of New York into Alexandria and to be murdered by a civilian while hauling down the flag of the Confederacy. From Maine, as an observer, came a young editor who many months before had published the prophecy that Douglas would defeat Lincoln for Senator, but that in 1860 Lincoln would defeat Douglas for President. He was at the threshold of a stormy and notable career and he will appear again in these pages, for he was James G. Blaine.

For candidates, it was Seward against the field. Seward was the eminent man of the party beyond a doubt, but, being the chief leader, he had also become the chief target. The rank and file of the party expected that his nomination was certain, but it became apparent to the delegates that he would be beaten if those opposed to him united on one of the other candidates. Prominent among these was Salmon P. Chase, able and honest but avidly ambitious and a little vain, next to Seward the chief Republican leader in the Senate. Various others had strong local backing and the supporters of each hoped their man would finally be turned to by a majority of the convention. These included Edward Bates of Missouri, Simon Cameron of Pennsylvania, Jacob Collamer of Vermont, and William L. Dayton of New Jersey, who had occupied second place on the Fremont ticket.

There was another candidate.

Not long after the election of Douglas to the Senate in 1858, Illinois leaders began to agitate for the nomination of Lincoln. At first Lincoln discouraged this and said he thought himself unfitted for the presidency. Probably no man ever occupied that office, with two possible and recent exceptions, who had not that misgiving at some time or another. These exceptions, of course, are Roosevelt and Woodrow Wilson. Washington had publicly expressed the same feeling when he accepted command of the continental army. Shortly after the senatorial campaign against Douglas, Lincoln was invited to make an address in New York. He went east, after the most careful preparation he had ever made for a similar effort, and made what is known as the Cooper Union speech. No address on the crisis of the times was clearer, better argued, or better tempered. It made a profound impression, which was enhanced by some speeches made in New England. When he returned to Springfield he found himself a full-fledged presidential possibility. Accepting the situation, he did what he could without loss of dignity to further his campaign. The effort of the inconsequential Drinkwater in his totally inadequate play to picture Lincoln reluctant while the convention was in session, may in its acceptance, by those who never bother to read deeply, turn this playwriting foreigner into as irresponsible and dangerous a litterateur as was Parson Weems. Therefore great stress ought to be laid on the fact that Lincoln was not only to prove himself a transcendent statesman, but that he was one of the keenest and subtlest politicians America ever produced. Lincoln sought the presidency and that seeking was ennobled by the sacrifices he had made for the great cause for which he stood. Many times he had yielded to others for the greater good and so, if circumstances demanded it, he could expect others to yield to him. No one can read the histories of that time and believe Lincoln was for long either doubtful or reluctant. He said that it would not hurt him to lose the nomination but that it would be injurious to lose the substantial support of his own state and wrote to Judd to ask, "Can you help me a little in this matter at your end of the vineyard?" It is on record that he offered to pay a hundred dollars towards defraying the expenses of a Kansas supporter at Chicago. When, less than a fortnight before the national convention, the Illinois convention met in Decatur, Lincoln's kinsman, John Hanks, and a neighbor bore down the aisle, amid the greatest enthusiasm, two rails with a sign attached showing that they were part of a lot cut by Lincoln and Hanks in the pioneer days at Sangamon Bottom. The rails were taken to Chicago and exhibited at the Illinois headquarters. This gave him the nickname of railsplitter, just as the fact that for years after a business failure he had struggled to pay moral obligations from which the law had freed him made his supporters refer to him as Honest Abe.

There was a picturesque and excitable throng in Chicago during the convention. The New Yorkers led in the noise and enthusiasm. Apparently the Seward men had unlimited money at their command, and they were not all prohibitionists. They brought a band and hundreds of supporters under command of a local prize fighter, Tom Heyer, to march and countermarch, to shout and serenade. So much of this prepared enthusiasm disgusted Schurz, although he was a Seward man, and it must have been embarrassing to Evarts and Curtis. But they were in a Lincoln stronghold and it was easy for the Illinois men to assemble crowds just as enthusiastic and quite as noisy.

When the convention was called to order, the venerable Wilmot was made temporary chairman and, after the organizing of the committees, the courtly George Ashmun was made permanent president. The platform declared in no uncertain sound for the restriction of slavery. When the question of its adoption was before the convention, the venerable and leonine Giddings moved to add a reference to the Declaration of Independence, but the delegates were impatient and voted it down. The picture of dejection, the old fighter started to withdraw from the convention, but later, with beautiful phrase and faultless oratory, George William Curtis, the incarnation of cultured enthusiasm and inspired earnestness, pleaded with the convention not to allow itself to go before the country as being afraid to reaffirm that immortal document. In a whirlwind of enthusiasm the motion was adopted and Ohio's grand old man returned to his seat the picture of happiness.

At the end of the second day it was certain that balloting would begin on the morrow. There were conferences of delegates until the early morning. To elect a Republican President

71

it would be necessary to carry the Fremont states of four years previous and also Pennsylvania, Indiana and Illinois. It was not quite sure that the Democracy would stay divided, and if it did no one could then tell what the proportion of the two divisions would be. The delegates from these three states believed that Seward would not be able to carry them. They honored Seward but they wished to present a candidate who could be elected. At these conferences Davis and Judd represented Lincoln. They had the assurance in Lincoln's own hand that he endorsed Seward's "Irrepressible Conflict" speech, but that he demurred at the suggestion contained in the "higher law" assertion. They had been instructed by their candidate to make no contracts that would bind him, but in the stress of circumstances and with no opportunity to consult him, it afterwards became evident that they disregarded these instructions. Next morning it was clearly evident that, when the preliminary skirmishing was over, the contest would be between Seward and Lincoln.

Tom Heyer and his cohorts marched up and down the streets of Chicago in the interest of their candidate while the convention was assembling. Probably the inhabitants thought it was all over, for no Lincoln demonstrations were carried on in the streets. But the Lincoln men had played a trick on the redoubtable Heyer and had gone directly to the Wigwam, filling practically all the vacant space. When the Seward people arrived hardly any of their number but the accredited delegates could obtain admission. In the gallery sat the leather-lunged "Doc" Ames, a Democrat impressed for the purpose, who led the Lincoln ovations at signals given him by Burton Cook from his seat upon the platform.

The clergyman who made the opening prayer used these prophetic words: "We entreat Thee that at some future but not distant day the evil which now invests the body politic shall not only have been arrested in its progress, but wholly eradicated from the system. And may the pen of the historian trace an intimate connection between that glorious consummation and the transactions of this convention." This is perhaps the most completely answered prayer on record in modern times.

The candidates were named from their delegations without speeches, Evarts naming Seward, and Judd, Lincoln. Then the balloting commenced. The states were not called by alphabet but geographically. New England was supposed to be Seward territory, but its announcement wet blanketed the Seward enthusiasm, for he received only thirty-two votes, while out of the antagonistic forty-nine, Lincoln received nineteen. Seward led at the end of the ballot with a hundred and seventeen and a half. The absence of Seward votes from the doubtful states was ominous. Lincoln had been expected to receive a hundred on this ballot; he got two more. The complimentary votes out of the way, the swing now began to the two leaders. Seward gained eleven, Lincoln gained seventy-nine and was now within three and a half votes of the leader and fifty-two votes short of the nomination. On the third ballot Seward fell back four votes and Lincoln's total was two hundred and thirty-one and a half. Two hundred and thirty-three were needed to nominate, and Carter, the chairman of the Ohio delegation, immediately announced a change of four votes from Chase to Lincoln. Bedlam broke loose!—The western prairies were to furnish the country its first President dedicated to freedom. As the delegates left the hall, after naming Hannibal Hamlin of Maine as Lincoln's associate, Evarts remarked dryly to Curtis, "Well, at least we saved the Declaration of Independence."

What of these two candidates, one successful, one defeated? They both received the returns in their home towns. Lincoln, as the trend to him became certain, left his office to tell the news to "the little woman down the street." Seward, when his heart-broken friends could find no one to write the usual com-

73

plimentary editorial for the Republican newspaper of the town, smilingly took pen and paper and wrote it himself. Heroes both!

The Democratic convention reconvened in gloom. Already once divided, it suffered further disintegration, and its chairman, Caleb Cushing, joined the second revolt. Finally Douglas was nominated by resolution, and when Fitzpatrick, the original nominee for Vice President, withdrew, Herschel V. Johnson was named for that office by the national committee. The bolting, or so-called Southern, wing nominated John C. Breckinridge of Kentucky, then Vice President, and Joseph Lane of Oregon.

All four parties entered manfully upon the struggle but the result was evident from the first. Lincoln did not leave Springfield, nor did he make campaign speeches, though Schurz records that when he spoke there, Lincoln, clad in his old high hat and a linen duster, marched with him to the hall and sat on the front bench listening to and applauding the speech. Thousands of young men all over the North banded themselves into battalions of campaign Lincoln Wide Awakes, perhaps with a premonition that they would do more serious marching ere long.

As the campaign progressed, the result, if all the candidates stayed in, was seen to be so certain that Jefferson Davis made an effort to get Bell, Breckinridge, and Douglas to agree to withdraw, that some other more promising candidate might be substituted. Douglas refused. He said it was now too late, that he could not hold his supporters for another, that compromise would be deemed surrender to slavery, and that his followers would go to Lincoln. Douglas deserves a word. He was a brilliant, eloquent, rough-and-tumble fighter, not too temperate either in speech or habit and with a conscience that was sluggish but determined. It did not trouble him to help set aside the Missouri Compromise but once his party went beyond what sluggish conscience would permit he could not be moved to go with it. He was destined to exercise great influence for the Union in the few stormy months of life which were left him, in which he showed himself a great patriot.

Lincoln was elected. Breckinridge carried eleven states and Douglas only one, though he picked up a minority of New Jersey's electoral vote through an anti-Lincoln fusion that refused to fuse. However, he came in second on the popular vote, in perhaps the last election when the popular vote has been a free one in every state.

So the chapter was written. The blood-stained sequel was its bitter consequence. With the South in active secession, Lincoln after a pathetic and affecting farewell speech to his neighbors, most of whom he was destined never to see again, left Springfield for Washington on his fifty-second birthday. It was arranged that he was to make speeches in a number of cities en route. Finally he entered Washington secretly, having been reluctantly convinced that he should do this to avoid lurking assassination in Baltimore. Among the speeches which he made en route was one at a flag raising at Independence Hall in Philadelphia, pregnant with great thoughts and a touch of prophecy, and in which he proclaimed a faith that he was "willing to live by, and, if it be the pleasure of Almighty God, die by." And with these words he went his way to fulfill his destiny and that of the Republic.

CHAPTER EIGHT

THE GREAT DECISION

ON a November day in 1863 a distinguished party drove from the White House in Washington to the Baltimore and Ohio station. In the first carriage sat the President of the United States. As it turned a corner the cavalcade attracted the attention of a short, spare man, who made practical use of a stout cane to help him in his progress, for he had a club foot. There were bitter lines about his mouth and a grim humor on his face. This was Thaddeus Stevens, the leader of the President's party in the lower house of Congress, where it was then in a majority. Realizing that the party was en route for Gettysburg to dedicate the National Cemetery, he turned to his companion and in a jesting tone which did not disguise its acidity and conviction, cried out: "Let the dead bury the dead!" Thus was indicated by one of the party leaders the prospects of Abraham Lincoln in the election a year ahead.

Ever since Lincoln's first inauguration he had been the butt of the humorous and the sophisticated. On his way to Washington he had been caricatured by *Harper's Weekly* as a clown and a drunkard. His single refuge in his country's distresses, his sense of humor, was put down to be unfeeling clownery. This abuse continued through his life. He never lived to see it subside. It did not greatly trouble him. He was conscious of certain qualities which little men continuously misunderstood. He knew he lacked social graces and did not grieve over criticism. And now this much derided personality must again con-

76

front the hard test of the ballot box and in days more critical than any President had ever faced before.

To give an absolutely adequate picture of the election of 1864, a writer should narrate substantially the history of the Civil War. The failures and successes of the Northern arms; the support and lack of support given by the government; the dreary monotony of the struggle, under which many good and, as they believed, patriotic men grew weary; the relations of other nations to the United States, and their secret anxiety to recognize the Confederacy at the first safe opportunity; the draft; the activities of the enemies of the Union within the nation and the resulting extra-judicial acts which even suspended the writ of habeas corpus—all these had a distinct influence on the question of the President's re-election or defeat.

In the weary days at the White House Lincoln must have felt that he satisfied nobody. There was no question but that the liberty loving radicals, "judging each step as though the way were plain," thought him "slothful in well doing," and they lost no opportunity to bring their belief to his attention. On the other hand, men in Maryland, West Virginia, Kentucky and Missouri, the border states which, from military and diplomatic exigencies alike, the Union could not afford to add to its enemies, were constantly endeavoring to urge their conservatism upon him.

The high water mark of the Rebellion had been reached at Gettysburg and that victory, with that at Vicksburg, had greatly increased the enthusiasm and courage of the North. But the steady grind which followed, the monotony of the news of battles and the recurring lists of casualties which succeeded these victories, led to another period of depression. It was as if the cup of victory, almost at the lips, had been snatched away. Most of the so-called radicals were impatient men and found it difficult personally to understand Lincoln, who in the midst of great events and distressing disasters could outwardly solace himself with the rough humors of Artemus Ward and Petroleum V. Nasby.

There was the self-important Chase, the Secretary of the Treasury, who with the vital but too little valued aid of Jay Cooke had kept the nation solvent in this perilous hour. He was pure, but one of the vainest and most ambitious of statesmen. This vanity led him into secret but patent intrigue to undermine his chief. Then came Cold Harbor and the Wilderness. The longing for peace and the specious cry that it was the governments at Washington and Richmond which alone were keeping the war-worn people of the sections apart became almost irresistible. The hammering policy of Grant with its tremendous losses was the right policy to pursue from a military point of view, but it was a perilous thing for a political administration to sustain at a time when it was seeking re-election. Lincoln never wavered in his duty, though he is known to have believed at times that he was contributing to his political undoing.

The opposition came from two powerful but diametrically opposed groups. One was composed of radicals, the other of Copperheads. It was a strange thing to view the possibility of Lincoln's defeat ripening into probability in the summer of 1864, the result of opposition of men like Stevens and Andrew on one side and Vallandigham and Voorhees on the other. He was apparently to fall between two stools. Each of these opposite elements crystallized around a military figure. The discontented radicals rallied to Fremont, the nominee of eight years previous. He had received a major general's commission and shown himself vain and pompous and without real military ability. He had, however, taken an unauthorized attitude toward the slave question in the district he commanded and thus attracted the favorable attention of the violent abolitionists, while Lincoln, who could not allow him to usurp presidential functions and so reversed his acts, suffered correspondingly in their esteem.

The other element of opposition which controlled the Democratic party turned to McClellan. Here was a general to whom the government owed much and whom Lincoln had removed from his command. With many good qualities he was imperious, conceited above most conceited men, and with many petty traits of character. He was president of the railroad in Illinois over which Douglas and Lincoln had had to travel in the days of their famous senatorial canvass, when Douglas, whom McClellan supported, traveled like an operatic prima donna, though Lincoln could get no favors whatever, even having at times to travel in the caboose of a slow freight to reach engagements to which Douglas was carried by special train. Soon after the war began it became evident that McClellan was the man for the immediate hour. To his wonderful organizing ability was owed that fighting machine, the Army of the Potomac. That, after Bull Run, he welded the disorganized and quite generally undisciplined units which had hurried to the defence of the Union into an efficient military organization should never be forgotten. Soon it became a question whether McClellan was the man to shoot the bolt which he had forged. He was obsessed with his own idea of military science and was cautious, perhaps timid, to a fault. He always considered his disadvantages, the condition of men, of horses, or commissariat, of the weather, of the terrain, and he never gave adequate consideration to similar handicaps affecting the enemy. He magnified their numbers and minimized his own. It is said that Lee, on the eve of a great battle when his council of war pointed to the fact that the Union forces greatly outnumbered his, remarked, "But you forget. McClellan will be there." This undervaluation of his resources was the general's great military fault, for when engaged he fought his battles intelligently and gallantly.

His attitude toward others was arrogant. Toward Lincoln it was abominable. On one occasion when the army was near the capital and McClellan was making his headquarters at his house in Washington, Lincoln, accompanied by Seward, called to discuss the situation. Not finding the general he waited in an ante-room. In an hour McClellan strode by and mounted the stairs and when, after another wait, Lincoln made inquiries, he was told that McClellan had retired and could not be disturbed. Any European officer would have been cashiered next day, but when Lincoln's enraged friends fulminated at this and similar slights, he responded that if McClellan would win victories he would be willing to hold his horse. In his relations with McClellan he showed impatience but once. In an answer to McClellan's excuse for his inactivity, because his cavalry horses were fatigued, he sent him a despatch requesting information as to what the Army of the Potomac had done in the previous fortnight which could fatigue anybody or anything.

When all is said, it is probable that the Union cause could not have survived in the early days of the Rebellion without a McClellan! It is almost equally certain that in its latter days it could not have survived with him. Although Lincoln had to make several unhappy experiments in finding a successor, history justifies his removal of the general when, after Antietam, Lee out-maneuvered him and escaped without molestation. McClellan was aggrieved. He was a Democrat and his party assumed to believe, and perhaps did believe, that he had been hampered whereas a Republican would have been encouraged and assisted. This gave him a great strength in his party. He had been zealously considerate of the welfare of his men and "Little Mac", as they called him in terms of affectionate endearment, had a warm spot in their hearts and consequently in the hearts of their folks "back home." That he would be the strongest man his party could present was early foreseen.

Although Lincoln refused to interfere with Chase either in

his cabinet office or his equivocal semi-candidacy, saying concerning the presidency, "I hope we shall never have a worse man," the candidacy of the Ohioan soon flickered and went out in spite of a circular issued in his behalf by Senator Pomeroy of Kansas. The Pomeroy circular brought matters to a head and the action of the Union members of the legislature of Chase's state of Ohio put the final quietus on the movement and left the Secretary in an uncomfortable and somewhat ridiculous position in the cabinet of the chief whom he had endeavored to undermine.

A mass convention of anti-slavery, anti-Lincoln radicals, comprising over three hundred malcontents, met at Cleveland early in June to nominate Fremont. Those powerful elements which disliked Lincoln and were represented by Stevens, Wade, Winter Davis, Andrew and similar leaders, kept out of the movement, believing that different tactics might force Lincoln to withdraw if nominated and realizing that affiliation with this motley group would be a waste of power.

A week later the Republican convention, which had been called as a Union body, renominated Lincoln, who received every vote but those of the Missouri delegates, who, under instructions, and with entire good feeling toward the predestined nominee, cast complimentary votes for Grant. The convention supported a vigorous prosecution of the war. In its desire to compliment the Southern and border loyalists it performed an act of far-reaching consequence when it abandoned Vice President Hamlin and nominated in his place Andrew Johnson of Tennessee, rough-fibered, patriotic, coarse and stubborn.

At this time things began to look more propitious for the Union party, and the Democrats, who had expected to celebrate the Fourth of July by nominating the "next President," postponed their convention till the last of August, in the Micawber-like hope that something might turn up which would be favorable to their ambitions. They were wise in this, for another slump in public confidence soon set in. When the Republican National Committee met in New York it met in gloom. Lincoln himself at a later date spoke of this period as a time when "we had no adversary and seemed to have no friends." The last complication for which Chase could be responsible occurred when the President, probably greatly to his Secretary's astonishment, accepted one of the pique-laden resignations which Chase was in the habit of tendering when he met with any executive opposition.

On August 12, Thurlow Weed, generally an expert in feeling the public pulse, told Lincoln that his defeat was inevitable. The radicals who were ostensibly with the party seriously proposed that Lincoln leave the ticket and that a compromise candidate be selected.

It would make a splendid picture to draw Lincoln as never losing his high faith in the success of his cause, but it would not be a true one. There is a true picture and an even finer one. Six days before the Democratic convention, at a cabinet meeting, the President produced a sealed paper and asked each member to write his signature across it. He then put it in his desk. Not until after the election did any man know what he had written. The paper contained these words:

"This morning, as for several days past, it seems exceedingly probable that this Administration will not be re-elected. Then it will be my duty to so co-operate with the President-elect as to save the Union between the election and the inauguration; as he will have secured his election on such ground that he cannot possibly save it afterwards."

In all the history of human leadership is there anything finer than this? Here we see perhaps the greatest act of unselfish statesmanship in a great life, which had included the yielding of the Illinois senatorship to Trumbull in 1855, the sacrifice entailed by the Freeport question, and many other acts of pure patriotic sacrifice. Abraham Lincoln, in the midst of his Gethsemane, abused and belittled, rising above pettiness, forgetting self but not forgetting the weakness of human nature, put his duty into writing so that after the bitterness of defeat, his lacerated heart might not lead him into resentments and away from the path which he then so plainly visualized.

When the Democratic convention met it did its best to upset its own "apple cart". It nominated McClellan, but its resolutions were controlled by the Copperheads. Although Vallandigham lost the election to the chairmanship of the committee on platform, he dictated the principal plank, which declared, in effect, that the war was a failure. There could be no doubt that either Lincoln or McClellan must be elected and Fremont could not decently take to himself votes which might be used to defeat such a declaration as this and he withdrew though with ungracious references to Lincoln.

No candidate was ever more abused than was Lincoln in this campaign. The New York *World* called the administration ignorant, incompetent and corrupt, and said, with an abominable viciousness that is luckily forgotten except by students, that the claim of Lincoln's personal honesty would not bear examination. Daniel W. Voorhees, "the tall sycamore of the Wabash," on the floor of Congress gave voice to this pure gem: "Genghis Khan and Tamerlane, preserved by the pen of the historian for universal execration, found no pursuit so pleasant as calling for more men, more men, more men for the harvest of death, and, like our present Executive, snuffing with jests and ribaldry the warm taint of blood upon every gale."

At last the situation cleared. Events not speeches were to dictate the result of this election. The stars in their courses fought against McClellan. Sherman captured Atlanta. Sheridan, resolute, dashing, picturesque, and a thorough and accomplished tactician, made his great campaign in the Shenandoah.

To the cry from the Democratic platform that the war was a failure came the deep tones of cannon and the sharp staccato of musketry. The policy of Grant had begun to justify itself. The crumbling of the Confederacy had begun. The war was *not* a failure. The administration had justified itself and just in time. Lincoln's re-election was triumphant. Above all, the vote of the soldiers, whose love for "Little Mac" had been so great a factor in his candidacy, and which by special enactment was taken in the field, was overwhelmingly for Father Abraham.

And so by the staunchness of the gentle and inflexible President, by the efforts of hundreds of thousands of wise and patriotic voters, and at last by the votes of the wavering balance of power impelled by Grant and Farragut, Sherman and Sheridan, the American people made the greatest decision in all their history, that slavery should go down in ruin and that the American Union should be maintained.

CHAPTER NINE

ANYTHING TO BEAT GRANT

WE have seen how the Republic in the past has regarded the men who have served her on the battlefield. Her first President was her first great commander. Jackson, Harrison, Taylor, were all eminent soldiers. Even Pierce was a Mexican War general, though without important military reputation. When, after the bitter struggles of the Johnson administration, the time for the presidential election approached, there was one name which transcended all others. From that April day when, in McLean's plain brick house at Appomattox, he accepted the surrender of Robert E. Lee, General Grant had been the favorite figure and the predestined choice. He could no doubt have had either nomination. He had no strong political affiliations previous to the war. He supported Buchanan in 1856 because he distrusted Fremont, and had he voted in 1860 it would have been for Douglas, but these were personal rather than partizan choices. Grant had quarreled with President Johnson and naturally was in sympathy with the Republican leaders of that day. He therefore stood for the Republican nomination and there were none to say him nay. After a wearisome convention, the Democratic party drafted, apparently against his will, Horatio Seymour of New York. Grant was elected, but although he received two hundred and fourteen electoral votes to eighty for Seymour, he received only three hundred thousand majority in a popular vote of five million, seven hundred thousand.

It was easy to see that the new President was not trained

85

in statecraft. No one today doubts Grant's honesty, but few even of his greatest admirers would claim that his administration was not sadly marred by his lack of political acumen, by his inability to deal skillfully with honorable opposition, by his disposition to look on his office as a personal reward for his military· achievements and by his reliance on bad men rather than good men to guide him. He showed his lack of grasp immediately on taking office. He appointed Alexander T. Stewart, the New York merchant prince, Secretary of the Treasury, and, on finding that the original act establishing the department forbade one "engaged in trade" to hold this office, he nonchalantly sent a message to Congress asking it to "suspend" the law for Mr. Stewart's benefit. He belittled the Secretaryship of State by giving it to Elihu B. Washburne as a plaything for a few weeks before making a serious appointment, in order that Washburne might carry the prestige of that office to France, where he was finally sent as minister. He saw no difference between his relations as a general with his military subordinates and as a President with his civil subordinates and tried to get rid of a territorial judge, whom the territorial governor did not like, because, as he said, "The Governor is entitled to have control of his staff." He once sent for Senator Schurz and, after finding he could not secure his vote on the important San Domingo treaty, asked him, with quite as much earnestness, to vote for the confirmation of a Mr. Jones, whom he had appointed to a foreign mission. On investigation it was found that this appointee was—as Senator Morton put it—"about the most elegant gentleman that ever presided over a livery stable." After his removal of Motley, he appointed as minister to England General Schenck, a gentleman who became known as the exploiter of the Emma mine and as an authority on draw poker. He looked out for his family and that of his wife and, according to Sumner, had forty-two such relatives in the public service, including his brother-in-law, who received a foreign mission. He accepted gifts as if he were an Eastern potentate receiving tribute. It was said that he knew exactly the amount of the money grants made to Wellington after Waterloo and the inference is that he considered his position, emoluments and perquisites in the light of a military reward.

There is no doubt that Grant admired, consorted with and envied rich men. His disastrous financial career in New York during his last years proves that, and his cordiality at this time toward characters like Jim Fiske and Jay Gould was unfortunate. He was close to two political adventurers, Babcock and Belknap, who held high office under him, the one his private secretary, the other Secretary of War. The members of the Senate who were the closest to him were of the most "practical" type, Carpenter, Conkling, Morton, Chandler, Logan, while the redoubtable Ben Butler was undoubtedly more influential than any other member of the lower house.

Grant was neither a bad man nor a weak one, but he had a peculiar conception of his functions and a tenacious confidence in his friends, good or bad. Not all his familiars were his friends in this sense, and Grant and Boutwell, his Secretary of the Treasury, took such action to end the Black Friday panic as made Fiske understand that a sword had been thrust through his schemes.

The effort which Grant made to annex San Domingo was frustrated by the ablest and most patriotic men in Congress, but Grant never forgave them, especially Sumner, who led the opposition. Here were two men between whom in the nature of things sympathetic understanding was impossible, and through most of Grant's first administration they faced each other in mutual contempt and scorn. Engineered by Conkling and his machine, the demotion of Sumner from his leadership of the Senate Committee on Foreign Relations was accomplished. This caused great feeling, as had the removal of

Sumner's friend Motley from the position of minister to England. Although there may have been good cause for this move, it synchronized significantly with Sumner's stand on San Domingo.

Above all, Grant seemed to many grave and honorable leaders of his own party unfitted for the presidency because of the rapacious and unbridled horde that surrounded him.

One great accomplishment of his administration cannot be overlooked. This was the settlement of the "Alabama claims". Grant's point of view and that of his Secretary of State, Hamilton Fish, looking toward a peaceable adjustment, as distinguished from the more truculent attitude of Sumner, was admirable, and the final award became the greatest achievement of his administration. But the man to whom the greatest honors of the arbitration fell, Charles Francis Adams, was ready to oppose Grant for the presidency.

During the second half of this administration the opposition to Grant within his own party began to crystallize. The organized element, typically represented by Roscoe Conkling, vainly cracked the party whip. Carl Schurz replied, "I stand in the Republican party as an independent man." The term Liberal Republican began to be applied to the congressional coterie that stood apart from Conkling in the Senate and Butler in the House. While the quarrel between Grant and Sumner was terribly bitter and they were not on speaking terms, the Massachusetts senator was not in opposition on Grant's Southern policies and was not, in its early days, absolutely affiliated with the anti-Grant movement. The senatorial group was small and consisted of Schurz, Trumbull of Illinois, Ferry of Connecticut and Tipton of Nebraska, all vigorous, enlightened men. They were greatly re-enforced by journalistic allies. The most formidable Republican newspaper had for many years been the *New York Tribune*. Next in influence, perhaps, was the *Springfield Republican*. Then came the *Boston Journal*, the

Chicago Tribune and the *Cincinnati Commercial*. Every one of these papers, except the *Boston Journal,* unhesitatingly joined the attack on the hungry horde, who, misusing the confidence of their unseeing chief, were fastening themselves on a great party and on the nation itself. Toward the end of 1871 it became evident that the party could not at that moment be regenerated from within. Schurz and the others conceived the idea that, if at a Liberal Republican convention a proper candidate could be nominated the Democratic party would be forced to accept the nominee and thus the country would be purged of a menace. As the campaign progressed this seemed increasingly feasible. A large element of tariff reformers, whose affiliations on other matters were with the Republicans, and who, like the originators of the movement, were opposed to the Grant administration, made common cause. The convention met in Cincinnati on May 1, 1872. The chief candidates were Charles Francis Adams, Lyman Trumbull, Horace Greeley and David Davis. Davis had already been nominated by a labor reform convention, a nomination which he had neither declined nor accepted, but kept in cold storage to influence the delegates at Cincinnati. Both he and Greeley were in active quest of the nomination and in some ways were the least in sympathy with the far-reaching ideals of those who had organized the movement. Their only deep concern was epitomized in the phrase—"Anything to beat Grant!"

A dinner party of eminent editors met at the house of Murat Halsted of the *Cincinnati Commercial.* Bowles of the *Springfield Republican* was there, so were Watterson, Horace White and Whitelaw Reid of the *Louisville Courier-Journal,* the *Chicago* and *New York Tribunes.* They determined to refuse to support Davis should he be nominated. With the exception of Reid, they scouted the possibility of Greeley's success. They let their action concerning Davis be known and thus put him out of the running.

89

As was fitting for candidates whose fortunes were to go before a gathering composed of the type of men that were expected to control the convention, Adams and Trumbull held aloof from active campaigning. Another candidate, supposed to be merely a "favorite son" was B. Gratz Brown of Missouri.

No convention called in so high a spirit as that of the Liberal Republicans ever came to so inglorious an end. Schurz, the permanent presiding officer, struck a noble keynote in his speech. But, unfortunately, as is always the case, men no better but less fortunate than the worst elements of a party against which a protest is being made, men who cannot get the patronage away from spoilsmen no worse than they would be, attached themselves to this movement from motives no more exalted than those which kept the prosperous henchmen in enthusiastic support of the old régime. These men had no interest in tariff reform, no desire to apply the principles of civil service. To them Greeley, the fighter of the old régime, with no new-fangled administrative ideas, was the most attractive candidate. With this element Brown was in entire sympathy. Though he and Schurz represented Missouri, they were mutually antagonistic, and the fact that Schurz was for Adams was enough for Brown. He determined to defeat Schurz and hastened to the convention. The first ballot gave Adams two hundred and three votes, and Greeley—who was not looked upon seriously as a candidate by the sober element —ran second, fifty-six votes behind Adams. Brown was fourth, with ninety-five, a little behind Trumbull and a little ahead of Davis. After this ballot was announced, Brown mounted the platform, withdrew his name and urged the nomination of Greeley. On the sixth ballot Greeley was nominated and Brown was quickly added to the ticket in the second place. When the convention adjourned the reformers were in a daze. Rhodes says in his history—"Greeley's was a preposterous nomination. Thoroughly honest himself, he had nevertheless been long associated with the worst set of politicians in the State of New York outside the Tammany ring." Greeley was an ardent high protectionist and held the tariff reform element in contempt. The regular Republicans were delighted with the nomination. Adams was the man they had feared. For a long time the moral leaders of the Liberal movement were doubtful what course to pursue and even contemplated calling another convention, but they finally accepted Greeley as offering relief from the injustices of the administration. The editorial conference did the same, largely because of Reid. Later on the Democrats joined the endorsement. The Southern delegates remembered Greeley's attempt to organize a peace commission during the last year of the Civil War and above all his signing the bail bond of Jefferson Davis.

Of course the regular Republicans nominated Grant. Certain irreconcilable Democrats nominated Charles O'Conor of New York, a patriotic man and a great lawyer, who neither accepted nor declined the nomination. Davis withdrew from the labor ticket. It was a campaign of many peculiarities. Grant, in a letter to Washburne, said that in the Liberal movement no one was satisfied but Greeley himself and that they had harmonized the regulars by removing the "sore heads", and he was right. The Republicans were solidified and enthusiastic. With Grant for their candidate they glorified the hero and ignored his administrative defects and those of the men surrounding him. The Liberals who had started out so well had to speak in qualified terms of a candidate who was opposed to so many of their principles, and some Democrats showed a visible effort in swallowing a candidate who had more than once intimated in the *Tribune* that while not all Democrats were rascals, all rascals were Democrats. General Sherman wrote to his brother, the senator, that Grant had never been a Republican nor Greeley a Democrat. *Harper's*

Weekly, despite the generally independent tendencies of its proprietors and of George William Curtis, its editor, had never effectively opposed Grant's policies or the men surrounding him. Now Nast, the cartoonist, entered the campaign with a bitter vigorousness. He caricatured Greeley most unmercifully, making much of the old white hat and the long gray coat, to one of the rear buttons of which he attached an insignificant tag labeled "and Gratz Brown." He was unsparing of Sumner and Schurz, and even Curtis could not restrain him though he wrote him that treating such men as he would Tweed showed "a lack of moral perception." These cartoons, while not necessary to turn the election, distressed Greeley immeasurably.

Poor Greeley! He had been put at the head of a motley and disorganized army and he led it to a disastrous defeat. He could not get himself taken seriously. The campaign which began as a farce ended in tragedy. Greeley fought with the last atom of his strength. No one doubted his honesty but the electorate knew he was erratic. He knew he was a beaten man when he returned to New York just before election. His wife was dying and he watched, almost without sleep, by her bedside. She passed away on October 30 and he "laid her in the ground with hard dry eyes." A few days later Grant was elected by a tremendous majority. Out of the wreckage there were found only sixty-six electoral votes for Greeley. The "old white hat" had been kicked out of the ring. The broken editor went back to his desk, but the combined misfortunes overwhelmed him. Before the month was over he had a nervous breakdown which probably affected his mentality, and he died in a sanatorium on November 29. His successful opponent attended his funeral.

The electoral count necessarily showed for the first time a change of votes from the candidate to whom they were pledged. Had Greeley been elected by the vote of November, a real problem would have arisen. Had the Greeley electors voted unanimously for the vice-presidential candidate a precedent might have been set. Three votes were cast for the dead candidate. They were rejected by Congress. That did set a precedent. Apparently no vice-presidential nominee will reach the presidency by a dead presidential candidate being elected. The minority vote split between Hendricks, Brown, Jenkins and Davis, with Hendricks far in the majority.

So on March 4th, 1873, Grant rode to the Capitol and was reinaugurated. He was still the same man to whom Lowell had referred as showing a "puzzled pathos" in a situation to which he was not adapted.

He had doubtless been touched by the tragedy of Greeley. It was fortunate he could not penetrate the veil of the future. He would have seen an administration stained by all the corruption which his opponents feared, a triumphant tour of the world, a political defeat, a terrible financial disaster, and finally a dying man sustained by an indomitable courage which reached the heights of heroism, writing his memoirs so that his family might not want, and passing into the beyond with the love of all Americans upon him, his faults known to be those of trust and guilelessness, his virtues resplendent in his country's history.

CHAPTER TEN

WAS THE PRESIDENCY STOLEN?

WHEN Grant's administration drew to a close there was greater hope in the Democratic ranks than had existed since the summer of 1864 when, before the final Union success set in, a change of the national administration seemed inevitable. The scandals of the Credit Mobilier, the Whisky Ring and the proven dishonesty of Grant's private secretary, Babcock, and his Secretary of War, Belknap, were a heavy burden and it behooved the Republican party to put its best foot forward. At its convention Blaine was the leading candidate. While distrusted by many, he had just made his audacious defence in the matter of the Mulligan letters and the meretriciousness of the display was not so evident then as later. Perhaps, had he not suffered a sunstoke just before the convention and his physical condition not been a matter of doubt and rumor, he might have been nominated. He led until the final ballot. Conkling and Morton were apparently heirs to the Grant strength and the former was ready to make any personal sacrifice to defeat Blaine, who had characterized him and his "turkey gobbler strut" with all his brilliant sarcasm. The most promising candidate, if the party was to keep its skirts clear of the "old crowd", seemed to be Benjamin F. Bristow of Kentucky, the Secretary of the Treasury, who had overthrown the Whisky Ring, in spite of what appeared to be Grant's personal opposition. These three diverse elements were unable to do more than to prevent either of the others from carrying off the palm. Bristow's forces might possibly

94

have nominated Blaine, or Blaine's supporters have finally gone to Bristow if Bristow, who courteously called at Blaine's home after the sunstroke, had not then encountered antagonism and discourtesy. The truculence of Blaine's family more than once did harm which all Blaine's diplomacy could not repair and in this instance Blaine and Bristow, who might have made common cause, were driven far apart.

The convention finally turned to Governor Hayes of Ohio. His qualities were good, his character high, his associations excellent and he had won a remarkable campaign in Ohio on a sound money platform, against "Honest Bill Allen", one of those popular, picturesque and plausible types, better fitted to run for office than to occupy it. There is no question but the choice of Hayes, unexpected as it was, was a wise one. Grant would have thrown all his strength against Bristow, while on the other hand those citizens who were disgusted with the corruption of the times would have voted against either of the administration men and, when the significance of the Little Rock transaction had sunk in, against Blaine as well.

There was only a semblance of a contest in the Democratic convention. Governor Tilden of New York had had his eye on the nomination for a number of years and carried it off handily. Tilden was one of those plausible, shrewd politicians with a seemliness, discretion and quiet taste for and tact in wire pulling than which even the pure air of Plymouth, Vermont, can hardly produce a better. He was forty-seven years old when the Civil War broke out. He did little if anything for the Union cause. Lacking the frankness of Vallandigham, he was one of the committee on resolutions of the National Democratic Convention of 1864, which declared the war was a failure, and he wrote to William Kent in that year, "The Southern States will not by any possibility accept the avowed creed of the Republican party as the permanent policy of the federative government as to slavery, either in the states or territories," and further: "Elect Lincoln, and we invite those perils which we cannot measure; we attempt in vain to conquer the submission of the South to an impractical and intolerable policy; our only hope must be that as President he will abandon that creed, the principles and pledges on which he will have been elected.

"Defeat Lincoln, and all our great interests and hopes are unquestionably safe."

A few months after this letter was written men were not proud of having said this sort of thing. But for the most part, Tilden, during the war, sought to make as few enemies as possible and spent most of his time trying cases. There was good reason behind Nast's famous cartoon in which a Union and a Confederate soldier confronted the candidate with, "Which side were you on?" to receive the answer, "I was in court trying a Railroad Case."

Tilden managed to get a reputation as a "reformer" without much hurting his status with the faithful. Just how much this reputation was deserved may be indicated by the famous "private and strictly confidential" letter of October 27, 1868, during the Grant-Seymour campaign. Tilden was chairman of the Democratic State Committee, and William M. Tweed was boss of New York. This letter was written by the secretary and sent out over Tilden's name. It requested the members of the committee to "communicate with some reliable person in three or four of the principal towns and in each city of your county" and to have "at the minute of closing the polls, not waiting for the count, such persons' estimate of the vote" wired to William M. Tweed at Tammany Hall, "Expense duly arranged for this end." That meant just one thing. Tweed was to be advised of the probable "up-state" vote early enough to know just how much to "deliver" by fraudulent count. Tilden denied authorship or even signing this letter, but when Greeley probed further and charged him with knowledge and responsibility, Tilden stood mute. Before an investigating committee he admitted seeing bundles of these letters and seeing his signature.

Although Tilden stood for financial political reform so far as the stage setting and footlights were concerned, he never took a single step in favor of purity of elections.

He did take part in the downfall of Tweed. But he was not the backbone of the movement. That credit belongs to Thomas Nast and above all to George Jones of the *New York Times,* who faced real danger in the cause and refused a bribe of five million dollars to cease his activities. When the investigation was under way Tilden, who had always hated Tweed, did take part in it. Whether this was for political purposes or not, it turned out to be good politics, for it prevented the Republican party from claiming all the credit, but it is significant that once Tweed was in jail Tilden discouraged any effort to go further. The Tweed ring had stolen on a perfectly enormous scale. Benches, nearly fifteen hundred of them, purchased at five dollars apiece and sold to the city for six hundred dollars apiece were but an indication of the magnificent proportions with which Tweed and his associates carried on their predatory activities. Comparatively few were punished. Many hundreds of thousands of dollars passed through the ring and were apparently sunk without trace. Tweed offered to reveal all, if he might be allowed to go home to die. But this did not suit Tilden, who was then Governor and who controlled Fairchild, the Attorney General, although the rugged, honest and patriotic Charles O'Conor, one of the great lawyers in the history of the American Bar, who had led the Tweed prosecution, favored it. But the beneficiaries of the ring had voted for Tilden and he never played "bad politics" in his life. Still, he had made a name for himself as a reformer, which did him no harm with his cohorts who winked the other eye. Although his connection with the Ring prosecution made him conspicuous, he did not rely alone on this good deed in a naughty world. He thought the Lord still had a predilection for the heaviest battalions, and built an organization which was remarkable in the way it functioned. It is said that when running for Governor he had his majority figured out within a few hundred at noon on election day, so admirably had his organization made its reports and so completely did it "deliver the goods." He had nearly the required two-thirds on the first ballot of the Democratic convention and was nominated unanimously on the next.

On the whole the nominations were considered excellent, although non-partizans like Mark Twain preferred Hayes. Asked to give counsel at a Tilden flag-raising, he sent it by letter, "Do not raise the flag." The Ohioan had an open frankness of manner that contrasted oddly with the shrewdness and craftiness of Tilden. Although both had what were esteemed admirable public records, Tilden, like many other wealthy men, had apparently been somewhat less than frank on matters concerning his taxes. Tilden did not stand up so gloriously as a candidate once his plausibility and lack of real vigor was analyzed, but there was one thing tremendously in his favor, the corruption of the Grant administration. And although the little known Ohio governor was to show himself "without fear and without reproach," this was a heavy burden to carry. Hayes on his honor and character deserved to win, but quite as surely on its recent record the Republican party deserved to be beaten.

One does not even need to make a discount for the usual redundancy of political platforms to see that the following plank was worth more to the Democratic party than was its candidate:

"When the annals of this Republic show the disgrace and censure of a Vice President; a late Speaker of the House of Representatives marketing his rulings as a presiding officer;

three Senators profiting secretly by their votes as law-makers; five chairmen of the leading committees of the late House of Representatives exposed in jobbery; a late Secretary of the Treasury forcing balances in the public accounts; a late Attorney General misappropriating public funds; a Secretary of the Navy enriched or enriching his friends by percentages levied off the profits of contractors with his department; an American Ambassador to England censured in a dishonorable speculation; the President's private secretary barely escaping conviction upon trial for guilty complicity in frauds upon the revenue; a Secretary of War impeached for high crimes and misdemeanors—the demonstration is complete, that the first step in reform must be the people's choice of honest men from another party."

Here was the backbone of the Democratic campaign and it was no wonder that thousands of voters who believed that reform could only come from the outside, refused to vote for Hayes, even though they respected and admired him.

As the campaign progressed, the practical souls who figured the chances unemotionally gave slight betting odds on Tilden.

The election returns seemed to have vindicated these wiseacres. In the early evening and all along toward midnight it seemed tolerably certain that Tilden had been elected. Both candidates retired with that belief. The doubtful states whose votes were considered vital were all for Tilden. Toward the wee sma' hours the *New York Times* received a telegram from the financial head of the Democratic State Committee asking for returns from South Carolina, Florida and Louisiana. These states had been assumed to be Democratic and this telegram roused the suspicions of the *Times*. It found reason to believe that there was ground for dispute on these states. On the morning after election this paper announced that Tilden had received to a certainty 184 electoral votes, that Hayes had received South Carolina and Louisiana, giving him 181, and that the four votes of Florida were claimed by both sides. If these four votes went to Hayes he would be elected by one vote. The *New York Herald* also admitted that the election was in doubt. The other papers, both Republican and Democratic, announced Tilden's election. The final Democratic claim was that these states had gone for Tilden and that an informality in the Republican electoral ticket in Oregon had given him one more, making the vote stand Tilden 204, Hayes 166.

When the smoke had cleared away, it was found that Tilden had the three contested Southern states on the face of the press returns, but that intimidation and fraud were charged. In Oregon a federal official had been chosen elector and as such he could not serve. Did this give the next man in the list—a Democrat—his place or could he resign and let his fellow electors choose his successor who would be a Republican?

Soon it developed that neither party would concede the election. President Grant invited a partizan group of statesmen to go to Louisiana, where it was evident that the greatest contest would take place, and there witness the proceedings of the returning board. Abram S. Hewitt, the Democratic chairman, requested an equally impressive delegation to represent him. Among the Republicans were Sherman, Garfield, Quay the General Lew Wallace, while a few of the Democrats were Senator Trumbull, now returned to his former allegiance, Henry Watterson and Speaker Randall. There was considerable testimony on both sides and the news as it came north was met with great partizan feeling. To the Democrats it seemed that they were being defrauded out of a well-earned victory, while the Republicans inquired whether, simply because Tilden's friends had tried to steal three states and probably more, that entitled him to steal the presidency. It seemed evident that neither candidate wished to occupy the office unless it belonged to him, but it was also evident that, being human, each thought the other the defeated man. Congress was in a furore. Men confidently predicted blood letting in the House Chamber. In a debate a Democratic representative stated that there was danger of reaching a point where one of the parties must make an ignominious surrender or fight. He turned to the Republican desks and said, "Are you gentlemen prepared for the latter alternative?" and from the Republican seats arose a tremendous shout of "Yes!" On his return from Louisiana, Watterson in a public speech called for the appearance in Washington of a hundred thousand peaceable citizens exercising the right of petition. Joseph Pulitzer, who followed him, suggested that they be "fully armed and ready for business." Another civil war was among possibilities by no means remote. Finally the returning board, fully Republican, gave the state to Hayes. The only honest question was—did the Negro voters have an opportunity to register their will in the contested parishes? Although there was some attempt to show a Negro defection from the Republicans it was negligible. More whites—carpet-baggers though they were —voted for Hayes than Negroes voted for Tilden. Louisiana at that time contained about ninety-three thousand whites and a hundred and fifteen thousand Negroes. In a single parish with twenty-one hundred colored voters not a single Republican vote was cast. In all probability the returning board was not a body of high standards. It may have been for sale, but nobody bought it. Above all, the evidence on which it decided showed intimidation very plainly.

The returning boards of Florida and South Carolina declared the Hayes electors elected and in Oregon the electors met, the ineligible elector resigned as elector and the survivors filled the vacancy by re-electing him, he having resigned his Federal office. The Democrat, who had received the certificate from a Democratic governor, organized himself in good

Gilbertian fashion, elected two colleagues, and returned a vote of two and one.

All these contested votes must now be canvassed either before or by Congress. If the Vice President, who must open the vote, was the deciding party, it meant that Hayes was to be declared elected. If Congress had the authority as a single body in joint session, Tilden was the man. If Senate and House were to act separately and concurrently it meant a deadlock, for the Senate was Republican and the House Democratic. Finally the two bodies appointed committees to consider the matter. Both committees were exactly the same size and each committee was made up in opposite proportion as regards majority and minority, therefore, when sitting jointly, the committees were equally divided. No proposition was offered which would not clearly result in the seating of one candidate or the other, therefore no proposition could receive more than half the votes of the committee. It is to the everlasting credit of American politics that, in spite of the impasse, Senator Thurman could say that in the meetings of that joint committee "there never was an unkind, or short, or harsh remark or word." Finally it was proposed that a tribunal carved out of the Supreme Court should decide all disputed questions. Out of this proposition came the act establishing the Electoral Commission. At first it was suggested that it contain four judges and that the Senate and House should each name five men, one of whom should be excluded by lot. Of this proposition Tilden is said to have declared—"I may lose the presidency but I will not raffle for it." Finally a bill was drawn—as nearly perfect in its balance as human ingenuity could devise. This provided for a commission of fifteen. Four judges, definitely designated, two of whom were Republicans and two Democrats, were to elect a fifth and each branch of Congress was to appoint five commissioners. To them were to be referred all contested matters concerning the count.

This finally passed both branches of Congress, but not without the opposition of Democrats like Proctor Knott and Joe Blackburn, and Republicans like Blaine, Morton and Sherman. But Conkling, Bayard and Thurman carried it through the Senate and Hoar and Lamar through the House.

There was one man on the Supreme bench who claimed to belong to no party—David Davis of Illinois. He was expected to be the choice of the other judges. Because he was so independent that it was thought he could not vote twice consecutively with any party, and because Tilden needed only a single electoral vote, his selection was looked upon with complacency by the Tilden men. There is no doubt that the Electoral Commission bill was at bottom a Democratic measure, as they felt sure Davis would serve and be with them. The Republicans accepted it because something had to be done to preserve the country. But Davis was suddenly elected United States Senator by the Democratic party in Illinois and he felt that his serving on the board as a Justice would be an impropriety, and the choice of the judges fell on Justice Bradley, a fair and honest man but a Republican. The Congressional commissioners of course were equally balanced between the parties.

When the electoral count was held and the vote of Florida was reached, objection was made to its being counted. Under the act it was sent to the commission. Before this august body many eminent counsel appeared. For Tilden there appeared Charles O'Conor, Lyman Trumbull, Jeremiah S. Black, Montgomery Blair and among others—and in a minor capacity— William C. Whitney.

The Hayes counsel included Samuel Shellabarger, personal counsel for the candidate, Stanley Matthews and, first and foremost, William M. Evarts, whose leadership in great arbitrations was universally admitted. He did not look beyond the law and, as he knew the case must finally be decided by the judges on the commission, he was wise. The proposition on which he relied was that once the returning boards made their returns there was no going behind it. Justice Field, whose brother, by the way, was with doubtful propriety among Tilden's counsel, pressed him closely on this but he could not make him waver. At last the commission decided. Florida must be counted for Hayes. The vote was eight to seven, each man, judges and all, voting with his party. It was so on every question, whether it concerned Louisiana or South Carolina. On the Oregon matter the commission voted unanimously not to receive the Democratic vote but in the old proportion to receive that of the Republican. And so Hayes was declared elected and took his seat peacefully.

Whichever candidate had been seated the sympathies of the country at large would have been with the loser, but historians, even Mr. Rhodes among them, take too much the point of view of that popular reaction. They deplore the strictly partizan vote of the Commission, but that is a double-edged sword. Mr. Rhodes admits that in good conscience the Oregon vote belonged to Hayes and calls the Democratic contention a subterfuge. Mr. Rhodes further admits that Mr. Hayes won South Carolina. On these two points there is no question. This is particularly so of Oregon. All the other points were capable of argument, but not this, and yet the seven Democratic commissioners, including the two judges, voted against counting for Hayes a vote that clearly belonged to him. Judge Davis, from whom so much was hoped for Tilden, said to William Henry Smith concerning the course of Judge Bradley—the odd man—"No good lawyer not a strict partizan could decide otherwise." Field and Clifford were strong partizans in spite of their ermine. Every opinion that Tilden was elected is based on a belief that politically, in the South at least, a Negro has no rights that a white man is bound to respect. It is good old Ku Klux logic, nothing more, nothing less. Does any sensible man believe that, with an ostensible

Tilden majority of only seventy in Florida, that anti-Negro hotbed, a free expression would have given him the state? Does any sensible man believe that, in a single parish in Louisiana containing two thousand Negroes, an untainted election could be held without a single Republican vote being cast? Even Mr. Rhodes gives Hayes South Carolina and Oregon. It is sometimes suggested that all that should have been done in Louisiana was to throw out the votes of the state. That would have been a cheap and easy way of stealing the office for Tilden. But if every state where there was Negro intimidation—and where there still is—had been thrown out, Tilden would have got less than a hundred and thirty electoral votes and Hayes's popular majority would have been over fifty-five thousand.

As independent and pure a man as James Russell Lowell was an elector from Massachusetts and stated in a letter that had he had any doubt of the election of Hayes in the country, and that the claims were honest, he would have resigned his place.

Some subsequent circumstances may be referred to, which throw light on what seems to me to be the befuddled view which in so many quarters still insists that Hayes was a fraudulent president. There is the verdict, quite dependable, it seems to me, the verdict of 1887 of the American Congress in passing the present electoral act. Let us remember that this was passed substantially with unanimity by both parties and signed by a Democratic president. And this President came to his office practically because the country accepted the precedent of 1877 of not going behind the accredited returns, not going into the palpable frauds in New York, frauds achieved under the benevolent patronage of the notorious John Y. McKane, which gave Cleveland the state of New York, a state without which he could not have been elected and which he carried even then by only eleven hundred votes.

There were no protests when this Congress enacted into law the "crime of 1876," and it did just that. The law seeks to place the decision of the legality of the votes with the proper certifying authorities of the states. This was the basis of the Commission's decision. In a case where there is but one return, it must be counted, even if questioned, unless both Houses vote concurrently to reject it. If there are conflicting returns, that which is accepted by both Houses concurrently shall be counted. If the Houses fail to concur, the properly certified return must be counted. And such in spirit were the provisions of the Electoral Commission Act. A vindication indeed!

If a candidate is defrauded what ought he to do? If the fraud is under color of law and it would be unpatriotic to contest further, he ought to submit, but he ought also to declare in ringing tones that he would be a candidate at the first opportunity, to give the public defrauded along with him, the chance to set the matter right. Did the smooth and supple Tilden do this? Not he. And thereby hangs a tale.

A Democratic House in Hayes's day ordered an investigation of the whole matter. This was for the purpose of making political capital for the next election, if not of unseating Hayes. But the Potter Committee was hoist by its own petard. A flood of telegrams in baffling cipher were produced, telegrams which passed between the Tilden representatives in New York and their agents in the contested states. Two acute members of the staff of the *New York Tribune*, Grosvenor and Hazzard, discovered the key. At no time was any serious denial made of the genuineness of the translation. The only answer was the lamest of attempts to avoid responsibility.

Let me give a few evidences of the corruption in which Tilden took part, for take part in them he did, unless we are to believe the ridiculous claim that Pelton, his penniless nephew, who was closeted with Tilden every day, was carrying on negotiations on his own responsibility for the purchase of the presidency for his rich uncle, for large sums of money which the nephew did not personally possess, and unless we believe that Tilden resented the efforts of Manton Marble and Smith M. Weed, and the rest, high in his confidence, to make him party to a dishonest transaction. Tilden never withdrew from his relations with these co-conspirators and Weed was his candidate for the New York collectorship under Cleveland. There are many other despatches equally incriminating to be found in the *Tribune's* pamphlet, "The Cipher Despatches," which can be found in most public libraries. Not a voice was raised to deny their authenticity; no man in authority dared come forward with a key which gave them any other meaning.

It is fair to say that Tilden denied knowledge of the transaction, but it was the word of a cornered man, confronted with damning facts, words which he, as a lawyer, would have ridiculed to a jury if he had been analyzing the case in an argument. Even when his testimony is quoted by his admirer and apologist, John Bigelow, it is so evasive that one loses confidence in the entire book. When Tilden was pressed in a searching cross-examination by Tom Reed, he made an exhibition as pitiful as that of a malefactor on trial in a criminal court.

Some of these despatches were sent to Henry Havemeyer, who could not read the cipher. Actually all were for Pelton. Weed telegraphed from South Carolina after his arrival as Tilden's agent:

Columbia, Nov. 14

To Henry Havemeyer,
Nothing definite yet, but working. Things mixed here. Our party claims Hampden party are trading off Tilden. Proceedings in court don't seem to disturb Chamberlain party. Shall I increase to 50,000 if required, to make sure. Select good

man to send down if required, as that is the only way. Am watched and if as well think better to turn over the matter to Governor Randolph.

W.

Pelton, in his code signature of "Denmark" replied on the same day:

New York Nov 14

Smith Weed, Columbia.

Telegram here. You can go to fifty if necessary. Perhaps use future prospects for some part, but you must see that trading is not done. I doubt whether you can trust it to person you name. Kennedy and other should be able to assist. When do you think you can reach conclusion? Telegraph what majority is on Tilden. Friend will go through on train leaving here six tonight. See him.

Denmark.

Four days later we have this from Weed (Bavaria and Africa were never definitely translated):

Columbia Nov 18

Majority of board have been secured. Cost is 80000, to be sent as follows: One parcel of 65,000 dollars, one of 10,000 and one of 5000, all to be five hundred or one thousand dollar bills, notes to be deposited as parties accept and given up upon vote of land of Hampden [*i.e.*, S. Carolina] being given to Tilden's friends. The three packages should be sent without inscription and tonight unless you receive telegram from me countermanding. Shall try to secure everything by plan of deposit. The friends of Chamberlain and Bavaria [?] are here in force, and I fear their money and careful watching and intimidation of Board. For God's sake let it go if you can. Be safe in Florida or Africa. [?] Do this at once and have cash ready to reach Baltimore Sunday night. Telegraph decidedly whether it will be done.

W.

This was sent later on the same day:

108

Columbia Nov 18

Shall leave tonight for Baltimore. Meet me yourself if prudent. Returning board say they will do it sure, and it's worth trying, but result doubtful to my mind.

S.

But Mr. Weed was not quite so dubious when he sent his next:

Columbia Nov 18

Looks well now. You must have the money at Barnums early Monday morning. I go tonight.

W

The following signatures appear on Baltimore hotel registers of Monday morning, Nov. 22:

At Barnum's   Smith M. Weed of New York.
At the Mount Vernon House,   William T. Pelton of New York.

Now let us turn to Florida where Manton Marble was in charge.

Tallahassee Dec 3

To Col. Pelton
    53 Gramercy Park
    Proposition received either giving vote of [one?] Republican of Board or his concurrence in Court action preventing elector's vote being cast, for half hundred best United States documents.

Marble.

No one has even questioned, then or since, that "best United States documents" were thousand dollar bills. Pelton immediately replied:

N. Y. Dec 4

Manton Marble Tallahassee
    Telegram here. Proposition accepted if done only once. Better consult Wooley and act in concert. You can trust him. Time very important and there should be no divided counsels. [Unsigned]

109

But next day Marble [Moses in code] telegraphed that he had failed and was through:

Tallahassee Dec 5

Col. Pelton
  53 Gramercy Park
Proposition failed. Finished yesterday afternoon responsibility [as] Moses. Last night Wooley found me and said he had nothing, which I knew already. Tell Tilden to saddle Blackstone.

Nor was Oregon neglected. The single Democratic elector if the Democratic claims were recognized would give Tilden the office. Here the Tilden agents were J. N. H. Patrick and James K. Kelly. They jointly telegraphed Pelton:

Portland Nov 28

W. T. Pelton New York
  Certificate will be issued to one Democrat. Must purchase one Republican elector to recognize and act with Democrat and secure vote and prevent trouble. Deposit ten thousand dollars my credit.
  Kountz Brothers, 12 Wall St. Answer.

J. N. H. Patrick
I fully endorse this
James K. Kelly

Ashael Bush of the firm with which the money was deposited testified that more than fifteen thousand dollars in all was furnished to Patrick. The next telegram is unsigned:

Nov 29

W. T. Pelton New York.
  Will we lose any Democrat in conceded Democratic states. Answer.

Pelton answered both these telegrams together, the first word doubtless applying to the second telegram.

No. How soon will governor decide certificate. If you make obligation contingent on result in March it can be done and incremable [sic] slightly if necessary.

Patrick replies:

W. T. Pelton   Portland Nov 30
   No. 15 Gramercy Pk., N. Y.
   Governor all right without reward. Will issue certificate Tuesday. This is a secret. Republicans threaten, if certificate issued, to ignore Democratic claim and fill vacancy, thus defeat action of Governor. One elector must be paid to recognize Democrat to secure majority. Have employed three [lawyers] Editor of only Republican as one lawyer, fee 3000. Will take 5000 for Republican elector. Must raise money; can't make fee contingent. Sail Saturday. Kelly and Bellinger will act. Cipher them Must act promptly.

Pelton replies with a Tildenesque care that money shall not be wasted on undeliverable goods.

                 New York Dec 2 1876
J. N. H. Patrick Portland   8.30 A.M.
Deposit [ed?] eight for counsel fee as directed. They advised you at your home. Understand not to be used unless they carry out arrangements, recognizing Democratic elector and duly forward his vote to Vice President.

And once again to Kelly—

                 New York Dec 6
                 8.35 A.M.

Jas. K. Kelly Salem
   Is your matter certain. There must be no mistake. All depends on you. Place no reliance on any favorable report from three Southern States. Answer quick.

   These despatches and many others no less damaging finished Samuel Jones Tilden as a political possibility. At the time of the next election ill health forbade him to make the canvass. But no sane convention would have nominated him. He was far more valuable an asset, once this sorry business had slipped the public mind, as a martyr than he would have been as a candidate with the cipher scandal ready to be revived.

In conclusion it is worth while to quote from a Southern historian, a man who has been accused of placing the South once more in the saddle. If any man could with any good grace claim the election of Tilden and that the South was cheated, that man might be supposed to be Woodrow Wilson. He says in his "History of the American People"—"It was plain enough that in any case the returning boards would have given the vote to the Republicans, whatever the face of the returns, so long as the men for whom they acted felt that they could count on the support of the Executive at Washington in the maintenance of their authority. It was equally clear, on the other hand, that there was all but indisputable evidence of fraud, or at the least irregularity in the votes upon which the Democrats relied." Hayes went into the presidency with a clear title, and for the patriotism and restraint with which this was achieved the nation owes an everlasting debt of gratitude to the statesmen who evolved the Electoral Commission and to members of both parties in the American Congress during the session of 1876 and 1877.

Disregarding the legal points, which were all on the side of Hayes, the simple facts of the case are that stolen goods were pried out of the hands of the Southern Democrats, who then cried so loudly because they were despoiled of the loot that the Republican party never again had the courage to make this stealing impossible and abandoned its members with black skins to political and sometimes actual assassination by their late masters. The party had pitchforked the Negro into political responsibility, brought upon him the hatred of the master class, used him for its purposes, and then abandoned him. It is the darkest blot on the escutcheon of the Grand Old Party.

CHAPTER ELEVEN

THE OLD GUARD DIES BUT NEVER SURRENDERS

STALWART: *A Republican partizan who is never turned from the faith, who accepts party dictation as absolutely as a soldier obeys orders, to whom the one thing politically sacred above all others is party regularity, who never lets high principles interfere with political duty, to whom a Republican if he is one of "our crowd" needs neither the recommendation of character nor intelligence as against a Democrat or a Half-breed.*

HALF-BREED: *A term of contempt used by "stalwarts" to describe Republicans who carry their sovereignty under their own hats.*

IF a political dictionary had been published in New York during the last third of the nineteenth century without giving these two definitions substantially as they are given here it would have been incomplete.

Much of our political nomenclature has been evolved in the Empire State. The terms "Barn-burners" and "Hunkers" appeared there in Van Buren's day and the term "Mugwump", intended to be contemptuous but embraced by independents from the eighties on, first appeared in that state. Although Blaine appears to have been the first to use the word "stalwart", it came to be especially a New York appellation and to apply to Conkling and the members of his organization.

Here is the tale of "stalwartism" when, bursting out of state confines, it attempted to control the presidency of the United States. It is not an inspiring story. It is filled with useless and bitter contention. It culminates in tragedy, but if it is pitiful it is tremendously human and, so far as the futility of selfish and petty striving is concerned, it is one of the illuminating chapters in the history of American politics.

After the bitter election of 1876, after the natural sympathy which went out to Tilden, the loser in that contest, and after the election of a hostile Congress in 1878, one might fairly suppose that, at the next presidential election, the party in power would expect to be substantially defeated. But despite the fact that Hayes was but indifferently cherished by the masses and that the leading statesmen of his party nursed a dislike for him, amounting practically to animosity, he had given a remarkably able administration and made his party stronger rather than weaker. This was evidenced by the shrewd and canny Tilden, whose attitude to his party nomination was more indifferent than the matter of his health, never of the best, explained.

General Grant had spent a portion of the interim between Hayes's inauguration and the next Republican national convention in a tour of the world. He had been received as no American had ever been welcomed and had carried himself simply and modestly, his poise and dignity reflecting credit on his country as well as on himself. When he landed at San Francisco in September, 1879, his popularity was at its height. Meantime his political friends were making ready to wage a vigorous and promising campaign to return him to the presidential chair. Chief among these friends were three senators, Cameron of Pennsylvania, son of Lincoln's first Secretary of War, Logan of Illinois, a famous volunteer Civil War general; and, strongest of all, the imperious Roscoe Conkling of New York. Grant was early receptive to the suggestion. He

wrote letters which show that studied indifference, that qualified acquiescence, which covers desire. Blaine was his chief
competitor and his friends were positive and active. There
were others, notably John Sherman of Ohio, then Secretary
of the Treasury, and Senator George F. Edmunds of Vermont,
to whom was turned the negative support of those who,
remembering not only Belknap and Babcock but the Mulligan
letters and the Little Rock bond issues, cried to the two leading candidates, "a plague on both your houses."

Early Cameron, Logan and Conkling carried through their
program in well regulated and thoroughly supervised state
conventions in Pennsylvania, Illinois and New York, but there
were recalcitrants in each state.

Elsewhere numerous delegates were elected pledged to
Grant. But the people at large were doubtful. No President
had ever had a third term. Although the irregularities of
Grant's trusted friends and his unwillingness to recognize and
deal with such irregularities, his manifest executive gaucheries,
the "puzzled pathos" which Lowell discerned, and the general
tone of his former administrations seem to scientific students
of government at least as great a bar, this unwritten custom
was more dangerous to his candidacy among the rank and file
of the voters. "No third term" became a rallying cry, the
most potent of any slogan directed at Grant's candidacy.

Much depended on securing the adoption of the unit rule
in the national convention. Under such a rule, a state would
cast its entire vote for the candidate having a majority of the
delegation. Thus the anti-Grant minorities in the states controlled by the "big three" would be "hogtied" for him. Cameron was Chairman of the National Committee but the
majority of that committee was anti-Grant. Cameron by virtue
of this office would call the convention to order. He was suspected of intending to apply the unit rule to the question of
election of a temporary presiding officer. On appeal he would

still apply the same rule and a second point of order would be futile. The chairman thus elected would act in the same way and the permanent organization would also be elected to carry out the same high-handed policy. The anti-Grant men of the committee could get no assurance that this cold-blooded brigandage would not be put in play, until they threatened to depose Cameron and he learned that the Sergeant-at-Arms, who represented established authority and the convention police power, would, in such an event, recognize the new chairman. Then a compromise was made. George F. Hoar of Massachusetts, opposed to Grant and Blaine alike, was named as the candidate for temporary chairman and the matters concerning the conduct of the convention were left to be regulated by the usual methods, the unit rule not to apply unless adopted. This left the Grant forces somewhat at a disadvantage. But Grant had a solid phalanx of delegates who followed their leaders and stood by their candidate with an enthusiasm and faithfulness that has almost immortalized them.

When the convention opened it became Grant against the field. Each army had its general. The Stalwart Old Guard was marshaled by Conkling. He had the dash and fire of a Rupert joined to the self-consciousness and attitudinizing of an actor. The opposition was generaled by the senator-elect of Ohio, the Sherman leader—James Abram Garfield. He was as good a tactician as Conkling and a cooler and calmer man. On all preliminary matters, in which there was a difference of opinion, these leaders confronted each other. There was nothing conciliatory in Conkling's air or speech. He was holding and inspiring his faithful three hundred and six, but nothing that he did brought a single opponent closer to his candidate. The "turkey gobbler strut" was again in evidence. Impatient and contemptuous, he flaunted into battle. He courted the homage of his cohorts and, invariably waiting until the convention was in order, he swept histrionically down the main aisle to his seat to the accompaniment of the cheers of his followers.

Garfield on the other hand was a model of tact and courtesy. He argued to those who were undecided, Conkling to those whom he already controlled. The Ohio man might have quoted Shakespeare and said:

> "I do oppose
> My patience to his fury; and am arm'd
> To suffer, with a quietness of spirit,
> The very tyranny and rage of his."

Only once did he depart from this method. While Conkling was making a pompous speech at a morning session, Garfield came down the aisle, and the convention burst into applause which caused Conkling to give over, until the member from Ohio was in his seat.

A typical instance of Conkling's truculence came when three delegates from West Virginia refused to vote for a resolution pledging the members of the convention, in advance of nominations, to the support of its candidates. He offered a motion declaring that these delegates had forfeited their right to participate further in the deliberations of the convention. Garfield's strength and leadership was invoked in this crisis and he made a speech so conciliatotry and fair that Conkling, seeing the unmistakable temper of the convention, withdrew his motion. Grant had about two-fifths of the convention. The other three-fifths was not solidified, but as all the preliminary struggles centered around efforts to make Grant's nomination certain, the followers of all other candidates made common cause with Garfield. Thus Garfield made many friends. A leader of these elements was absolutely necessary and Garfield's actions do not justify the strictures in Colonel McClure's "Our Presidents" in which he states that Garfield "illy concealed his efforts to advance himself while ostensibly struggling for Sherman." Of course it was inevitable that the possibility of a final compromise on this brilliant and tactful man should enter the minds of many. Even Conkling during the clash just alluded to, sarcastically penciled him a note congratulating him on being "the dark horse". The effort to adopt the unit rule was defeated, a body blow to Grant, but if his compact two-fifths stood unwavering, there would be no ballot, after the earlier ones, on which his nomination would not be strongly possible. If the resourcefulness of his leader had been re-inforced by the spirit which Garfield showed it would have been almost humanly impossible finally to defeat him.

When the hour for nominations was reached Conkling and Garfield again came into comparison. Probably no Republican national convention has heard two nominating speeches so good as those made by these two leaders. Standing on a reporters' table, imperious, truculent, commanding, Conkling made a superb figure, radiating insolence and confidence. He began with the oratorical tinsel which so often distinguishes such efforts, but it was tinsel of the sort that made the blood of his followers dance and compelled even the admiration of his opponents. In a moment of impulse, said to be unpremeditated, he seized Myles O'Reilly's lines, which were to become famous by this use, and opened his speech in verse.

"And when asked what State he hails from,
  Our sole reply shall be
He hails from Appomattox
  and its famous apple tree."

Here was a lightning flash for a keynote and it aroused the Grant battalions to frenzied enthusiasm. But as the speaker progressed he approached more legitimate oratorical effectiveness such as may be typified in a single sentence: "His fame was earned not alone in things written and said but by the arduous greatness of things done." He referred to the charges against Grant's earlier administration and the revolt of 1872 and to the curious psychological fact that such charges once used are seldom thereafter effective: "Calumny's ammunition has all been exploded; the powder has all been burned once its force is spent." Finally he pictured the party "advancing, with its ensigns resplendent with illustrious achievement, marching to certain and lasting victory, with its greatest Marshal at its head." But even in this speech the orator had flaunted the alleged weaknesses of the opposing candidates in the faces of their supporters and, though it was a remarkable effort, it only made it more difficult for those delegates not originally for Grant to come to him on any subsequent ballot.

Garfield's oratorical problem was a hard one. Had he possessed the spirit, fire and disdain of Conkling, he could not have made the same type of speech without leaving the honors with the man who preceded him, if only for the reason that the earlier speech would have been fresher. A later effort along those lines would inevitably have been tarnished. Garfield chose to go along other lines. Sherman, whom he was to nominate, was no chieftain about whose brow clustered the laurels of glory plucked from the teeth of danger. He was a plain, hard-working, prosaic, executive statesman. Garfield chose, in persuasive phrase, to warn the convention against its own enthusiasms. Probably the occasion which Garfield confronted has never been more ably met in speech than in his first phrases: "I have witnessed the extraordinary scenes of this convention with deep solicitude. Nothing touches my heart more quickly than a tribute of honor to a great and noble character; but as I sat in my seat and witnessed this demonstration, this assemblage seemed to me a human ocean in tempest. I have seen the sea lashed into fury and tossed into spray, and its grandeur moves the soul of the dullest man. But I remember that it is not the billows, but the calm level of the sea from which all heights and depths are measured.

. . . Not in Chicago, in the heat of June, but at the ballot boxes of the Republic, in the quiet of November, after the silence of deliberate judgment, will this question be settled." These sentences were heard with profound attention. Then a voice cried, "We want Garfield!" Quickly the scholarly speaker, who had been a college president at the age of twenty-six, summoned Shakespeare to his aid: "Hear me for my cause and be silent that you may hear." Then he went on to describe his candidate whose monument was "twenty-five years of National Statutes" and who throughout all opposition had "remained unmoved until victory crowned him" and stood in "that fierce light which beats against the throne" whose fiercest ray had found "no flaw in his armor, no stain upon his shield."

According to Conkling's nephew, the New York senator turned his sarcasm upon this speech, and remembering Garfield's opening simile he left the hall saying he felt sea-sick.

When the balloting commenced it was quickly seen that the Old Guard could never be wooed from its choice. Its boots were nailed to the floor. Ballot after ballot, whatever the shifting of the votes among the opposition, the Grant phalanx stood solid. No exhibition of political loyalty was ever greater than that of the men who followed Conkling's lead. Never below three hundred and four, once reaching three hundred and thirteen, with a usual total of three hundred and six, they stood unmoved, awaiting the break which, in the absence of some skillful maneuver on the part of their opponents, exhaustion must finally bring about. They even stood together, without aid from other delegates, on a motion to adjourn for the night. Blaine's forces mustered two hundred and eighty-four votes on the first ballot and on the thirty-fourth he still held within nine of that total. But during all these trials it became evident that the supporters of other candidates would not vote for either of the leaders. There came a defection from

Edmunds to Sherman but it did not avail and Sherman's vote began to fall again. It was evident then as it is evident now that Sherman's bolt had been shot. On the thirty-fourth ballot seventeen votes were given to Garfield. He endeavored to decline the honor but his remarks were cut short by the chairman, who ruled his explanation out of order and directed him to resume his seat. On the next ballot eighteen votes were detached from Blaine and fifteen from other sources making his total an even fifty. This was the beginning of the end. Conkling's sarcastic prophecy had been fulfilled. Three hundred and seventy-eight votes were necessary for a nomination. On the thirty-sixth and last ballot there was a stampede from every candidate but Grant. The man whose supporters led in this movement, James G. Blaine, describes the scene in which "the banners of the Senate were caught up and massed in a waving circle around the head of the predestined and now chosen candidate, who sat pale and motionless in his seat with the Ohio delegation." He had received three hundred and ninety-nine votes but not one had come from the unwavering three hundred and six.

What sort of man was this which the convention of a great party had declared worthy of the highest office within the gift of his countrymen? James Abram Garfield was then about fifty years of age. He had begun life as a canal boy. A constant and consistent love of learning had been onerously gratified and at last he had graduated from Williams College. He was a Campbellite by religion and taught in Hiram College, the denominational school of this faith, and soon became its president. As a lay preacher he was eloquent and successful. Finally he went in for politics, served in the Ohio senate and at the outbreak of the war joined the defenders of the Union, rising to the rank of Major General. In the Army he proved a brave soldier and a competent commander. He resigned his commission to enter Congress, to the lower branch of which he had been elected. No member of that body, not even Blaine himself, had a more copious mind, wider learning nor greater debating ability. Garfield was a remarkable legislator and if Ohio turned to Sherman rather than toward him as its presidential candidate it was because it felt, honestly and properly, surer of Sherman's demonstrated executive ability. The newly named candidate had a fine presence and an open and affectionate nature. He was prone to put his arm over the shoulder of those with whom he was engaged in private consultation, calling them by their Christian names, and his being radiated cordiality. He had a kind, warm heart and disliked to give offense and there was a sense of wavering about him that was his worst quality. The physical courage of the soldier was not entirely duplicated in the moral grit which could make an Andrew Jackson stand immovable and alone. Backed by the opinion of a party, he was a great force on the floor of Congress. Elected United States Senator, he was apparently just entering a new phase of eminence when he was nominated for President.

But Garfield was not scrupulous in advance of his day. He had been in the Credit Mobilier and his dividend had been three hundred and twenty-nine dollars. He had received a large fee as attorney for certain contractors who dealt with the government, a fee much too large merely for his legal attainments. And, although he claimed it was because it could not be dissociated with the general appropriation bill, he voted for the notorious "salary grab" of 1873. Those were the days when the public servant was worthy of his perquisites.

Of course the East must now have second place on the ticket. Also the Grant faction must be placated if possible. It was soon known that the choice of imperial New York was a peculiar one. Against the wishes of the bosses of the convention, a civil service resolution, twice defeated in committee, had been adopted by the delegates, in spite of a member's glorification

PUCK.

FORBIDDING THE BANNS.

THE BRIDE (Garfield): "but it was such a little one!"

of office seeking and his honest, if naïve, question, "What are we here for?" Now New York, flouting all this, and especially showing its disdain for Ohio, which through Sherman and Garfield had helped to wreck the Grant candidacy, presented for Vice President Chester Alan Arthur, the one time Collector of the Port of New York, removed from spoilsmanship by President Hayes and John Sherman, his Secretary of the Treasury. Arthur was nominated and the convention adjourned, the Old Guard defeated and grim, almost defiant.

James A. Garfield had taught school in his younger days in a little town in Southern Vermont. After his relinquishment of the place, the town engaged Chester Alan Arthur as his successor. It was a strange coincidence but in the enthusiasm of the time there was no cynic prophet to point to it as a sinister portent.

The Democratic convention which met in Cincinnati was a vivid contrast to that of the Republican party. At Chicago nearly all the delegates had settled choices of candidates, at Cincinnati few were enthusiastic for any particular aspirant. At Chicago there was vigorous leadership, in Cincinnati there seemed to be none. These facts made it fairly sure that the candidate, however half-hearted his early support, who should succeed to a fair lead, would quickly get from the indifferent delegates the two-thirds necessary to success in Democratic conventions. This candidate proved to be General Hancock, who, although he was less than twenty ahead of Senator Bayard of Delaware, his nearest competitor, and had less than a quarter of the votes cast on the first ballot, more than doubled it on the next roll call, a fact which precipitated a landslide of announcement of changes which concluded with only thirty-three votes against him. The second nomination went to William H. English, true to the type of vice-presidential candidate of that day.

The ensuing struggle was not an inspiring one. Professor

Lingley in his admirable "Since the Civil War" says concerning it: "Since each side was loath to press forward to the solution of any real problem facing the nation, the campaign was confined, for the most part, to petty or even corrupt partisanship." The Republicans met an unexpected reverse in Maine in September through fusion which resulted in the election of the Greenback candidate for Governor. This aroused the party to redoubled effort in the "October States." They were carried, largely by such processes that Arthur, then broadly tolerant of "practical" methods, referred at a dinner after the election, with good-natured but pointed sarcasm to the campaign in Indiana and the distribution of "tracts and political documents all through the State."

The great danger to the Republican cause came from the aloofness of the Old Guard. Garfield had traveled from his home in Mentor, Ohio, to New York City in order to be present at a conference of leading Republicans, primarily no doubt, to meet Conkling, but "Hamlet" was enacted without the presence of this particular moody Dane. Finally Grant's good offices were sought and he persuaded Conkling to enter the campaign. Together they addressed a large meeting in Warren, Ohio, Grant presiding and speaking briefly, Conkling making an elaborate campaign speech. It is evident that Conkling had satisfied himself, as well as he could, that Garfield, in his administration, would not be unfriendly to the New York senator, although he never viewed Garfield entirely without distrust. The attitude of Conkling and Grant was undoubtedly of great help to Garfield. So also was the fact that Hancock was in no wise a politician. He blurted out the truth that "the tariff is a local issue" much to the disgust of his followers and the contentment of his foes. Garfield's record in Congress was scrutinized and his opponents commented unfavorably upon it. It was better than some, worse than others. It should not have attracted the supporters of Edmunds but they had accepted and assisted in the solution of the convention problem which his nomination brought about and supported him vigorously. Toward the end of the campaign a forged letter, said to have been written to one Morey by Garfield, taking the locally unpopular side on the Chinese question was circulated on the Pacific Coast. This lost Garfield Nevada and all but one electoral vote in California, but he carried New York, Connecticut and Indiana of the doubtful states and Maine came back to her allegiance. Hancock had to be content with the now solid South from Florida to Delaware, from Virginia to Arkansas, to which were added the two anti-Chinese states and only New Jersey of the so-called doubtful group.

Here ordinarily the narrative of the election would come to a close but the tragic aftermath is so inextricably blended with the politics of the campaign that the story can end only at Elberon. After his election Garfield was forced to consider the claims of two men for his cabinet. He had been the manager of John Sherman's campaign. He had received the nomination himself. Sherman had assisted in making that possible, sending word to his delegates to join in the Garfield movement. Although Sherman believed he had been badly treated, he blamed Governor Foster rather than Garfield. He was Secretary of the Treasury in Hayes's cabinet and had administered its affairs with consummate ability. He was willing to continue in that office and his appointment would have been an earnest of Garfield's good faith toward the civil service declaration of the convention which nominated him.

On the other hand there was the brilliant Blaine, among the active chiefs "first in honor and in hope." It had been easy for Blaine to urge his delegates to vote for Garfield. Although local considerations had bound the latter to Sherman, he was a warm and affectionate admirer of the Plumed Knight. Although congressman and senator-elect from Ohio when he was chosen delegate-at-large pledged to Sherman, he had either been unwilling or unable to prevent Blaine's carrying the district delegates from his own bailiwick. Politically he was for Sherman, but he would have been personally delighted to have seen Blaine the winner. Both Blaine and Sherman were dominant types and it seemed probable that the cabinet would be too small for both of them. Conkling was antagonistic to both but of course preferred Sherman to Blaine. When Garfield announced his cabinet Blaine headed it as Secretary of State and Sherman's name did not appear. To the civil service reformers this was a blow. To the average citizen it seemed gross ingratitude. Conkling was greatly disgruntled. He had visited Garfield at Mentor, before and after election, both times by invitation. That Garfield gave the somewhat incredulous Conkling reason to believe that he would not be ignored in matters concerning New York seems certain. One Sunday in March Conkling called at the White House and is supposed to have been told by Garfield that he was not ready to consider the New York appointments. And yet two days afterwards Garfield made open war on Conkling and upon the element that honored Sherman. The term of Hayes's Collector of the Port of New York, E. A. Merritt, who had been appointed on the removal of Arthur, had two years to run. He had been a most exemplary officer. He suddenly found himself kicked upstairs, into the pleasant and lucrative London consul-generalship, to make a place for Conkling's dearest foe, the Blaine leader of the Empire State, William H. Robertson. This was opening old sores with a vengeance. Even a calm and phlegmatic leader would have remonstrated, and Conkling had neither calmness nor phlegm. Some observers acquit Blaine of inspiring this move, although it was charged to him at the time. It would seem to have been so impolitic and so evidently fraught with evil party consequences, that it does not seem like the work of so shrewd a politician as Blaine. Whether it came from Blaine's advice or was an impulse of Garfield, the Secretary had now to stand by his chief and to a great degree accept the onus of his act. Conkling was furious. Aided by his junior colleague, Thomas C. Platt, he went to work to prevent senatorial confirmation of the appointment. Garfield's Postmaster General, Thomas L. James, the New York member of the cabinet, and Vice President Arthur joined the Senators in protest. Finally it became known that Garfield had said that Senators who opposed his wishes in this matter would need letters of introduction in future visits, which of course meant a willingness of the administration to enter upon a patronage war with the Senate if Robertson was not confirmed. Garfield's attitude was not commendable to wise and tolerant citizens. The degrading spectacle of such a struggle on the part of the Senate would have been pleasing to Conkling and Platt but their colleagues were not prepared to enter such a battle and confirmed the appointments. Then the New Yorkers haughtily withdrew from the Senate, returned to their constituency and sought a vindication at the hands of the legislature. This grotesque and childish performance was destined to bear bitter fruit. No historian can take a view in any degree favorable to the Senators. No matter how ill-timed and poorly advised was Garfield's policy, the action of Conkling and Platt was beneath the dignity of members of a city council. Not a single policy or principle was in issue, nothing but the pursuit of place. Can anyone imagine a Bayard or a Morrill of that day or a Borah or a Walsh of this, precipitating a party crisis on such a pretext, no matter how much his prestige was injured? Not Quay or Clarkson, in the Harrison administration, made their disappointments the cause for so unpatriotic an outburst. The administration was now in a whirl of patronage dispute. Tariffs, revenue, public improvements, foreign relations must be forgotten until it was determined to which faction or, if to both, in what proportion, the jobs belonged. Meanwhile before the New York legislature, the running fire of attack and defense of the administration was being carried on by members owing allegiance, ostensibly at least, to the same party.

The ending of this feud was terrible indeed. Gaunt murder walking abroad in the busy paths of men took its toll. An assassin, a disappointed office seeker, shot the President as he was passing through the railroad station to go to the commencement of his Alma Mater at Williamstown. This was no assassination coming from a misguided, if wicked, national sense after a great civil war. It was no murder arising from the effect of anarchistic doctrines and villainous cartoons on a weak and vicious mind. It was a murder fanned by lust for office and abuse of those in power. It was a murder committed, by a small politician, a proclaimed "Stalwart" whose mind, however eccentric, had been inspired to action by the ignoble struggle of the hour. It was a crime done to make one of the murderer's faction President of the United States.

Thus was brought to a bitter conclusion a battle that never should have been fought. Both Conkling and Platt were ignominiously defeated by the New York legislature. While Garfield lingered, the unhappy Arthur bore himself with dignity and unpretentiousness. In so far as there was an active head of the government it was the brilliant Secretary of State. Documents were signed by a rubber facsimile of the President's signature. Let Blaine, to whom on the day of inauguration Garfield had written referring to "the love of comradeship of eighteen years" and the "faith in the next four" complete the picture.

"As the end drew near, this early craving for the sea returned. The stately mansion of power had been to him the wearisome hospital of pain, and he begged to be taken from his prison walls, from its oppressive, stifling air, from its homelessness and its hopelessness. Gently, silently, the love of a great people bore the pale sufferer to the longed-for healing of the sea, to live or to die, as God should will, within sight of its heaving billows, within sound of its manifold voices. With wan, fevered face tenderly lifted to the cooling breeze, he looked out wistfully upon the ocean's changing wonders; on its far sails, whitening in the morning light; on its restless waves rolling shoreward to break and die beneath the noonday sun; the red clouds of evening, arching low to the horizon; on the serene and shining pathway to the stars. Let us think that his dying eyes read a mystic meaning which only the rapt and parting soul may know. Let us believe that in the silence of the receding world he heard the great waves breaking on a further shore, and felt already upon his wasted brow the breath of the eternal morning."

So came Chester Alan Arthur, in circumstances of great pathos and difficulty, into the Chief Magistracy of his nation. Then emerged from the chrysalis of machine politics, a character of dignity, ability and honesty, one of the greatest examples of the steadying effect of responsibility in history. In spite of the exclamation of one who had known him in his lesser political days: "Chet Arthur President of the United States. Good God!" the White House has few finer memories than that of this cultured gentleman under the burdens of a bitter heritage, serving his country in a manner that she is proud to remember. And in that service the bickerings of place were not allowed to enter. As far as Arthur could make it so, the assassin's arm was impotent. Conkling and Platt were ignored by the man whose oath and duty transcended his inclinations of a time not long past, as men count time, but dim enough when looked back upon through a blood-stained vista. They then declared puny war upon their old associate and those who saw it realized that the wheel had come full circle.

CHAPTER TWELVE

UNHORSING A PLUMED KNIGHT

AS the election of 1884 approached, the name of Blaine loomed larger and larger. His close connections with the dead Garfield and the unquestioned fact that it was the vociferous antagonism of the "Stalwarts" which brought murder into the diseased brain of the assassin, strengthened the man from Maine tremendously. Arthur had been made President by this crime and had belonged to the Conkling group. This was a terrible handicap. He had been a city politician and had been removed as Collector of the Port of New York because of undue political activity in that office. When Garfield was shot in the Baltimore and Ohio Station on that July day in 1881, his murderer had boasted that he had made Arthur President. Arthur proved himself to be a remarkable type of man. He rose splendidly to his responsibilities. He possessed a fine dignity. He refused to allow Conkling to use him and even Grant, who in Conkling's behalf asked favors, was refused. No man ever confronted a tragic situation more nobly. But the public could never forget that Garfield was shot to make Arthur President. Arthur would have been wise had he foregone the ambition to be elected in his own right. On the eve of the national convention it was evident that only a great revulsion of feeling could bring about his nomination. The original Blaine men were against him. Conkling now hated him as only a disappointed man can hate. The reformers could not forget his early career and brought forward their usual stalking horse, Senator Edmunds of Vermont. Blaine for the first time since 1876 clearly held the pole at the start and, what is more, was more likely than ever before to profit by the breaks in the ranks of other candidates. But in the minds of many enlightened Republicans and of the Independents who generally voted the Republican ticket the Little Rock affair and the Mulligan letters made his nomination undesirable. Prominent in this group, as delegates, were Henry Cabot Lodge, George William Curtis, Theodore Roosevelt, Andrew D. White, George F. Hoar, John D. Long and Frederick T. Greenhalge. They were resolved to do everything within their power to prevent the nomination and they were supported by some of the most influential newspapers in the United States. They contested every point manfully and vigorously.

The vital force behind the opposition to Blaine, both in the convention and afterwards, went back to the days of his speakership fifteen years before. Then had occurred those indiscretions which dogged him all his life. When a bill was reported, renewing the land grants of the Little Rock and Fort Smith Railroad, he had saved it by properly ruling that a hostile amendment was not in order. The point of order which this ruling supported was made by Logan at Blaine's direction. Later Blaine became interested in the road and promised Warren Fisher, Jr., who was exploiting it, that he would not "be a deadhead in the enterprise," and at a later date recalled to Josiah Caldwell, also active in the road's affairs, that he had once "unwittingly" done the corporation "a great favor." It is conceivable that Blaine meant no more by his "deadhead" phrase than a reference to his services as a broker, not pretty in themselves, of the roads securities, but it seems almost impossible that a public man so clear-headed as Blaine should innocently write a letter so capable of ill construction. Blaine sold certain Little Rock securities to his friends in Maine. The road sold its first mortgage bonds at par, but included a bonus of the same amount in common stock, in preferred stock, and in land grant bonds; in short, for every dollar paid, the investor received stocks and bonds aggregating four dollars at par. Now Blaine brokered the bonds to his friends and in the principal transaction, amounting to a hundred and twenty-five thousand dollars, retained, besides a commission, the land grant bonds, or a third of the bonus which would have passed to the buyers had they dealt with Boston stock brokers. Finally the road went to smash. Either from honor or political necessity, Blaine felt under obligation to make good the losses of his friends. He borrowed money, paying 8½% a year for it. Then three other railroads bought the Little Rock first mortgage bonds. A fiery controversy arose over the question whether or not Blaine, the powerful political leader, profited by this purchase.

Finally in 1876 the matter was so much talked of that an investigation by a committee of the Democratic House was held. At this investigation one Mulligan let fall the fact that he had in his possession letters of Blaine to Fisher, which Blaine had thought destroyed. That Blaine was greatly embarrassed by this information was evident to all present. He whispered to the Republican member of the committee to move an adjournment and it was done. Then in interviews, dramatically described next day by Mulligan, he urged that gentleman to return the letters and, that being unavailing, got them into his possession to read and refused to part with them. All attempts by the committee to get them were abortive. Never again did these letters go out of Blaine's possession. But of course Blaine could not leave the matter here. One day in the House he rose to a question of personal privilege and, after an admirable and vigorous speech vindicating his right to withhold the letters, he cried, "I invite the confidence of forty-four millions of my countrymen while I read those letters from this desk." Whether he read them all, or in the proper order, will always be an open question. His political colleagues at the time were satisfied that their leader had cleared himself triumphantly. But Blaine was not through yet. Most remarkably, most adroitly, he carried the war into Africa. Proctor Knott was the chairman of the committee having the investigation in charge. Josiah Caldwell, no particularly convincing witness, had telegraphed him in Blaine's favor. Knott should have given this telegram to the committee to be considered for what it was worth, but he said nothing about it. This is an example of the vicious partizanship which was pursuing Blaine. He had learned of this telegram and concluded his speech by a charge of this suppression, of which he dramatically made the most, and for the time being his foes were unhorsed. But cold analysis soon changed the opinion of many thinking men. Blaine might not have been guilty of intentional dishonesty, but he had not been convincingly vindicated. "Burn this letter" and similar phrases would not down. But Blaine persisted in his long pursuit of the presidency and his supporters were tremendously loyal and enthusiastic. They entered this convention with a great confidence which proved well founded.

On the first ballot Blaine received 334½ votes, Arthur 278, Edmunds 93, and all others 113½. Blaine needed only seventy-seven votes to win. No very substantial change came on the second ballot, but on the third Blaine received three hundred and seventy-five and was within thirty-six votes of the coveted prize. Logan, who had received about fifty votes, then withdrew his name and his state gave Blaine thirty-three of the necessary votes. Then two votes from Kansas that had been given to Logan, and one that had been given to Hawley were registered for Blaine. This settled the matter, if the votes he had been receiving did not waver. They stood solidly and the final ballot, after the rush to his standard had ended, gave him five hundred and forty-one votes. Arthur received a little over two hundred. The Edmunds men, forty-one of them, on this final ballot now sat ominously silent. Logan received the reward of his withdrawal by being given the second place on the ticket.

What would the reform element do? Nearly all those who had participated in the convention swallowed the nomination, although some of them, including Theodore Roosevelt, if rumor is to be believed, made rather wry faces while they did it. Among the delegates George William Curtis was the most conspicuous bolter. He and the Harpers had accepted the corruption of the Grant days complacently enough, but now they became stern moralists indeed. It is curious to recall the veneration which Curtis received for this act and to contrast it with the vituperation that used to be poured on the shoulders of Lodge because he did not break with his party. Opinions may possibly differ as to Lodge's duty in this instance, but men like William Walter Phelps, John Hay and William McKinley, who were for Blaine from the start, and Andrew D. White and John D. Long, who were among the reformers who supported the convention's nominee, against none of whom was criticism leveled, were indeed a goodly company with which to be associated. There is no good reason for praising Curtis and the Harpers. They "reformed" twelve years too late. A different and more consistent figure was Carl Schurz, who had not entered the convention and who opposed Blaine as he had opposed Grant. There was a formidable revolt against Blaine; Curtis and Schurz were joined by James Russell Lowell, Henry Ward Beecher, General Francis C. Barlow, Colonel Thomas Wentworth Higginson, Charles J. Bonaparte, Benjamin H. Bristow, William Everett, John F. Andrew (son of the war Governor of Massachusetts), Moorfield Storey, Roger Wolcott, James Freeman Clarke and George Fred Williams—then embarking on a very stormy political career. They had powerful allies in some of the ablest newspapers and periodicals in the United States. In Boston the *Advertiser, Transcript* and *Herald* were against Blaine. In New York the *Times, Herald* and *Evening Post* took the same position. So did the *Springfield Republican* and leading journals in Philadelphia and Chicago. The bolters were called Mugwumps. They came from a class whom Blaine had characterized in a letter to Garfield, "They are," he said, "noisy but not numerous; pharisaical but not political; ambitious but not wise; pretentious but not powerful." The chief force of the movement was in Boston and New York. There was considerable conscious virtue in the Mugwumps, but the movement was honest, fearless and public-spirited. These men and newspapers all hoped that the Democrats would nominate Grover Cleveland, then Governor of New York, and that party was wise enough to gratify their wishes.

In Grover Cleveland we find one of the finest examples of individual honesty and strength in the history of American politics. He was, in his early days, a simple, stolid, unimaginative, provincial lawyer. A bachelor, he was fond of the society of men and his amusements were utterly commonplace. He had been the sheriff of his country and later he had been elected mayor of Buffalo in one of those elections which follow administrations of a majority party when it becomes arrogant and intolerable. He had plenty of backbone and his fame went over the state as Buffalo's veto mayor. The Republicans were in the midst of one of those bitter disagreements which occurred periodically between "Stalwarts" and "Half-breeds," and when Arthur's Secretary of the Treasury, Judge Folger, was nominated for Governor, the Democrats beat him roundly with Cleveland. As Governor, Cleveland had been emphatically his own man, and his refreshing and untrammeled honesty had become a byword. Such contest as there was in the Democratic convention was between him and Bayard of Delaware. Cleveland represented the immediate day. Bayard was a reminiscence of the past. Cleveland led on the first ballot and on the second achieved the required two-thirds, but not until

General Bragg of Wisconsin had leveled his finger at the recalcitrant Tammany delegates and told the convention that men loved Cleveland for the enemies he had made.

The Mugwumps were delighted. Here was a man after their own heart. They prepared to enter the campaign with vigor. The first step was to prepare a pamphlet giving the circumstances of the entire Little Rock scandal. They had just the man in their ranks to write such a circular. Moorfield Storey then, as now, was a cold, scrupulous, analytic lawyer. He could no more be touched with sympathy or find excuse for wrongdoing than he could perform on the flying trapeze. He could be trusted to focus the white light of clear morals upon his subject and ignore all else. It is fortunate that Mr. Storey has never been made a judge. With him there would be no extenuating circumstances. Calmly, relentlessly, Mr. Storey analyzed Blaine's relations with the Little Rock Road, with Mulligan, Fisher and the rest. He came to the irresistible conclusion, falling short of absolute proof, that Blaine had used his office of Speaker to advance his personal fortunes.

Something had to be done or Blaine's defeat was sure. The Republicans decided to appeal to the "good Christian people."

Cleveland was a bachelor. He had apparently been "bound in the flesh as all men are." He was charged with the abduction of one Maria Halpin, whom he was alleged to have seduced, and to have imprisoned in an asylum. It was further claimed that he had kidnapped and hidden her child and his. These accusations made his supporters stand aghast. But from the executive chamber at Albany came the words, "Tell the truth." The shiftiness of Blaine, as shown in the reports of the testimony of the investigation of 1876 quoted in the Storey pamphlet, ill contrasted with the unflinching demeanor of Cleveland. Those who wished to vote for Cleveland caused the matter to be investigated. The lurid embroidery of the tale was stripped away, but "the kernel of truth," as the investigator reported, remained. It lay in the fact "that when he was younger than he is now he was guilty of an illicit connection. . . . After the primary offence, which is not to be palliated . . . his conduct was singularly honorable, showing no attempt to evade responsibility and doing all he could to meet the duties involved, of which marriage was certainly not one." Even this residuum cost Cleveland many thousands of votes and by many the charges were believed and reasserted in all their exaggeration. Although the candidates held honorably aloof and Cleveland in particular is known to have suppressed certain scurrilous charges against Blaine, which had been in his possession, it was the vilest personal campaign that has been waged in recent years.

Another element entered into the campaign. The "Bloody Shirt" had been waved most dramatically by Blaine on the floor of Congress in 1875, when he made his bitter and unfair attack on Jefferson Davis. An episode in Cleveland's early life gave his opponents an opportunity once more and for the last time effectively to raise a war issue. When the Civil War broke out, Cleveland and his two brothers recognized their duty to the country and to their widowed and dependent mother. They merged their responsibilities and decided that two should volunteer and the other support the home. They drew lots and it fell to Grover to remain behind. Later the draft was established and was carried out with no such discrimination as marked the conscription of the recent war. Cleveland was drafted and, rather than take refuge in the exemption which his assistant district attorneyship might have afforded him, he hired a substitute. The Blaine men took instant cognizance of this and misinterpreted it to their advantage, although Blaine himself was not a veteran. Cleveland's substitute plagued him, not only during this campaign but during his entire career, but he never stooped to explanation or apology.

Blaine was attacked as dishonest, Cleveland as impure. At

one time the regularity of Blaine's marriage was questioned and the attack met and disproved. The cartoons were savage. Blaine was portrayed as a tattooed man from whose skin the soap of editorial exoneration could not scrub the marks of dishonesty. The tariff, which the Republicans originally sought to make the chief issue, had often to give place to personalities.

Blaine had always been admired by Irish-Americans. His mother had been a Roman Catholic and he had more than once encouraged the Irish cause. Cleveland had alienated a large number of this element by vetoes of measures in which they were interested. To carry New York for the Democrats the defection of the Irish vote must be minimized as much as possible. Patrick A. Collins of Boston, an Irishman of national reputation, was brought on and made a series of vigorous speeches which did something toward recalling the Irish vote to its customary allegiance. William C. Whitney used his great influence to placate Tammany and succeeded in a measure. Still the destination of many of these votes was in great doubt.

Blaine went on the stump. He was weak in his explanations of the personal charges against him, but he had a fascinating and magnetic personality which gained him votes. In October Ohio gave an enthusiastic Republican majority and the omens were favorable.

But things were not going well in the Empire State. Not only had the Mugwumps made great progress, but the old Grant stalwarts held somewhat aloof, although Platt had supported Blaine both for nomination and election. Then there was labor trouble between the employees of Blaine's chief organ, the *Tribune,* and its owners, a circumstance of which the Democrats took instant advantage.

It was known that a cordial word from Roscoe Conkling would have been worth thousands of votes. It would have made New York surely Republican. He was known to despise the George William Curtis element and once said, "When Dr.

Johnson said that patriotism was the last refuge of a scoundrel, he quite overlooked the possibilities contained in the word reform!" Admiring and sympathetic friends asked him to make just one speech for the Republican nominee. Conkling had a long memory. He remembered Blaine's attack upon him and his influence over Garfield which had culminated in Garfield's death and his retirement. As a lawyer he only responded, "Gentlemen, I have long since given up criminal practice." That door was closed.

On his return from his campaign tour, the week before election, Blaine stopped in New York for a day. Great preparations had been made for his reception. On October 29, a committee of clergymen waited on him at his hotel to assure him of their support. The spokesman of this committee was one Dr. Burchard. Blaine, exhausted and preoccupied, stood listlessly on the stairs while Burchard made what Blaine assumed would be a commonplace and flowery panegyric, to which he paid no attention. But Burchard slipped in a fatal sentence: "We are Republicans," he declared, "and do not propose to leave our party and identify ourselves with the party whose antecedents have been rum, Romanism, and rebellion." Blaine replied briefly, taking no notice of the offensive sentence. He claimed not to have known it was delivered till told of it afterward. This is no doubt true. Had he been willing to allow the religion of his mother to be subjected to insult, his political acumen would have shown him the possibilities of his tacit acceptance of these words when used as a weapon against him. On the next Sunday fliers giving Burchard's words with the statement that Blaine had heard and not rebuked them were distributed in the closest proximity to the Catholic churches in New York. Denials came too late. Burchard had crippled Blaine, how much remained to be demonstrated.

On the afternoon of Blaine's unlucky Wednesday, he reviewed a tremendous business men's parade, which marched down Fifth Avenue in a pouring rain which did not dampen its enthusiasm. It was a spectacle which must have greatly heartened the candidate. But that night another tactical error was made, Blaine was allowed to be the guest of honor at a banquet at Delmonico's, which became known as the "millionaires' dinner." Here were represented nearly all the great financial interests of the country. At this dinner sat H. H. Rogers, Russell Sage, Cyrus W. Field and H. D. Armour. Here also was the most notorious railroad wrecker of his day, Jay Gould. After the postprandial exercises there was a private conference. This in the popular mind meant only one thing, more money. It was after this affair that the *New York World* made this inquiry. "Is there a workingman now who believes that James G. Blaine is sincere when he pretends to be the friend of labor?" The Democratic party could have well afforded to shoulder the bills for this expensive and spectacular entertainment.

The following Tuesday four candidates went to the polls, Blaine, Cleveland, ex-Governor St. John of Kansas with the Prohibition nomination, and the gyrating Ben Butler, who had desired the Democratic nomination and now ran on a "greenback" platform. These last two candidacies were not unimportant. St. John was sure to be a refuge for thousands who shied at Blaine's financial record and would yet have accepted him rather than vote for any Democrat, while the congenial blatherskitery of Butler was a refuge for certain elements who detested the rugged honesty of Cleveland.

After midnight it became known that New Jersey, Indiana and Connecticut were for Cleveland. Of course the solid South was for him, whatever the wishes of its majority might or might not be. With New York this would give him the election. There everything was against Blaine. Burchard had hurt him. Gould had hurt him. Tammany had been placated. The Republicans near the end of the campaign had issued an affidavit

140

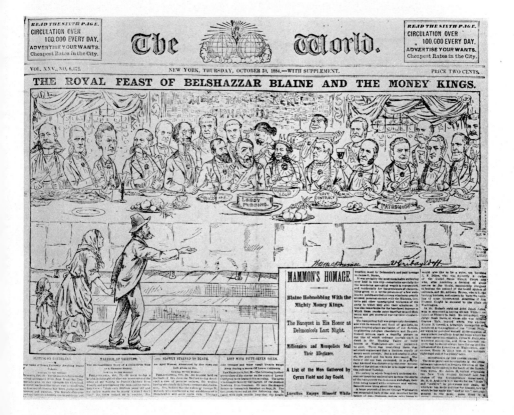

The "Millionaires' Dinner"

from Maria Halpin attacking Cleveland, an act which affronted all men of nice taste. At last, there was a rain storm on election day, always deemed a bad omen for Republicans, who were strongest in the outlying districts where the polling places were at a distance. It became evident that the result depended on a few thousand votes, in the territory just outside of New York City, places like Long Island City, then under the domination of the notorious John Y. McKane. For nearly a week the matter was undecided. During this time the country seethed with excitement, similar to that following the balloting in 1876. Jay Gould was in control of the Western Union Telegraph Company. A New York mob believed that the news was being manipulated by this company for fraudulent purposes. On Thursday it paraded the streets singing "We'll hang Jay Gould to a sour apple tree," and on the next morning that timid and pusillanimous gentleman telegraphed his congratulations to Cleveland. Finally it was decided that Cleveland had carried the state by the plurality of 1149 in a total vote that went well over the million mark. These returns were perfectly regular on their face. The precedent of the electoral commission not to go beyond the regularly certified returns left no alternative to the Republicans but to accept the results. No one today can be sure who was honestly elected. Of one thing we may be sure. Blaine had the honest majority of the popular vote. On the figures it belonged to Cleveland by only twenty-three thousand and no sane man believes that the Southern Bourbons did not eat up at least three times that amount.

The "Mugwumps" were the chief cause of Blaine's defeat. While without Burchard, the "millionaires' dinner," or St. John, Blaine would have squeezed through, they would not have injured an unweakened Republican to an extent sufficient to have brought about his defeat.

Now, nearly forty years afterwards, we can stand aside alike from the marble and ruthless morality of Moorfield

Storey and the great partiality of Gail Hamilton and estimate Blaine as history ought to estimate him. On the matters concerning the Little Rock Railroad and the Fisher-Mulligan letters, no careful and honest friend can give him anything better than a Scotch verdict. That he "played politics" to catch the public fancy cannot be reasonably denied. But he was an absolute patriot. He had great qualities. He never was charged in his subsequent career with being venal. He was only half demagogue—the other half was clear statesman. Americans can and should remember him affectionately.

The career of his great rival, Grover Cleveland, is one of the finest heritages which American political life gives us. His fiber was the fiber to stand strain. His honest frankness, his inability to be shifty, even if he would, his strength of character and inflexibility, his growth with his responsibilities, all make him loom up among his fellows like a great boulder on the side of a green and fertile hill.

CHAPTER THIRTEEN

GOLD OR SILVER

NEVER did an American party take over the government with greater happiness or higher hopes than the Democracy on March 4, 1885. But for all the completeness of its victory, it had been largely personal and won by a stiff necked, unimaginative, rather commonplace country lawyer, who had elements of greatness without ever attaining certain needed elements of statesmanship. He was honest with himself and with the public. He had a curious combination of strong partizanship and political independence. He was not conciliatory. The mailed fist was there and it was never covered by a velvet glove. He was fair and honest in his administration of the civil service and made enough progress along those lines to anger the practical members of his party, but not enough to satisfy all the complacent idealists who bow before this particular idol. Little more than twenty years after the close of the Civil War, he affronted all the Union-veterans, not only by vetoing an unprecedented number of personal pension bills after careful investigation, all of which deserved to be killed, but by vetoing in language so frank as to be offensive, a dependent pension bill and then seeking, prematurely, to return the captured Confederate battle flags to the states from which the regiments losing them had come. He had an excellent mind, stubborn and prosaic withal. After his election he confessed to Carl Schurz that he knew nothing about the tariff, but with Schurz's guidance he put that stubborn and prosaic mind to work and mastered it. It was probably easier for Cleveland to do this than to have read "Paradise Lost" with any intellectual pleasure.

In December, 1887, less than a year before election, he sent to the convening Congress a message which discussed the tariff and only the tariff. Then came the Mills bill. There was a wide gap between the President's ideal theories of a revenue tariff and the schedules which came out of the selfish local interests which had to be considered in the Ways and Means Committee if any bill was to be produced. The Mills bill fell between the House and Senate, but the message had focused the campaign on the tariff.

After eight ballots the Republicans nominated Benjamin Harrison of Indiana and Levi P. Morton of New York. It was a brisk convention with a number of nearly equally strong candidates. Probably Senator Allison of Iowa would have received the nomination if the Iowans had not shown a distrust of the railroads and an especial hostility to Chauncey M. Depew (who had 99 votes on the first ballot) as a railroad man. Depew later reciprocated and held his delegates away from Allison. A coalition without New York was fruitless and so Allison was dropped and Harrison carried through.

It was a close election, somewhat lacking in the excitement of four years before. The personal attacks were lessened, for there was nothing to be said about the honesty and political morals of either candidate. Cleveland had been married during his term to a very sweet and beautiful girl and although one heard "God forbid that that should happen to a daughter of mine" from the unofficial guardians of what they thought was the national conscience, and while that composite lady whom Mr. Beers in his "Mauve Decade" has called the Titaness, pretended to believe that "the poor dear" was dreadfully abused, Mr. Cleveland, with his past all discovered and behind him, now living in domestic tranquillity, was not so

144

open to attack. Besides, the scandals of the former election were all burned powder.

The campaign was generally dignified and evolved around protection and free trade, as the Republicans *would* call it, or tariff for revenue as the Democrats rightly termed the Cleveland policy. Towards the end some Republicans pulled a rather dirty but very neat trick. The innocent British Minister, Sir Sackville West, was lured into answering a decoy letter and advising, somewhat guardedly but no less surely, his correspondent to prefer Cleveland to Harrison in his vote in the interest of Great Britain. Cleveland moved slowly, too slowly for good politics. But at last he asked for the recall of the offending Minister. Salisbury, who, until Richard Olney taught him a needed lesson some years later, had a contempt for American diplomacy, refused. Then Cleveland sent Sackville West his passports and Salisbury, thoroughly angry, kept the legation under a second secretary as Chargé as long as Cleveland held office.

On the final decision, the country, by its electors, accepted the Republican panacea rather than the Democratic. Cleveland, however, held the popular vote by a small margin. But that was in a period following reconstruction when the popular vote had no real meaning and when the wisdom of the federal election system was fully demonstrated.

So Harrison came in. Mutually antagonistic as these men were, they had one thing in common. They had a coldness which irked their followers. No party leader likes to advise a President and have his words greeted with slight but unmistakable signs of indifference and boredom. In the next campaign when they were facing each other again, "Bob" Ingersoll wrote a friend that each party would gladly defeat its own man if it would not thus elect the other fellow. Cleveland had been gruff; Harrison was glacial. Cleveland could be genial until he realized his visitor wanted something; Harrison suspected his visitor the moment he laid eyes upon him. He told Quay, who had managed his campaign with positive genius, that God had put him where he was. The irate Pennsylvanian, after responding "Let God re-elect you then", stamped out of the White House for good and all. Tom Reed, the Speaker who held Congress in line, counted a quorum from the silent Democrats who were present and brought about a needed reform in the face of what was almost a riot and so made it possible to enact legislation, said he had only two personal enemies in Maine and that Harrison pardoned one out of the penitentiary and made the other collector of the port of Portland. Like Quay, Reed let the President shift for himself.

Harrison's administration was marked by the "Force Bill," attempt to bolster up the universal manhood suffrage amendment to the constitution, blocked in the Senate by a minority of Republicans. Another panacea for universal prosperity became pressing. More money, which is after all a fictitious medium of exchange, is an attractive cry. The greenbackers finally receded from the free coinage of paper and fell back on the free coinage of silver. A silver dollar represented, as it does today, a gold dollar's worth of silver, the surplus bullion being entombed in the vaults of the Treasury. Free silver at sixteen to one meant fixing by law two standards of value, that gold could only be sixteen times as valuable as silver. Natural laws are the only things that cannot be regulated by statutes. What the silver men proposed was that Congress should repeal the law of supply and demand. In vain did the opponents conjure up the fable of the newsboy who should sell papers until he earned half a dollar (they used round figures), then he could take it to a silver mine and get fifty cents worth of uncoined silver, then he could go to the nearest mint and have it made into a silver dollar, then with the dollar he would go back to the mine and invest it in twice as much bullion as he had before, take that to the mint and emerge with two dollars and in twenty-one such round trips, he was to become a millionaire. This was no true picture, of course, for the value of silver could not stay as it was under this artificial respiration if it was tried. But it had enough truth to make a reasonable political parable. But the silver men persisted and at last it became evident that Congress must do something for silver or silver would run away with the administration, and that is why so sound a financier as John Sherman backed the silver purchasing act which bore his name and why he voted to repeal it with the very next administration. And then came the McKinley Bill. We shall have something to say of the bill and the man whose name was attached to it. His time is to come. It passed only five weeks before the mid-term congressional election and the contest went strongly against the administration. As in all such cases, party legislation then ended and Congress became a sham battlefield in which to fight with phrases, as a preliminary to the national campaign.

Neither convention in 1892 was spiritless. Cleveland's enemies under the lead of Hill tried to get rid of him and through a snap convention held at an early day and on brief notice, Cleveland was for a short time supposed to be eliminated but the popular reaction kept him in the field even with the votes of his own state against him. Blaine, restive under Harrison as his Secretary of State, sick, unhappy, at last succumbed to pressure, resigned a short time before the convention and contested for the nomination.

Both the President and ex-President emerged successful on the first ballot. The Populists had come forward and reached almost major proportions. There was nothing in common between a Cleveland Democrat and a Populist. Cleveland had, in this campaign, an opportunity to do his party a tremendous service perhaps at a great sacrifice. In state after state in the far west, the Democrats and Populists went into an anti-Republican fusion. If Cleveland had refused to permit this, he might have lost the election, though the probabilities were the other way, but he won with a party infected with the Populistic views and during his whole term he was fighting his party and his party was fighting him. What is to be told now might have been a very different story had Cleveland won or lost without this entangling alliance.

As President Cleveland's second term drew to a close it was evident that it had been a failure. Just as history records the futility of the Johnson administration and at the same time gives its head credit for sound patriotism, honesty and right thinking, so Grover Cleveland emerges from the stress and storm, the first figure of that day. None the less the fact remains that the President and his party were at odds and that no man elected to the presidential office ever left it so absolutely hated by the party which elected him. The Republicans in Congress sat aloof and amused. A tariff bill had been forced through Congress. Its provisions were not those which Cleveland believed the party stood pledged to carry out. Nor were they those which the majority of the Ways and Means Committee of the House, under the leadership of William L. Wilson of West Virginia, had incorporated in the bill. Passed by the House it went to its fate in the Senate. It was returned for enactment amended in some instances beyond recognition. Then occurred one of the most amusing of parades in American politics. Grandiloquently, vociferously, with much use of the word "Courage," the majority defied the Senate and Wilson produced a letter from the President terming the action of the Senate "party perfidy and dishonor." The House without division sustained Wilson. When, however, in a few weeks it was proposed to terminate the conference between committees of the two bodies, which meant no legislative action whatever, Mr. Wilson and his colleagues, like Bob Acres, felt their courage oozing out at the palms of their hands. They passed the bill, amendments and all, and then tried to save their faces by a pitiful display, passing individual bills placing on the free list articles which the Senate rejected and which they knew it would reject. The bill became a law without the signature of the President. Cleveland stood like a rock against radical financial legislation but restrained it only by the aid of the great bulk of the Republican opposition. Hard times came on apace. So-called industrial armies, commanded by visionaries like Coxey, set out for Washington to complain to those in authority. Industrial conditions were menacing and Cleveland sent United States troops to Chicago, technically to protect the mails, during the great Pullman strike. As the administration entered upon its last year, nothing seemed more certain than that the Republicans with a high tariff platform would take substantial control of all branches of the government.

There were several candidates for the Republican nomination. Senator Allison of Iowa had his supporters. Governor Morton of New York, who had been Vice President under Harrison, had the always potent influence of the Empire State. Matthew S. Quay, put forward from Pennsylvania, was sure of some votes; even ex-President Harrison had his "ear to the ground." But there were two men to whom the country at this moment looked as eminent statesmen and popular leaders, Thomas B. Reed of Maine and William McKinley of Ohio. When Harrison's first Congress convened, they were the most eminent members of the House. Reed's long service and brilliant talents secured him the party nomination for the speakership. McKinley was his nearest competitor and when Reed was elected speaker in a contest into which acrimony had not entered, his rival was made chairman of the Committee on Ways and Means, an appointment that had far-reaching consequences. The preëminent piece of legislation of the Harrison administration had been the McKinley tariff bill. Although other members of the Ways and Means Committee and certain influential senators had borne a great part in the framing, as well as the enactment of this measure, it took its name, as was the custom, from the chairman of the committee reporting it. Seldom has a bill been so appropriately named. Whatever influence others had exercised in its framing, McKinley was one of the most stalwart protectionists in America and was glad to give his name to a great protection measure. But if he had been elected speaker, it is perfectly sure that the protective measure of Harrison's administration would have been known as the "Reed tariff." But whatever the feeling on the abstract question of protection and free or freer trade, "tinkering with the tariff" is always a dangerous thing for the party in power. The McKinley tariff only became popular after the passage of the Wilson bill. It was the greatest factor in defeating the Harrison administration. McKinley himself was defeated, although in a district which had been so shaped as to make him confront a Democratic majority. Then along came the Wilson tariff, Democratic disorganization and hard times. The call "Give us back the McKinley bill" made its sponsor the incarnation of what the people wanted. First he was elected Governor of Ohio. During his administration a very unfortunate happening, the failure of a friend for whom he had endorsed much paper, ruined him financially. He decided to resign the governorship and restore his shattered fortunes by practice of his profession. Certain wealthy friends, in such a way that the most sensitive of men could not refuse, restored him to financial solvency and he continued his career.

From the first McKinley had a natural advantage, because the party in power seemed to have greatly injured the welfare of the country by having reversed the policy for which he stood. He was to be the "advance agent of prosperity." Although Reed was perhaps the most brilliant man of his time with a far more opulent and original mind than his rival, and although in the teeth of the most abusive opposition he had wrought a congressional reform which was to be of tremendous consequence to ordered government, though he was wise and witty, a fascinating figure and a man of absolute sincerity, he had had the misfortune, by carrying off the speakership, to place his opponent in a position of great psychological advantage. Still, if this had been all, Reed might have made a strong fight and by his splendid parts have impressed himself strongly enough upon the country to have been nominated.

Alas, beyond personality, there is another factor in campaigns—organization—and McKinley's friends formed an organization that was superb. Mark Hanna of Cleveland was at its head. So far as the great bulk of the public knew, here was a new figure in politics; but he had been active in Ohio and in certain national conventions. In 1884 and 1888 he had been an active supporter of Sherman. He was inordinately desirous of taking a large part in making a President. He was fond of McKinley and after the first Harrison convention, when he saw that McKinley under certain conditions might have had the nomination, he hitched his wagon to this particular star. Hanna's sporting desire one day to make a President turned gradually to an affection for the amiable and delightful gentleman of his choice that was intense in its devotion. Hanna was brusque, vigorous, active, outspoken. He had had experience with the cold fastidiousness of those reformers who are quite willing to lead but never to walk abreast with any but those they fancy their equals. They were not his kind. Furthermore, he believed in the use of money. There seems in the minds of most writers upon this period a belief that the lavish use of money which he sponsored did not include bribery. None the less it must be remembered that the party organization in the South, where it never elected anybody, was largely held together by hopes of reward. During the winter preceding the convention McKinley's cousin William M. Osborne of Boston, once a member of the Boston Common Council and later police commissioner, made a tour of the Southern states under Hanna's direction and when the Reed people began to take interest in the situation they found that region "all buttoned up." Reed's managers in Vermont were also nicely gathered into camp through the bland treachery of Redfield Proctor, as mild a mannered man "as ever scuttled ship or cut a throat." New Hampshire, the adjoining state to Reed's, gave McKinley equal endorsement with Reed. The solidarity of New England was gone. Even in Massachusetts the leading Republican newspaper is said to have had a McKinley editorial in type, its publication being prevented only by a sudden change of ownership in the interest of Reed's campaign.

Efforts were made to defeat McKinley by supporting various candidates in the communities in which they were strongest in hopes of merging the opposition. One anecdote of this stage of the campaign is of interest. Platt, who had assisted in the nomination of Harrison on an alleged promise which if made certainly was never fulfilled, is said to have been willing to aid McKinley if he would make him Secretary of the Treasury, but McKinley, in spite of Hanna's protests, returned answer that if that was the price of the Presidency he would remain a private citizen. And so New York was for Levi P. Morton. Well before the convention McKinley was so far in the lead that the certainty of his nomination was uniformly admitted.

Even Joseph Manley, in charge of the Reed interests before the national committee, publicly admitted giving up hope a week before the meeting of the convention and was told with some asperity by another Reed worker that "God Almighty hates a quitter." Manley, however, had only stated an absolute fact with no belief that more enthusiastic and less discreet managers would continue to batter a stone wall.

More and more public attention centered around the coming declaration of principles. It had been certain for many months that on an old-fashioned protectionist platform the Republicans would surely win. But the unrest in the silver states caused agitation for a free silver declaration. That the party would go as far as that few believed, but many wanted to "do something for silver," and others wished to let well enough alone. There is no doubt that McKinley was among the latter. His friend H. H. Kohlsaat was stubbornly for gold. Hanna seems to have wanted a gold standard and was for getting it along the lines of least resistance. Of course the eastern seaboard was for gold. Henry Cabot Lodge and Edward Lauterbach were the prominent Eastern factors. Finally the controversy resolved itself to the question of inserting the words "existing gold standard" in the financial plank. Even if hostility to free silver was only thinly veiled, the tariff would pull the Republicans through no matter if the Democrats adopted a straight "sixteen to one" financial plank. If the Republican convention declared outright for a gold standard, party lines, once vertical, would become oblique and no one would be exactly sure of the outcome. Never was the issue clearer between expediency and honor. By dodging the issue they were practically sure of a "walkover"; by meeting it they were sure to encounter a bitter battle with the possibility of defeat in the end.

The convention met on June 16 in St. Louis. The platform was not presented until the third day. In the meantime there had been tremendous excitement. The Republicans from the silver states were as solid for their financial theory as the Easterners for theirs. Telegrams passed between Hanna and the predestined candidate. Threats of a possible bolt which could be avoided by equivocation were heard on every side. At last Hanna consented to the use of the specific words "existing gold standard." Lodge, Lauterbach and Kohlsaat had won. Who was most influential, what Hanna said to Lodge, what Lodge said to Kohlsaat, and all the rest is of little importance. The fact remains that an unequivocal plank safeguarding the financial honor of the country was presented to the convention.

As the platform reading was finished, Henry M. Teller, the white-haired senator from Colorado, honest and high-minded leader of the silver forces, offered as a substitute an out and out free silver declaration. There was something fine and pathetic about this venerable figure as he stood there, pleading, as he knew, in vain. It was not a question for compromise. The new alignment must begin then and there. The gold platform was adopted and with genuine emotion Teller, who had been at the birth of the party, honorably following the dictates of principle, withdrew at the head of thirty-four delegates from the silver states.

Parties rise to heights and sink to depths. Here was one of the great moments of Republicanism. In meeting the test of a great issue it reached the greatest height it has reached between the days of human aspiration in which it was born and the days when during the war with Germany it showed what in such a time the stand of a minority should be. It put by a certainty of success to meet courageously a great issue. Nor ought Teller to be forgotten. As conscientiously for silver as was Lodge for gold, his heart wrenched by parting from loved associates, he walked in deep sorrow the path which his conscience dictated.

When the vote for President was taken, it was shown plainly that Manley had been right and that holding Reed in the field for a humiliating defeat had been little less than cruel. Omitting fractions, McKinley received six hundred and sixty-one votes, while Reed's total was eighty-four. Garrett A. Hobart, who had shown himself an able parliamentarian as president of the senate of New Jersey, was nominated for Vice President. Reed was the greatest parliamentarian living and would have presided over the Senate admirably. Three delegates voted so to nominate him. No doubt the majority would have been delighted to have so strengthened the ticket, but it was not to be expected that Reed would consent to such a nomination. And yet if he had, how it would have changed history! He would have been too great a figure to deny a re-nomination. He, not Roosevelt, would have succeeded McKinley and as he died only fourteen months later, the Presidential succession law would have probably put John Hay, McKinley's Secretary of State, in the White House. Like Webster, Reed missed being President by refusing to consider the lesser office.

Now all eyes turned to the Democratic convention, which met in Chicago shortly after the Fourth of July. A similar contest to that which had torn the Republicans asunder was imminent, but in this instance the strength lay with the silver delegates and the gold men bid fair to be in the minority. This was somewhat increased by the fact that while the chances were none too rosy, the Democrats might win with silver and that they could not win if, by taking that issue out of the campaign, they left the tariff the predominant question. Their one hope was in forcing the currency issue on the Republicans. The Democratic convention was different from the Republican in that no avowed candidate seemed to have the remotest chance of being the nominee and at the time of gathering there seemed to be no drift toward anybody in particular. All interest centered on the platform. It was East against West and South, although the picturesque George Fred Williams, Republican, Mugwump and sound money Democrat, who had been one of the foremost champions of gold in Congressional debates which seemed to be even then ringing in the delegates' ears, a man who had been elected on a gold pledge, shifted suddenly while on the train, to the great disgust of ex-Governor William E. Russell, whom Massachusetts hoped to present to the convention in the remote event of a satisfactory platform being adopted.

Never was a political body more certain as to its intent. It was an untamed convention, in which Altgeld, the fiery governor of Illinois, and Tillman, the equally fiery senator from

South Carolina, were, in a great degree, to ride the whirlwind and direct the storm. At the outset it threw aside the Democratic national committee as then constructed. It defeated the committee's choice for temporary chairman, David B. Hill, and elected a warm free silver advocate in John W. Daniel, the lame senator from Virginia. Then and there, as a writer for the *New York World* said, the political scepter passed from East to West. That the new régime intended to dissociate itself from the only President the party had elected since Buchanan, and from all his works, was evident from the fact that only in the galleries was there anything but stony and eloquent silence at the mention of Cleveland's name. At last the crucial moment arrived. The platform which was reported was as unequivocally for free coinage as that of the Republicans was decisively for the gold standard. Then the East submitted its minority report. First in debate came Tillman. He raged through his allotted time with such violence that he was almost incoherent. In reply came the cold, unimpassioned and utterly futile reasoning of Senator Hill. He was followed by Vilas of Wisconsin and Russell of Massachusetts, both abashed by the passionate impatience of the convention. Then there modestly came forward a young delegate who, as a congressman, had not been beneath the notice of Tom Reed, and who had been seated at the head of the contesting silver delegation from Nebraska, William Jennings Bryan. With his opening sentences he roused the interest of the convention. As his speech progressed, as he told his listeners that "The farmer who goes forth in the morning and toils all day . . . is as much a business man as the man who goes upon the board of trade and bids upon the price of grain," as he declared that cities might be destroyed and that if the farms were spared the cities would spring up again, but that destruction of the farms would cause grass to grow in every city in the world, he became the outstanding figure of the convention. Then in his final outburst he declared, "You shall not press down upon the brow of labor this crown of thorns—you shall not crucify mankind upon a cross of gold." At last the delegates saw their views gloriously and humanly incarnate. Although after adopting the platform, the convention adjourned over night, and although pledges and obligations made five ballots necessary, from the moment of his peroration Bryan was the predestined nominee. Not long afterwards the Populists, refusing to listen to the "middle of the road" group among them, nominated Bryan as a man who stood for all that they did, though they rejected the Democratic candidate for Vice President, Arthur Sewall of Maine, and selected the fiery Tom Watson of Georgia.

The Republicans at first affected to think little of their opponent, whom they called "the boy orator of the Platte." They pretended to be shocked at the "sacrilegious" simile with which he closed his speech, although some of them referred to it as plagiarism and named Samuel W. McCall of Massachusetts, then a congressman, as the original user of the figures. Such attempts were abortive. Bryan kept boring in. His perfect good temper charmed even those who opposed him. His genuine poise and his undoubted honesty made him friends everywhere. In his tour of Ohio he stopped at Canton and referred to McKinley most courteously and felicitously.

The Republicans found there was something the matter. McKinley, the child of destiny, was being stubbornly opposed. These Democrats were acting as if they expected to win, which was not at all on the programme. A campaign where both parties went through the motions for the edification of their members was all that was expected, but these Democrats were taking themselves seriously and, what was worse, the voters seemed to be taking them the same way. Mark Hanna was at the head of the Republican national committee. He thought in terms of dollars and cents. He went out after money and he got it. If the amount to which he thought the committee entitled was not forthcoming, he expressed himself so vigorously that the remainder was almost immediately donated. Men who had stood aghast at the "blocks of five" episode of former years felt that the threat to stability was so great that though it was a pity to buy votes, after all, in this instance, it had better be done. But Hanna knew a far better trick than bold bribery. Next to Bryan the greatest asset to the Democrats was one Harvey who wrote "Coin's Financial School," a pamphlet full of sophistry, but in such simple language and with such everyday illustrations that it was doing untold harm. Hanna was bound to force public attention upon his side. Never had there been sent out so many spellbinders, never had a staff been so remunerated. Simply written pamphlets were printed and circulated by the hundreds of thousands. No little parish where votes might be got went without careful and repeated attention. So strong are party names in America that it was not deemed safe to allow the sound money Democrats to wander about loose, lest the word Democrat should cause them to fall into the Bryan bag. Therefore a convention was called to make a Gold Democratic nomination and presented the famous Blue and Gray ticket, consisting of General John M. Palmer of Illinois, a Union veteran, an old personal supporter of Lincoln, and General Simon Bolivar Buckner of Kentucky, the Confederate veteran who had surrendered to Grant at Donelson. This was a refuge for the Democrats who could not vote for McKinley, but although the Cleveland administration was nominally for this ticket every department was honeycombed with McKinley workers.

Bryan toured the country continuously. His phrases—which history has proved mistaken—were impressive, honest conviction shone in his face, and his attractiveness and good nature made him friends everywhere. McKinley remained at Canton and day after day spoke lucidly, eloquently, and with great variety of thought, to various delegations who visited him.

Meanwhile Hanna's campaign of education became more and more complete. The result was that Bryan gained thousands of friends and admirers who afterwards became convinced that they ought to vote against him.

By election day Hanna's work was done. The country was safe for the Republicans. Everywhere the Republican election machinery was organized to profit to the last vote by the campaign of education. Soon after ten o'clock it was known on the eastern seaboard that Bryan had been substantially defeated. When all doubtful questions were settled it was seen that McKinley would receive 271 votes from 23 states, while Bryan would get 176 votes from 24 states, including one from California, which gave McKinley the other eight.

But Bryan had made a great fight. His popular vote was six and a half million, a phenomenal number for that time, while McKinley received half a million more. Bryan sent entirely good-tempered congratulations to McKinley and the President-elect responded in kind. So ended one of the most important and hard-fought political battles in American history As we look back on it today we cannot help taking pride in one phase of this contest. It showed the American people two contestants for high honor supporting their party policies actively and ardently, yet able to do it in manner that should make the phrase "an American gentleman" one of deep significance. One, the successful candidate, was destined to head the administration of his country in days of tremendous stress, and at last to lay down his life in her service; the other was to become one of the three strongest personal leaders of his time, to be twice more the candidate of his party, and finally to become a President maker and cabinet head, only to leave his chief in deep sorrow. History has much to say about both these men, but it can never picture them more favorably than in this campaign, setting an example which some of their successors have fallen far short of approximating.

CHAPTER FOURTEEN

FEUD AND FACTION

ON the 4th of March, 1908, during the inauguration of William Howard Taft, a cavalcade drove briskly through the blizzard, down Capitol Hill to the beautiful new Union Station. In its center, in a closed carriage, rode Theodore Roosevelt, twenty-fourth President of the United States. Much speculation followed him. Why had this artist in publicity forgone his opportunity to play the incoming President off the stage? Was it as a service to the successor he had created? Did the owner of the "big stick" efface himself so that Taft might not be so forlorn an object as sensitive John Adams, whose inauguration had seemed to him only a fond farewell to George Washington? It did not seem so to those who had most shrewdly observed the conduct of the Colonel during his career since the Spanish War. Many of these observers thought they could sense a rift in the lute. Be that as it might, Taft, as the inheritor of Roosevelt's station, was made to face one of the least enlivening tasks which a man can confront. He had been an indefatigable supporter of McKinley and Roosevelt. Their policies he had set himself, both in the Philippines and in the Cabinet, industriously and wholeheartedly to carry out. He had always been known as a faithful subordinate. Now he set himself honestly and resolutely to the task of making a good executive. He had the judicial temperament and had always desired to make a great judge. As President he refrained from jumping at conclusions. Perhaps he was too little in the habit of immediately settling points for himself and then devoting all his energy to beating down opposition, honest or dishonest. It may be that he had too open a mind. He does not go down in history as any man's man, but he may have listened too much and to too many. He probably carried judicial habits of thought too far. But he did not, nor did he intend to, substitute his will for his oath. When Gifford Pinchot had his quarrel with Ballinger, Taft found it incompatible with his nature to dismiss his Secretary of the Interior. Conviction by public opinion, and Ballinger seems to have been properly convicted, was repugnant to him. Too long he gave the Secretary and not the public the benefit of the doubt. He proceeded, not sensationally, but with business-like intelligence and without fear or favor against those parties whom his predecessor had denounced as "malefactors of great wealth." It probably seemed to him that so to proceed without favoritism was better, on the whole, than rabid denunciation.

Taft's most delicate job concerned the tariff. Cleverly, persistently, Roosevelt had evaded meeting this dangerous but necessary reform. The Dingley bill was still on the books. It had been there since early in McKinley's first term. It was now archaic. Tariff changing is the most dangerous kind of party legislation, especially after a long term of years without such legislation. This Theodore Roosevelt knew as well as any man. He resolutely set himself to evade action. It might mean a political deluge. Very well, let it engulf his successor, but not at the close of the Roosevelt administration. Taft faced the music. The bill produced was unpopular. Taft had done the best a man of his temperament could do in influencing Congress from the White House, and it was due to his influence that certain forward-looking features were put into the bill, but the Aldriches and Warrens had not been put down. Taft defended the bill because of the good in it and also because of the necessity for a change, but did not endorse such objectionable clauses as the woollen schedule. At Winona he used words which, separated from their context, seemed unqualifiedly to praise the bill. This speech was quoted against him with deadly effect. As Mr. Taft's term progressed he seemed destined to be a single term president.

In the meantime Roosevelt was in Africa. He had made Taft his successor. With a facile use of all the political weapons in the armory of the most resourceful politician who had held the office in recent times, he blighted the hopes of all who dared aspire. If there had been no hot-house forcing, the Taft movement would never have blossomed, for its beneficiary had never attracted public imagination. In the contests for delegates, the big stick was always busy. When the national committee sat to decide contested seats for the preliminary roll, the anti-Taft men were loud in their denunciations of the steamroller tactics of the Roosevelt-built machine.

When Taft had been safely nominated and elected there began to be, as now seems clear, a slight disturbance in the happy relations between the men. Taft is said to have written Roosevelt what was intended to be a grateful acknowledgement. In it he used these words: "Next to my brother I owe more to you than to any other man for my election." This brother was Charles P. Taft, who had financed the campaign. The gentle blundering of the amiable President-elect is very well typified by this sentence. To think that he owed more to Charles P. Taft than he did to the man who had appointed him his political residuary legatee was silly, but it must have been gall and wormwood to Roosevelt, and even those who detest Roosevelt's subsequent actions must sympathize with his disgust. Then came the question of the new cabinet. Roosevelt's statement that Taft gave him to understand that he wished the old cabinet, except Bonaparte and Cortelyou, to hold over, and that this was announced to the members in Taft's presence, must be believed inasmuch as it seems never to have been contradicted. If this arrangement was made, it was, of course, overturned. One must doubt, however, Roosevelt's statement that he expected Taft would recede from his promise. Roosevelt's whole career both before and after Taft's election proves that he expected to dominate him, and he had not found out so soon that this expectation was vain. As time went on the little group of Roosevelt admirers known to the newspaper men as "fair-haired boys" and the "tennis cabinet" found the White House atmosphere distinctly chilly. Taft was to be President in his own right. Then came the Ballinger imbroglio. Gifford Pinchot sped to Italy to meet his mentor when he emerged from the wilds. Although the amenities were kept up, Roosevelt returned ready ultimately to oppose Taft. That he intended at that day to be a candidate, however, cannot be fairly assumed.

There was no doubt that the "Old Guard" was in the saddle. Many of the Progressive group of the Republican party had turned to LaFollette as a candidate. Their hopes were never high. They intended to get a good minority of the convention vote for the Wisconsin Senator and then four years later, after the Republican defeat, to reorganize the party and elect either La Follette or another. Little by little the talk of Roosevelt's candidacy grew. He had said on his election in 1904: "Under no circumstances will I be a candidate for or accept another nomination." He is said to have told a friend that he would give his right hand to recall these words. Past question this was at first a restraining influence. Finally the governors of seven states, the most notable of whom was Hadley of Missouri, invited him to run and he responded, "My hat is in the ring."

From that minute his popular strength with all sorts and conditions of men began to assert itself. Taft's friends had the machinery. He was strongly intrenched with a very large block of early elected delegates. The only question was whether the Roosevelt tide would quite or only almost sweep him into the

nomination. With such a bitter contest all possibility of the
election of either disappeared. The Colonel took the stump.
Never had he been more truculent. Never had he disregarded
the arguments against him with such utter sangfroid. He
grasped at issues with which he had never before been in
sympathy and with which he never concerned himself thereafter, including the initiative and referendum, the recall of
judges and the recall of judicial decisions. Certain of these
tendencies he had denounced as "a species of avatism" in 1896,
as his friend Henry Cabot Lodge stated to a body of law
students in 1913 in an address on Abraham Lincoln which was
really a defense of the judiciary. The great Massachusetts
politician further quoted his friend as writing in the same article: "Savages do not like an independent and upright judiciary.
They want the judge to decide their way, and if he does not
they want to behead him."

Among Roosevelt's personal supporters was George W.
Perkins, one of that class whom the Rough Rider was supposed to long to punish. He was a partner in the house of
Morgan and his connection with the Harvester trust and the
fact that that corporation had not been prosecuted under the
Roosevelt régime when it might have been, became an issue of
the campaign. Another supporter, well equipped with the
sinews of war, was Frank A. Munsey, owner of many maga-
zines and newspapers. Then there was Gifford Pinchot, another not wholly unblessed with this world's goods. Roosevelt
denounced the big bosses, and little bosses climbed upon his
shoulders. He excoriated Penrose, although he had been cheek
by jowl with Quay. Penrose's bitterest foe was Boss William
Flinn of Pittsburgh, hardly an altruist, and to his charge were
committed the Roosevelt interests in Pennsylvania. Senator
Crane of Massachusetts was anathema, but although the
Roosevelt followers included men like Charles Sumner Bird,
of great honesty and a most lovable character, its organization

contained several strategic local leaders who reflected no especial credit on any cause they might espouse. There were plenty of excellent men in the Roosevelt ranks and an equal number of politicians who showed that they appreciated certain of their leader's characteristics. The radicalism of his present principles also brought supporters from what their leader is said to have referred to as a "lunatic fringe."

Meantime Taft stood in dumb surprise. Finally Roosevelt, who had always been a "practical man" and had not hesitated to let Addicks of Delaware control patronage when he was in the Senate, tried to tie Taft up to the discredited Lorimer. This was a blow below the belt indeed. Taft favored the expulsion of Lorimer from the Senate, but he was a kinder and gentler man than his predecessor, and the Illinois Senator in taking a stand between the two had nowhere else to go than to Taft. Taft said plainly that he disapproved of Lorimer. Roosevelt continued his attacks. Then he began to couple himself with Lincoln and not even that disgusted his followers. He had some high-minded supporters who believed in him, others who thought that the stagnation in the party needed this remedy, but he became as much a mob candidate as ever Jackson had been. He denounced W. Murray Crane, of whose great help he had availed himself in the past, whose advice had given Roosevelt the tremendous prestige of the coal strike settlement and whom he had invited into his cabinet. He maneuvered for votes every minute. He was clever, alert, hot-blooded in his manner and cold-blooded in his ruthlessness.

Roosevelt swept Illinois and Pennsylvania. In April the campaign began in Massachusetts. This conservative state might turn the tide by leading a swing back to Taft. If it went for Roosevelt it would be a terrible, perhaps a final, blow to the Taft campaign. Roosevelt entered upon a systematic attack. Reluctantly the President took the stump. He made a calm, able speech in the Boston Arena. He met the charges of

Roosevelt temperately and honestly. That he had been deeply wounded by the attitude of a once dear friend was evident, but he certainly met his rival's allegations admirably. To those who walked away from that hall in the cool air of a New England spring, it seemed as if the end of the Roosevelt pretensions had come. It moved neither the fiery candidate nor his supporters. He might have been Jack Cade and have cried, "Away, burn all the records of the realm, my mouth shall be the parliament." Such men as Albert E. Pillsbury, a great lawyer and no special admirer of Taft, and Edwin D. Mead, than whom no gentler or more just soul has sought to serve his fellow men, condemned Roosevelt without qualification. Pillsbury wrote that the ex-President had "thrown public faith and private honor to the winds." Mead commended Taft, who had "remained silent so long, under the grossest attack to which a President of the United States was ever subjected or likely to be subjected."

When the Taft league began filling its list of Massachusetts delegates, a young German-American politician, a local character never distinguished for logic, tact or polish, went into the headquarters and offered himself or some other German-American to the manager as a delegate-at-large. His proffer was declined, probably in an arbitrary manner. This declination had far-reaching results. The politician ran as a Taft candidate for delegate-at-large, although the full number of delegates had been put forward by the Taft league. There were eight men on the ballot for delegate-at-large with Roosevelt designations against their names. There were nine Taft men so designated. A vote for more than eight was invalid. The voters also could express their preference directly, an expression which had no binding influence on the delegates. On the question of preference the names of Taft, Roosevelt and La Follette appeared. Not only eight delegates but eight alternates were to be elected in the state-at-large. Massachusetts declared her preference for Taft by over two thousand majority. She elected eight Roosevelt delegates-at-large, defeating among others Senator Crane, ex-Governor Bates and John W. Weeks. She elected the eight Taft men as alternates to the eight Roosevelt delegates. Enough men had voted for the nine Taft candidates for delegate, and so invalidated their ballots, to bring about this anomalous condition. This prevented the clear-cut mandate which might have aided Taft.

Roosevelt continued to make gains. He won successes in Maryland, New Jersey, and even in Taft's home state of Ohio. When all the delegates were elected the claims were so confused that no one really knew anything except that the result would be close. With the proclivity of the average politician to look towards the rising rather than the setting sun, Roosevelt seemed to wise observers to have rather the best of it. There were others who believed that a compromise candidate might be chosen. To most politicians it seemed like a suit for the right to bury a corpse.

Finally the Roosevelt managers filed over two hundred contests before the National Committee. So wholesale an effort was spectacular and done to affect public sentiment. This was admitted in Munsey's Washington organ. Less than seventy-five contests had real merit. If the intent of the voters was worth anything, the eight Taft candidates from Massachusetts could well have been seated, for a convention is the judge of its own members and the certificates were not of election to a public office where the question of intent of voters cannot go beyond the face of the ballots. The intent of the voters was clear but the Massachusetts Taft men made no contest.

Before the national committee the Taft machine steam roller got to work. Four years before, when the Roosevelt machine thought it was putting into the presidency a pale echo of its chief, it had shown how to do a very neat job. The present committee was willing to better the instruction. The

167

opposition four years before had suffered, if not wholly in silence, at least without effective protest. But when the Roosevelt organization found itself hoist with its own petard it shrieked to Heaven. Any possibility of a Roosevelt victory was dissipated by the tactlessness of his supporters. Senator Joseph Dickson of Montana, the Roosevelt manager, made on the very first day of the committee meetings this ingratiating statement: "By fraud and misrepresentation and brutal control of political machines the Taft managers have stolen district and state conventions; with the eyes of the nation centered on Chicago they will fail in the brazen effort to steal the presidential nomination itself." Heney, the San Francisco attorney, who had done great work in the graft trials, was utterly without any appreciation of the amiability and *savoir faire* of the gentlemen who were doing their best to defraud him in a seemly and affable manner, and he hurt their feelings by the things he said about them. Then there was the placid Ormsby McHarg, who predicted a political revolution and added: "We have had offers by telegraph of one thousand crack shots from Oklahoma to march right down to the Coliseum and clean out the whole caboodle." What wonder that when the convention met the hall was strongly guarded by police!

One contest deserves especial note. The Republican party called for the election of delegates in a certain manner. The election laws of California prescribed another. Two Taft delegates were elected as the party call had dictated. The Roosevelt delegates were elected as the California election laws prescribed. Could a single state dictate the policy of a national party? The committee declared, soundly we think, for the party system. But if the Roosevelt delegates had been thus elected and the Taft delegates by the state system there is no doubt that the committee would have declared for the state system. It is significant that the Taft forces made no election contest in California.

Carrying out the program, an old, old program among political parties it is too, the committee, being a Taft committee, decided all the contests that it possibly could in favor of the Taft delegates. A competent newspaper observer, who has no bias toward Roosevelt, thinks that he lost fifty votes that he should have had. Roosevelt, being Roosevelt, and being acutely conscious that this time it was *his* ox which was being gored, rose to a high moral plane and talked about "naked theft." The contests were to be taken to the floor of the convention. The first battle was for temporary chairman. Elihu Root was the Taft candidate. Though Root had been his Secretary of State, Roosevelt in his present temper would not accept him, though he had paid him compliment after compliment in the past. Governor McGovern of Wisconsin was backed by the insurgents. The effort was made, on the question of seating the delegates, to prohibit any delegate whose seat was contested from voting on any other contest. That this did not prevail was one of the chief Progressive grievances. The proposition was absurd. A candidate had only to contest enough delegates, as fraudulently as the Roosevelt machine had contested over a hundred, to invalidate the voting power of properly elected delegates, make the body practically a rump convention and dictate his own nomination. He might be met by the same tactics and, let go to its logical end, there might finally be a totally delegateless convention. No unprejudiced lawyer would consider this tenable for an instant.

Governor Hadley of Missouri was in charge of the Roosevelt interest. He conducted himself with such poise, efficiency and good nature, that he might possibly have been nominated himself, but Roosevelt declared against any compromise. When the delegates were finally seated, Roosevelt, who was in Chicago, repudiated the whole thing and urged his followers to take no further part but to organize a new party. That left Taft's managers in charge of the convention and

169

spoiled any chance, however remote, of making a compromise nomination.

The last episode which raised the cry of fraud concerned the now famous Massachusetts eight. They sat in their seats on the roll call for President and responded "Present but not voting." Massachusetts had expressed her preference for Taft. These men had been elected by a clear mistake. They had a mandate, not compelling, it is true. Their alternates had been intelligently elected and were present. Chairman Root ordered the call of these alternates. Against protests he declared that if delegates elected to perform a duty refused to perform it and they had alternates ready to act, those alternates could rightly do so. He is criticized because he called no other alternates when a delegation refused to vote; but the facts are, and both Root and his critics knew this to be true, that this was the only delegation where the alternates would not have remained as silent as their principals. Taft's margin over all, including the three hundred and forty-four who did not vote, and not counting a few absentees, was about fifty votes. Without enthusiasm Vice President Sherman was joined to the ticket and the convention adjourned. A long line of convention abuses running over many years thus culminated, leaving an honest, just and lovable man in the position of a wrongful beneficiary, and the man who should have been his friend in the position of a moral hero wrongfully despoiled. It is the least edifying spectacle in the history of conventions.

While these events were taking place the opposition party had been marshaling its forces. Among the Democratic candidates were Champ Clark, the Speaker of the House, Representative Oscar Underwood of Alabama, the Chairman of the Ways and Means Committee, and the Democratic governors of Massachusetts, Connecticut, New Jersey, Ohio and Indiana. Champ Clark was a magnificent figure with his large and well-proportioned frame, his mobile face and deep-set eyes. The conventional attire of the day sat appropriately upon him but it did not interfere with the impression that this man would be equally impressive in the pioneer hunting shirt and coonskin cap of other generations, or even in a Roman toga. He was an effective speaker and had been conspicuous in party councils for years. One who reads his memoirs finds few traces of any original thought. He was a serviceable war-horse but fell far short of being a great man. In Underwood we have another type. The son of a Union soldier who had settled there after the war, he would have made an especially sentimental appeal as a representative of the South. But his would not have been a sentimental candidacy. He was brilliant and at the same time acute and business-like. Few would deny that he was of presidential dimensions. Of the governors, Foss and Baldwin were merely negligible. Marshall of Indiana might possibly be turned to, to break a deadlock. Judson Harmon of Ohio was of more importance. He had been a cabinet officer under Cleveland and stood toward his party somewhat as Alton B. Parker had eight years previously, except that he was a more notable personality than Parker had been up to the time of his nomination. The other governor was Woodrow Wilson of New Jersey. Even then he was one of the phenomena of American politics. Six years previous no one would have thought of him except as a private citizen nor of electing him to any high office. He had been merely one of the hundreds of responsible men who are not politicians, but who perform their civic duties with deeper understanding than most and may be referred to as competent citizens. Throughout all his life previously more than this had not been discovered in him by those who exert real political leadership. He was of Virginian birth, of post-Revolutionary, Scotch-Irish ancestry. After being graduated at Princeton he studied and practiced law but had turned to collegiate teaching. In his college work he had had occasion to write somewhat on law, literature and government. He discovered that he had an admirably fluid English style and so wrote several interesting books. These books, not being on popular subjects, yielded him more reputation than profit.

Finally he produced a "History of the American People" in five volumes. This was published by Harper and Brothers in the days when that firm was under the control of the redoubtable Colonel Harvey. Every bit of publicity which was needed to assist in its sales was utilized for its benefit. As the days of 1908 drew near when a President was to be elected, *Harper's Weekly* began to contain editorials advocating this scholar in politics and literature. It reiterated them and it was through these editorials that Wilson became, in the popular mind, a presidential possibility. These editorials, however, made no impression on the Democratic convention of that year, but did somewhat stimulate the sale of the history. Meanwhile the author had been made president of Princeton University. The Democratic party of New Jersey was in a parlous state. The state machine, one of the worst in the country, had got into ruts. A new type of candidate must be nominated if it was to win. Here was the president of the great university of the state (it was not then generally known that he had worn out his welcome at Princeton), a man whom so notable a periodical as *Harper's Weekly* had vouched for even for the presidency. Such a nomination would be putting the best foot forward indeed. Nominated and elected, when he took his seat in the capitol at Trenton, Wilson's friends set about making the Harper prophecy true. The Govtrnor took a new view of some of the so-called liberal issues, notably the initiative and referendum. He quarreled fearlessly and profitably with the New Jersey bosses. He withdrew his interests from Colonel Harvey, who had been his chief sponsor, *Harper's* being too conservative a paper to make his can-

didacy attractive to the liberals. He trod his expressed desire
to see Bryan "knocked into a cocked hat" underfoot and extended a friendly hand to "the great Commoner." He gathered
around him a number of able and aggressive Democrats not
of the "Old Guard" type. His manager was William F.
McCombs of New York.

Of these candidates Wilson, Underwood and Harmon were
intellectually the best fitted for the presidency. Baldwin was
finical, Foss erratic. Probably Clark and Marshall furnished
the poorest caliber of all. Underwood and Harmon were considered the representative conservatives and Wilson and Clark
as the chief liberals. All the publicity which the Hearst papers
could give was given to Clark. At times during the convention Clark went from Washington to Baltimore and Hearst
was always present in the conferences.

Of course the convention met with high hopes. The Republican fiasco earlier in the month had made the Democratic
nominee the predestined winner.

There was one figure of tremendous importance and influence present. This was Bryan, the three times standard bearer.
He was always looming up in the background. He apparently
was for no particular candidate except so far as his instruction
for Clark might bind him. Of all the candidates before the
convention, Clark had been his most loyal friend and supporter. But Clark had an anxiety to win at all hazards, and
seemed, as the campaign for this nomination progressed, to
think little of the principles in the contest. When certain delegates known to Bryan as reactionary began to show an interest in Clark, Bryan became suspicious. Besides, the great
Commoner under his bland exterior still nursed a resentment
against those who had been either indifferent or lukewarm to
his candidacy in 1896, and their friendliness to Clark seemed
ominous to him. Perhaps he had a vision of a deadlocked convention finally turning to the old reliable journeyman candi-

date of the party. He first attempted to defeat Alton B. Parker of New York for temporary chairman, allowing himself to be nominated against him. In this he failed. He must have realized that a man who could not be elected temporary chairman of a convention could not be its nominee. No doubt he noticed that the Clark delegates, in their anxiety to offend no one, divided their votes on this question.

Just before the balloting for the nomination, Bryan made a sensational coup, the most spectacular act of a colorful life. Mounting the platform he offered a motion that the convention, "as proof of our fidelity to the people" declare itself "opposed to the nomination of any candidate for president who is the representative of or under obligation to J. Pierpont Morgan, Thomas F. Ryan, August Belmont or any other member of the privilege-hunting or favor-seeking class." Now both Ryan and Belmont were members of the convention and Bryan added a clause, which he finally withdrew, demanding the withdrawal of delegates representing their interests. "Bang!" This was an explosion destined to reverberate for years in political history. It was meant, in particular, to "hogtie" the New York delegation. In the history of conventions there is no more audacious, dramatic or fearless act. The convention was enraged. It was in a hole. It dared not reject the motion but it was angry at having to pass it. Bryan stood with calm courage under the most menacing threats of violence he had ever encountered. One lusty patriot screamed, "I'll give $25,000 to any one who will kill him." Another inquired at the top of his voice why some one did not hang him. A delegate rushed on to the platform, frothing at the mouth with rage. He was shaking his fist in close proximity to Bryan's face when his friends led him away. Bryan asked for a roll call. Charlie Murphy, then head of Tammany, sitting at the side of Belmont, said to him with a cynical smile, "Augie, listen and hear yourself vote yourself out of the convention," and then cast the ninety votes of New York for the resolution. Bryan's was an act of great moral and physical courage. Never had he been so near physical injury, but he was unperturbed.

When the balloting began it was evident that Clark had a great lead. Wilson was next but a long way behind. The ninety votes of New York were for Harmon. When, on the tenth ballot, New York, controlled by Murphy, shifted from Harmon to Clark, his nomination seemed probable; but for Bryan's motion it would have seemed certain. Clark now had a majority of the convention, which he held for eight ballots. The convention, however, was operating under the old Democratic two-thirds rule. Still everything seemed to favor him. There is now a dispute as to whether Wilson gave up the fight, or his manager McCombs lost courage. One or the other surely happened, and it remained for certain old stagers to hold them from immediate surrender.

In the meantime Bryan was maturing his plans. He was under instruction for Clark but he did not regard these instructions as longer binding. On the fourteenth ballot he announced that he would not vote for any man who was indebted to Wall Street for the vote of New York. He forthwith cast his vote "for Nebraska's second choice, Governor Wilson." Of course this helped Wilson tremendously. There are today those who believe that Bryan wished to create an impasse by which he might finally profit. It does not seem so to me; but whatever his wishes, Bryan's moment never came. Ballot after ballot was taken. Little by little the serene, unruffled college professor gained. Finally the forty-sixth was reached and the tellers announced the final result. The two-thirds having been achieved, there was a stampede to the winner. The final figures were Wilson 990; Clark 84; Harmon 12. Underwood, on almost any ballot, might have nominated Clark, but he held aloof. Clark declared that Bryan's treachery cost him the nomination, and undoubtedly Bryan stopped him. In his memoirs

Clark says with utter truth of Bryan's anti-Tammany attitude: "I never said, 'Great is Tammany and Croker is its prophet!' Bryan did. I never welcomed Mr. Murphy at a railroad station, and had my picture taken clasping hands with him. Bryan did. I never sent a trusted friend half-way across the continent to beg Mr. Murphy not to defeat my nomination under the two-thirds rule by refusing to give me the New York delegation after I received a majority. Bryan did." A very discerning and impartial newspaper observer of political events has said, "Politics is a game. Gratitude is often a by-word; honor an unknown quantity; loyalty and personal friendship disregarded. These things are expected in politics. But in a long period of political observation I never have known a case of political treachery equal to or even approaching that of William J. Bryan towards Champ Clark at Baltimore in 1912."

While this may be the fact, it is easy to see that Clark was willing to take the nomination on any terms and would have been perfectly willing to owe it to the reactionary elements of the convention, consisting of men who do not give something for nothing. Bryan in contrast, was willing to help to the nomination of any able progressive whose success might be secured. There is nothing in this incompatible with good political morals and when one judges this act in the light of the whole of Bryan's career, one may well class it as highly commendable and courageous.

In August the convention of the new party met in Chicago. It was one of the finest appearing bodies of men that ever convened. The rag-tag and bob-tail that assemble when there is a contest, that trade between the lines, that are carried as an accompaniment by delegation after delegation, sometimes an incubus but of which the old party delegations cannot rid themselves, were very greatly absent. These men had come merely to register a decision already made. Such an affair is not attractive to the practical gang politician. In a seemly but joyful and enthusiastic manner it sang hymns, nominated Theodore Roosevelt of New York for President and Hiram Johnson of California for Vice President. Then it adjourned and its members went to work to achieve second place in the poll for their candidate.

Never since the election of 1860 when the split between the factions of Douglas and Breckinridge made Lincoln's success sure had the election of a particular candidate seemed so certain. The real contest was as to who would be the second man. The Progressives were made up of vigorous, fresh, active and well-appearing enthusiasts who had come together from various motives. There were those who idolized the ebullient Roosevelt. There were those who really believed with fervor, almost with fanaticism, in the principles which he was now enunciating. There were those who believed that any house-cleaning in the Republican party would be a good thing. And last there were the camp-followers who, utterly discredited in the old parties, took hope that they might be influential in the new. This last class is always to be found in such a movement, and doubtless were as prevalent in the Republican party when it commenced its career in the fifties as were its members among the Progressives of 1912.

The old line regulars were almost numb. In every Republican state there were numerous local officers for which the Progressives had not made nominations, although they did put up many candidates. Would they vote for the Republican or Democratic nominee? When a Republican stump speaker raised his voice in opposition to the truculence with which Taft was assailed, the managers would say, "Hush! hush! Remember our candidate for the legislature!" This was not always the case, but it was so frequently, so that poor Taft seemed often deserted. If the Republican party had "gone after" Roosevelt as it might, many accepted beliefs would not have been created which are even today reiterated and honestly held.

The Roosevelt campaign was one continual whirl. He charged all over the United States. He knew crowd psychology as few men have known it, and played to it with great skill. He had superb courage, and when a madman shot him, he insisted on going to the hall and delivering his speech. He was painfully wounded and left the stump, but only temporarily. On his return he was, of course, a greater idol than ever. Vice President Sherman died during the campaign, but that hardly caused a ripple.

On election day both the expected and the unexpected happened. As expected, Wilson swept the country. The divided opposition gave him Republican states all over the country. He had four hundred and thirty-five electoral votes out of five hundred and thirty-one. The unexpected result was that the old Republican party went into third place. In the country at large Roosevelt had six hundred thousand more votes than Taft, who carried only two states, Utah and Vermont, and had only eight electoral votes or one-eleventh as many as Roosevelt received. Still more surprising is the fact that this terribly beaten party should in four years have become the contender against the Democratic, lose by only a hair, and four years after that sweep the country with the most tremendous victory in its history, while the party of a day proved not to be the party of the hour, but disappeared when its leader, ought we not to say its proprietor, returned to his old allegiance.

What did the Progressive bolt accomplish? Some think it elected Wilson. With the vote of Taft and Roosevelt combined against him, Wilson would have been defeated. But the best judges are satisfied that it could not have been so combined: Taft received votes given to him as a rebuke to Roosevelt, which would have gone to Wilson had it not been certain that he did not need them. Still greater strength would have gone to him from radicals whom Roosevelt held, had Taft been unopposed. What the Progressive split certainly did was to leave a wound which could not be healed quite sufficiently to insure Republican success four years later. It was the quarrel of 1912 which re-elected Wilson in 1916. Had Roosevelt remained passive after the Republican convention of 1912, it seems certain that nothing could have prevented his nomination and election in 1916. That this did not occur is one of the benefactions which come from circumstances. However able a war President Roosevelt would have made, his election for more than two terms would have broken down a restriction which is one of the wisest unwritten laws of the Republic.

How the three contenders for the prize and their futures stand out! Taft was to take his dismissal with rare philosophy and good humor and, after more than eight years of retirement, was to be called back to public service in the high office which of all others is most congenial to him, the Chief Justice of these United States.

Roosevelt was to stand as a strong bulwark in a bitter day, to preach a courageous evangel greatly to a great people and to fall at a time when his greatness was most visible and his mistakes of ambition and temperament were almost forgotten.

Wilson was to reach the very height of power and, after a period when he seemed greater than kings, to retire broken in body and repudiated as few men have ever been, but still nursing with pride and alertness the shadow of his great dream.

CHAPTER FIFTEEN

"HE KEPT US OUT OF WAR!"

WITH the election of 1912 over, it looked as if Theodore Roosevelt had demolished the Republican party. It had been beaten three times before, with Fremont, with Blaine, with Harrison, but it had never fallen to anything resembling a third party. But for the party of Lincoln to limp to the doors of the House of Representatives on the day of the electoral count with a pitiful eight votes seemed less like a temporary setback than like disaster and disintegration. It seemed bitter irony that the count fell on Lincoln's birthday. Just as Van Buren's candidacy had been fatal to Democratic success in Cass's day, so the one-time Republican idol, once the greatest favorite of his party (for Lincoln's recognition was posthumous) had thrown the party responsible for his career into the slough of despond. But T. R. had done a far more thorough job than had Van Buren. He, not the Republican candidate, had been the runner-up. It looked to many as if the durable Democracy which had seen the end of the Federalists and the Whigs was to see another great party go down and to confront as its fourth major opponent the new Progressive organization.

But the wiseacres, Democratic and Republican alike, were not so sure of this. The Republican machinery, though badly dented, was intact. The party which had been out of government control since 1897 was handicapped by the scarcity of men trained in government. Nothing proved that more completely than Mr. Bryan's deserving Democrats who were to occupy diplomatic posts. The tariff which the Democrats must pass would cause dissatisfaction, as all tariff bills do. There is nothing like a lean and hungry period to solidify opposition, and it seemed as if that opposition might enlist with the old organization and march under the old banner. It did.

Never had a President been inaugurated under what seemed more favorable circumstances. Woodrow Wilson had been the first choice of the plurality which elected him; he had been the second choice of practically every voter of the divided majority. A conservative Republican said in my presence as he entered the election booth on that November morning in 1912, "Here's a vote for Taft and a prayer for Wilson." All the voters of the former Republican group, much as they wished to win, cherished even closer the wish for the defeat of the man with whom their candidate had quarreled, whether that man was Roosevelt or Taft. There was little animosity against Wilson except in the hearts of those two redoubtable Democratic colonels, Harvey and Watterson.

But this modern era of good feeling was not to continue for long. The defects of Wilson's qualities were to bring quick antagonism on his head. For Wilson, who had great ability, great ambitions and—as his followers believed—great ideals, was without humility or magnanimity. In one way he resembled Roosevelt, and this resemblance was somewhat at the bottom of their mutual aversion. Each believed so thoroughly in himself that he could brook no disagreement and held in disdainful contempt not only the discretion but the moral character of any dissenter. In this respect Wilson was probably more sincere and therefore more bigoted than even the militant New Yorker.

There was one thing in the character of this complex and interesting man which was destined to work him especial injury in the public eye. He was self-sufficient, but he seemed to fear to put his views to the test in discussions with really great men. He was surrounded by satellites. Their agreement was a matter of course. Their admiration was sweet in his nostrils. He brought into his confidence no pre-eminent fellow leader who would contest with his opinions, for Wilson's own sake, and so he seemed never to have the other side of his views adequately presented to him. He quickly made up his mind, and, his mind made up, its decisions were gospel. To disagree with this mind, "a single track mind," he called it, was to sin against the light or break the heart of the world. His closest confidant was the amicable and unselfish but rather second-rate Colonel House. All morals and honesty were, as he seemed to think, in his own custody, and yet he took an oblique view of contractual obligations. This is made clear by his attitude at Princeton during the struggle of forces in that University. The dean had refused the presidency of the Massachusetts Institute of Technology, on representations concerning the future made to him by the Princeton authorities which were tantamount to the elements of a contract. This concerned the instituting of the graduate school. After Dean West's opportunity in Massachusetts closed, Wilson, then president of the University, reversed his position and at a meeting of the trustees, held on February 5, 1909, he said, "I wish to say to the Dean, somewhat grimly, that he must be digested on the processes of the University." When West referred to the pledges made him in 1906, Mr. Wilson's reply was, "We must not lay too great stress on commitments." This is certainly evidence that President Wilson was incapable of straight thinking when contractual morality was concerned. He disdained the obligations of his party platform and did the opposite of what it promised in two particulars, the second term pledge and the matter of the Panama Canal tolls. All these are matters of record.

Wilson was not insincere in his friendships, but he was quick to believe that these friendships had been betrayed. No two men ever served a chief more unselfishly than did Colonel House and Secretary Tumulty. Theirs was rare devotion, Tumulty's was akin to worship, but the time came when Wilson sent them both to Coventry.

In spite of Wilson's "single track mind," he conducted himself so that his opponents could refer to what they sarcastically called its "turntables." He had made in his early days scholarly and constructive arguments against the initiative and referendum. As a politician he embraced the principle. He once expressed a wish to see Mr. Bryan "knocked into a cocked hat," and later, though not permanently, took him to his political bosom. His brother-in-law, Professor Axon, in a campaign article published in the *New York Times* in October, 1916, explained this quality in these words: "He dealt with facts, and in crowded times like these, facts change chemically even while you are looking at them." Perhaps. Facts are ephemeral enough. But truths are permanent and it is truths which breed principles.

Wilson had a strong following, not born of personal association, but which followed him with an almost fanatical devotion. In their eyes he could do nothing that was not sacrosanct. They seemed to have the faith and fanaticism of dervishes. In spite of his very human faults, they saw in him a constant and an almost absolute perfection. On the other hand, he roused opposition that was powerful and bitter. To their minds he could do nothing good or (to some views) even decent. And in the days of Wilson's presidency it was hard to find anybody who took a middle ground. He was saint or satyr.

Woodrow Wilson had a passionate belief in himself as a leader. He believed the people needed him above all men of his time and in his own eyes he was true to them. He yearned for a warm-hearted popularity, a familiar affection which he had no power to attract. It was the superficial side of Roosevelt which had brought the mob to "Teddy," and Wilson had no superficial side.

But in the words of Charles William Eliot, an avowed admirer, "Woodrow Wilson, like most reformers and pioneering folk, had a fierce and unlovely side," and the great public sensed it.

Woodrow Wilson had at least one great vision, one noble and unforgettable ideal. Disagree, as we may, with the structure and availability of his plan; make allowances, if we must, for his ambition to have his name connected with it; remember, as we do, the little nations whose liberties he abandoned in his quest, the outstanding fact remains that Woodrow Wilson literally with the last ounce of his strength fought to save civilization from the probability of committing suicide by war. I hold no brief for the method or the panacea. I detest the autocratic refusal to counsel with men who could have safeguarded and perhaps made permanent his dream. I deplore the arrogance which his opponents calculated on when he walked into the pit they had dug and when in old Yankee parlance he "bit off his nose to spite his face." I grieve over the lack of that sweetness and conciliation with which Lincoln would have wooed support. But when all these things are said, the fact remains that if ever a really civilized peace descends upon mankind he must be remembered as the greatest of its early prophets. And so also the fact remains that his death came from the wounds of that battle. It was an ill-fought fight. The general's strategy was poor, the general's temper was pitiful and petty. Perhaps the very campaign was an error and the thing he sought would not have achieved his end. Let it pass. Statesmen and historians may, nay must, criticize with nice estimate and academic measure, but the multitude of men and women will remember the passion of his sacrifice and the white light of his ideal. He sought to turn men from a false and selfish understanding of patriotism and to fix their gaze on a world toleration and faith. And the tragedy of Woodrow Wilson does not lie in the death his battle finally brought him. It lies in those petty qualities which were in him and which made him fail.

Early in Wilson's administration the Republicans gained courage. The new tariff caused disturbance. For a brief period times seemed hard.

Then there was the Mexican fiasco. Wilson frankly meant, if he could, to drive Huerta, one of the greatest scoundrels unhung, from the presidency. But with all his detestation of the Mexican leader, he was hesitant and weak in his policy. He would not grasp the nettle. The leader with whose cause he sympathized, later turned out to be little better than Huerta and made capital of his hatred of the Gringoes, who, through the attitude of their President, had assisted in his victory. Many able men believed that the United States should have avoided taking sides between rascals and have observed the international custom of recognizing the *de facto* government without going into its method of seizing the title, as the nations of the world, including the United States, had done in recognizing Peter after the murder of King Milan of Serbia. But Wilson, always ready to decide world affairs, did not accept this position and made what at the time seemed a pretty bad mess of it. He toyed with an arms embargo, sometimes on, sometimes off. A boatload of American sailors was arrested at Vera Cruz, being taken from the boat, which was American territory, at the wharf. This was the act of a blundering Mexican official and was immediately countermanded. Huerta expressed regrets, but Admiral Mayo called for a salute to the flag. While this question was pending, news reached Washington that a shipload of munitions was on the way to Vera Cruz from Havana. At a conference with Bryan and Daniels, the President determined to prevent this. Here these three men of their own decision ordered what was an

185

act of war. War must be declared by Congress. These were not munitions slipped over our border in defiance of an arms embargo, but arms from a neutral country with which we had no right to interfere. Admiral Fletcher seized the custom house under fire and eighteen American sailors were killed. We were at war, not with a nation, but with a man. Vera Cruz was held until the abdication and flight of Huerta. The American flag was never saluted. The "turntable" in the "single track mind" was illustrated, said the President's opponents, by the failure to obtain this salute. In August, 1913, he had advised Congress that we could not be the partizans of either party, but at no time could the President disguise that he had become a violent anti-Huerta partizan.

After Carranza came into power, Pancho Villa, one of the most delectable and picturesque bandits who ever cut a throat, not receiving the power he expected, turned on his chief. Although Carranza had little respect or gratitude for the United States or its President, Villa had less. Calmly he rode into Columbus, New Mexico, and shot up the town, killing American soldiers. After a certain amount of palaver between Carranza and Wilson, in which the former's contempt for Americans was by no means invisible, Wilson sent a detachment under General Pershing into Mexico in pursuit of Villa. Pershing was hampered by instructions which were intended to conciliate Carranza. But the Mexican was highly incensed at the American invasion even in pursuit of his bitterest foe, and nearly annihilated a detachment of Pershing's troops at Carrizal in June of 1916. Pershing finally fortified himself in Mexico and the National Guard was sent to the frontier where it remained for some months on an irksome duty, but as it turned out a useful one, for the strength and defects of the system became visible before the great war. Finally Pershing and his troops returned across the border, the Guard came home and Villa, rumored defunct, was left as carefree as a mountain goat, and almost as lively.

The great issue of Wilson's administration rose of course from the great war. From the moment of the Austrian ultimatum the life of every neutral country was tinged with the great fact. It is impossible to enter into a discussion of its details, except as they had an effect on the presidential campaign of 1916. At first the war ended business depression. It immediately took the best man-power out of industry in Great Britain, France, Belgium, Russia, Germany and Austria, and so built up neutral prosperity. America was the greatest sharer and, although what we saw was a hectic flush, we mistook it for the glow of health. The "Democratic hard times" disappeared as an issue.

The moral questions involved in the war concerned every one but there was no agreement in the early days. There was a large German population which stood by the fatherland. Some of them, though naturalized or even American born, were Germans before they were Americans, but this was not often the case. Thousands of them were kindly Teutonic people who could not believe that the stories of German aggression and outrage in Europe, and of espionage and violation of diplomatic hospitality in this country were true. They accepted German denials, believed them and doubtless gave speciousness a credulity it did not deserve. Perhaps if we can put ourselves in their place and think of ourselves in Australia, for instance, with our native country rightly accused of devastating and despoiling Canada, but with those accusations denied by authorities of our own flesh and blood, we will not think hardly of this element. They were joined by a large body of professional and political Irishmen and their followers, who rejoiced at the prospect of England's being ruined at whatever cost to the civilized world. They did not carry

187

the entire Irish-American population with them, but their very audible vocalities made it seem so.

On the other side there were the eager citizens of French and English blood, angry, bitter, vehement, as they saw this country seemingly unmoved. They carried with them the great bulk of the old-time Americans, those whose generations had been in America at least as long as those of the President, whose grandfather had been born abroad. This was in part due to the unconscious bias of the English heritage of most of them, in a still greater degree to the absurd German war psychology, and in the greatest degree of all to their sympathy with Belgium and to their belief that Germany meant to impress a Junker dominion on the world and that, if she succeeded in Europe, she would soon be at war with us over the Monroe doctrine and a place in the sun.

The President kept his personal sympathies to himself. The pro-German element thought him pro-British; the pro-British thought him pro-German. He was deeply and honestly imbued with the belief that it was better for the world that America should not be embroiled. A strong, calm nation beyond the seas and aloof from bitterness might play a great part in pacification. But though the principle was enlightened, the President's methods were fumbling. Early in the struggle he urged the people to be neutral, not only in deed but in thought. This was asking an impossibility. While thousands on thousands of the flower of European manhood were falling on both sides, while the horrid efficiency of the new warfare was tearing its way through the flesh and blood opposed to it, mental neutrality was unthinkable. I doubt, carefully as he concealed it, if Wilson was neutral in his own heart and mind. If he was, he was one of the most remarkable mentalities that ever trod the earth. The public was not able to understand his position. It was, as the average man saw it, an invitation to be callous, to pass by on the other side.

188

Then came the German submarine campaign and at last the sinking of the *Lusitania,* to stir and enrage the entire heart of the Republic. And just then Wilson did a characteristic thing. He had been invited before the *Lusitania* outrage to address a festival given for the newly naturalized voters of Philadelphia. He had written his speech before the disaster. It was meant to be a philosophic speech. It contained a fling at the old native American stock. Wilson always had a complex that the old families looked down upon his comparatively short American background, and he wrote that the nation must be "constantly renewed out of new sources" lest it have "narrowness' and prejudice." But the most striking passage, probably the most famous he ever enunciated, contained these words: "There is such a thing as a man being too proud to fight. There is such a thing as a nation being so right that it does not need to convince others by force that it is right."

This had no reference to the *Lusitania* affair when it was written. In a way it was merely detached philosophy. The Philadelphia speech would have been a good speech if it had been delivered in a time of peace. But it was a terrible blunder to deliver it at that time. Here at any rate was a "crowded time" when facts "changed chemically" even while he was looking at them. But it was characteristic of his confidence in his own words that he did not write a new speech. The country stood aghast. The German War Office chuckled. They thought they had arrived at a complete estimate of the American President and his intentions. Even when Bryan resigned soon after, because he would not sign a stiff note, and it was a brave thing to do at that moment, the German Foreign Office interpreted the note which was sent in the light of the Philadelphia speech.

Thus the European War made issues for the next campaign. The war prosperity favored the party in power. The Presi-

dent's apparent lack of sympathy, which was galling to both
pro-German and pro-British, and the *Lusitania* disaster, followed by the words "too proud to fight," were of value to
the opposition. So was the inconclusive Mexican policy, which
made men quote,

"The King of France with forty thousand men
    Marched up a hill and then marched down again."

There was another element of weakness in the President's
chances. His wife had died during his administration and in
a comparatively short time he had married again. This was
emphatically his own business, but it did not have a happy
effect on the voters, especially on the enfranchised women in
the suffrage states. The inefficiency of many untrained office
holders also affected many who wanted "to see the country
run right."

But who would be Wilson's opponent? It would be a delicate task to bring together the discordant elements of four
years before. The Progressive party was still in existence. If
it insisted on continuing there was no beating Wilson. If it
amalgamated with the Republicans in the nomination of
Roosevelt, who was an ostensible candidate in both parties,
the chances were very little better. It would have taken almost
a miracle to have brought the vote of enough "old liners" to
the man who had kicked over the 1912 apple cart to defeat
Wilson. And if a prominent and active "old liner" who had
been in the thick of the fight four years before were to be
nominated, the breach would not be healed. The same result
would have been inevitable with Hiram Johnson, Albert J.
Beveridge, or any of the Roosevelt seceders. Herbert Hadley
would have been terribly cut by the old Roosevelt forces
because he had not joined the revolt, but had kept his "party
regularity." Neither would it do to nominate a man who had
stood aloof in 1912, unless for good reason. If a man had

refused, except for extraordinary reason, to bear a part in the battle of four years before, he would be looked on—and properly—as a timid, time-serving quitter. The problem was to find a man whose duty, not whose timidity, had precluded his taking part in the fray of four years before. In 1914 there were two such men. One of them was ex-Governor Curtis Guild, of Massachusetts. He had been Ambassador to Russia during the Taft-Roosevelt struggle. He could not have entered it. He was a man of great personal attractions, high gifts as an orator, and an indefatigable campaigner. He knew politics. He would not have made blunders which alienated votes, as did the candidate finally chosen. He was not so well known throughout the country as most presidential possibilities. But he was as well known at large as were Lincoln or Hayes at the time of their nominations. But when quiet consideration of him as a possibility had only just started, he died. If he had lived I believe he would have been nominated, for his availability would have steadily revealed itself and his nomination would not have uncovered a place on the Supreme Bench for a Democrat, and if he had been nominated he would have been elected.

The other justified non-combatant of the "War of 1912" was Supreme Court Justice Charles Evans Hughes. He was the candidate of circumstances which were beyond his control or that of the Republican and Progressive war horses. He had been an able and honorable reform governor of New York and had been supported for the presidential nomination in 1908 by his state and a large but inarticulate minority. He is a great lawyer and Taft had put him on the Supreme Bench, where he was rendering congenial and important service. He is said to be the only man who has never deviated a hair's breadth from letting "the office seek the man," where the presidency was concerned, though many have pretended to. The practical politicians detested him. Roosevelt detested him.

He had once been contemptuous of Roosevelt's support of a Hughes measure in New York, the race-track bill. Roosevelt had attempted to render aid, through presidential pressure, by withholding patronage from one of Hughes's opponents. This was not in accord with Hughes's theory of government, and he disclaimed responsibility. Hughes in those days could always make his theories and his acts walk hand in hand, an accomplishment in a statesman as rare as it is exemplary.

There were other candidates, most of them serious in their own opinion, but merely strategic choices in the hands of their supporters. Root was considered the most seriously, but the nomination of the chairman of the convention of 1912 was politically unthinkable. The Progressives and the Republicans met simultaneously in Chicago early in June. From the first there were efforts at conciliation. A conference committee was appointed, which included among others, Senator Smoot, Murray Crane, Senator Borah and President Butler of Columbia among the Republicans, and George Perkins, freight-payer par excellence, Hiram Johnson, and Charles J. Bonaparte among the Progressives. Gradually it appeared that the fullness of time might ease the situation, just as it had in the Lincoln-Fremont days of 1864, but that in the meanwhile nominations must be made. On the tenth of June, Roosevelt was named by the Progressives, with all the demonstrations of earnestness that can be imagined. John M. Parker of Louisiana was nominated for Vice President. On the day before two ballots were taken by the Republicans; Hughes had a substantial lead on the first ballot, 253½, against 105 for Weeks of Massachusetts, who was closely pressed by Root with only two less. Roosevelt had 65 and was in the eighth place, Fairbanks, Cummins, Burton and Sherman each distancing him. On the next ballot Roosevelt rose to fifth place, but he had only 81 votes to the 328½ of Hughes.

After adjournment for the night, Roosevelt made a frantic

but belated effort to stop Hughes. He offered to decline the Progressive nomination and support his old friend, Henry Cabot Lodge, if the Republicans would nominate him. Lodge might have been nominated if this proposition had not come too late, for he had not agreed with Roosevelt's principles in 1912, had taken his position with Taft, and presided at the Republican state convention in Boston in that year. In spite of this, he had maintained his warm friendship with Roosevelt and could have had a strong recommendation from the Colonel, which would have carried as many Progressives as finally went to Hughes. The fact that T. R. could suggest this shows how little he cared for the principles of the Progressive platform of four years before. He offered the Republican convention a conservative of conservatives. Lodge was very much affected by this and felt until the next morning that the presidency was within his grasp.

But it was too late. The Hughes torrent was already flowing over the dam. If Roosevelt wanted to take the responsibility of re-electing Wilson, he might. The Republican convention boldly put the issue up to him by nominating Hughes by a vote of 949½ to Roosevelt's 18 and Lodge's 7.

Hughes was a bitter pill for Roosevelt. He had a dignity, a nice sense of seemly conservatism, which irked Roosevelt. But, as with Fremont, there was nothing else to do but withdraw. True, he disliked Hughes, but he abhorred Wilson. His dislike of Hughes was temperamental, but his detestation of Wilson was not only temperamental, it was deep, honest, abiding and patriotic. Whether it was right or wrong, it went down into honest fundamentals. So Roosevelt declined with a cordial good grace. Parker, vice-presidential nominee, did not follow suit. Thus the new party was left in an anomalous position. It did not fill the vacancy at the head of the ticket nor present candidates for electors. So far as the party machinery went, the breach of 1912 had disappeared. The question was now what the rank and file would do. To many of the Progressive element the defeat of Wilson transcended everything else. Of course the Taft and Roosevelt vote, if wholly united, settled everything. But there was an element of the Progressive party which had not evolved a program in 1912 merely because it would give Roosevelt something to run on, but because they believed in the policies which the platform had enunciated. Wilson stood for more of these policies than did Hughes. These men were for the President. Bainbridge Colby and Matthew Hale were among them.

A few days after the adjournment of the Republican convention, the Democrats unanimously renominated Wilson, not because all the leaders wished to, but because they had no alternative. Wilson's mental isolation and sublimated ego were more difficult to bear if you were a supporter than if you were an opponent. But borne they must be, and meekly enough the party leaders kissed the rod.

Then the campaign began. It was perhaps the least creditable campaign in the history of presidential elections. There was little candor, little frankness. It seemed as if neither party was willing to be straightforward with the voters, so entirely were the leaders benumbed by the possibility of losing the Germans or the sympathizers of the Allies. In addition to this the Hughes supporters were riding behind a mettlesome team of regulars and progressives which at any moment might pull in different directions. Wilson still believed, in spite of the indignities Germany had been putting upon us, that our mission would be that of a peacemaker rather than a participant. He believed this, I think, until the revelations of the famous Zimmerman letters. But practically every other leader was convinced that war could not be avoided. And yet the Democratic slogan was, "He kept us out of war!" and the Republicans were busy explaining how they could keep the peace better than a man whose "too proud to fight" attitude had made the embattled nations believe that they could offer us insults which at last even Wilson must resent. To each Republican criticism of Wilson's European and Mexican policies the question would quickly come, "What would *you* have done?" And because any possible answer would have made antagonisms, none whatever was forthcoming. Hughes, a keen lawyer, made lawyer-like arguments and steadily fell in the estimation of the electorate. Wilson, at his summer home in New Jersey, made speeches in which he said that the Republicans were demonstrating the fact that if they were entrusted with the government they would make a mess of it. Roosevelt at the outset of the campaign made some frank, outspoken speeches. But even he, when he went into the middle west, walked discreetly.

Once during the campaign there came one ringing, sincere expression. It came from Woodrow Wilson. Toward the end of September, one Jeremiah A. O'Leary, president of the American Truth Society, a rabid anti-British and therefore pro-German organization, sent the President an insulting and abusive telegram in which he sought to show by certain primary results that the Democratic party in New York and New Jersey was opposed to his policies and inferentially threatened him with loss of votes. Wilson met the attack with a vigor that was startling. For once he decided that the "loftiest look" was the "subtlest armor." He responded almost instantly with this telegram:

"Your telegram received. I would feel deeply mortified to have you or anybody like you vote for me. Since you have access to so many disloyal Americans and I have not, I will ask you to convey my message to them."

This was not argumentative, but it was vigorous and swift. It was of course good politics, for the element which O'Leary represented, an element which had nothing at heart so much as the ruin of Great Britain, holding it even above the peace and dignity of the United States, would cast no votes for him and it attached many doubtful votes to his standard. But the O'Leary telegram was more than good politics. For a moment Wilson became passionately human. In its swift, frank anger the O'Leary telegram flashed like a sun-touched saber in a cavalry charge.

Hughes insisted on an active stumping campaign. He thought the people had a right to see and hear him. But he did not warm their hearts nor, with his careful abstinence from vigorously enunciating a constructive program, did he convince the thinking members of his audiences.

During the campaign he made a tour of the Pacific coast, invaded California, and made the great mistake of his campaign. California had been stirred to its foundations in 1912 by the primary campaign when certain Taft delegates, elected under the rules of the party authorities had been seated over those elected under provisions of the state law. Hiram Johnson, Roosevelt's running mate in 1912, was Governor and a candidate for Senator. He was for Hughes with entire heartiness. In 1912 Roosevelt had received over two hundred and eighty thousand votes, Taft less than four thousand. When it was decided that Hughes should go into California, it was seen that a delicate situation must be handled. The national committeeman from California, Crocker, was one of the fading "Old Guard." He meant to use Hughes not for Hughes's own benefit, but to bolster up the tottering cause of which he was the representative. Both Hughes and Willcox, the chairman of the National Committee, knew this. Telegram after telegram went from New York to California, urging that the two factions practically declare a truce and work together while Hughes was in the state. At long distance Crocker procrastinated and evaded. The first telegram to Crocker was the joint work of Hughes and Willcox, and

Hughes was fully aware of the danger. An effort from New York was made to have Johnson preside at one of the two Hughes meetings in the state, but Crocker merely replied, "We can handle the situation," and later, "All arrangements for California meetings are concluded." A single concession was made to the Progressives; a representative of that element joined Crocker on the Hughes train. Now it is the fashion to blame Willcox and Johnson for what happened; Willcox for not preventing the complication, and Johnson for reprisal. But Hughes was more to blame than Willcox, and Johnson made no reprisals. It was distinctly up to Hughes to see that his own attitude did not offend the Progressive elements. Willcox was not on the spot. Hughes was. But Hughes let Crocker have his own way, although he should have been aware of the danger. Johnson stood by the ticket, voted it, and never said a word against it. If he did not break through the isolation which Crocker had imposed upon him, and in which apparently Hughes had acquiesced, few who seek to comprehend human nature will blame him.

When Hughes entered California from the northern boundary, representatives of both factions were with him. But when he went to the rear end to speak to the crowds he was invariably shepherded by Kessling, Crocker's man. Any one with any imagination can imagine how Roosevelt would have handled the situation, how he would have slapped Rowell, the neglected Johnson representative on the back, and cried, "Come out, old man, we're all together in this thing!" Of course Hughes was undemonstrative, but he need not have been non-resistant. He was ignorant of Johnson's being at the same hotel with him at one time, but he was ignorant of nothing else. It was his permitting Crocker to make him an apparent ally which gave point to the hotel episode. If Hughes had shown any political acumen, Crocker alone would have been held responsible for that.

After this inglorious campaign, the country expected Hughes to win. Certainly Wilson was stronger than when the campaign began, but the odds still seemed too great to overcome. It was said that an electoral majority could not be figured for him with New York, Indiana, Illinois, New Jersey and Connecticut against him, and the Republicans seemed certain to carry them all. On election night the assembled crowds learned that all these pivotal states had gone for Hughes and went home, the Republicans jubilant, the Democrats hopeless. Next morning the papers gave Hughes 283 electoral votes and Wilson 248. But after they went to press the papers received news that was first annoying to the Republicans, then alarming. The decisive balance had gone from these pivotal states to the far West and many states counted surely for Hughes were showing probable reversals. On the tabulation printed that morning a large number of states were given as settled which soon turned out to be doubtful. By noon everything was in the air. By night it looked like Wilson. Within a day or two his election was conceded. Delaware and Minnesota had been given to Wilson. They finally turned out to be for Hughes, while Montana, North Dakota, Wyoming, Idaho, and Kansas had to be placed in the Wilson column. This was a great territory which had been considered surely for Hughes by Republicans and Democrats alike. Even New Hampshire went over to the Democrats. At last California became the deciding factor. It was terribly close, but it finally gave Wilson a plurality of 3773 votes and the presidency.

Wilson's unexpected strength in the country at large came no doubt from the cry, "He kept us out of war!" In little more than a month after the inauguration we stood, through the declaration for which he asked Congress, at the side of the embattled Allies, telling the world that we had come to make it "safe for democracy." The secondary cause, without which Wilson could not have won, was Roosevelt and the spirit of

1912. The factional bitterness was unhealed in Ohio, and for that reason and no other a state which had been Republican in every other normal presidential election went Democratic. And the California result traces to the same source. With either of these states Hughes would have won.

The election of Wilson, in view of what was coming, was best for the country. In the sixties his party, even in the North, had not distinguished itself as a minority party in war time. As President Eliot wrote after Wilson's death, "The Wilson family, in spite of their Scottish origin and long residence in the North, were thoroughly Southern in sentiment before the Civil War began. . . . The sufferings of the South during the War and the Reconstruction period were familiar to the young boy; and his heroes and exemplars were all Southern, like Calhoun, the antagonist of Andrew Jackson, and Robert E. Lee, Jefferson Davis and Alexander Stephens, leaders of the Confederacy."

The Democratic South found it easier to support one of its blood and faith in this crisis than it would a Northerner of Republican affiliations. As for the Republican party, its contribution to history as a minority party, supporting a President, arrogant, contemptuous and ungrateful for its loyalty, shines as brightly as any chapter in the history of American political parties. By the grace of God and the human assistance of William H. Crocker and Charles Evans Hughes, Woodrow Wilson was again to be the head of the American republic and for a time the most important personality in the world.

CHAPTER SIXTEEN

THE BEGINNING OF A SOLEMN REFERENDUM

BETWEEN the re-election of Wilson and the next presidential campaign a great gulf is fixed: our part in the greatest war mankind has ever known. A little over a month after Wilson's reinauguration, the man who had "kept us out of war" entered the Chamber of the House of Representatives and asked the Congress sitting there in joint session to declare war against the Imperial German Government. Nor does this show Wilson in the light of a hypocrite. He was pre-eminently a man of great visions. But they were not always true visions. Passionately did he believe in them. Most imperiously did he scorn any one who ventured, from the best of motives, to doubt their authenticity. When war burst over Europe Wilson believed it was his mission to guide the making of the peace. He was ruthless in his disdain and opposition toward any one who might make a gesture that did not accord with that hope. Hence for a long time he resisted and belittled any efforts for war preparedness, and when at last he came to it, he entered upon the movement as blandly as if he had been the first to propose it, and completely ignored those who had at first agitated the subject. Most tenaciously did he cling to his peacemaker idea. When men had given up hope, his faith was strong. But facts were facts. Germany was in reality warring on us long before the President admitted that we could not be neutral. He blinded himself as long as he could to anything which could remove him from the bench when the great cause was tried. But at last his eyes were opened. The Zimmerman letters proved Germany's proposed complicity in a plot to bring Mexico and Japan together to wage a war of conquest against us and so to keep two dangerous nations busy, one already a technical ally of the nations fighting her, the other a potential danger. This was borne in on Wilson's consciousness, and then the war came. Once more we were America the unready. Our air service was such that we made use entirely of French planes, and many other humiliating aids were we forced to accept from our allies. But our men, once they got across, were properly fed, and no man, so far as I know, was sacrificed needlessly for lack of possible medical and surgical care. With all the contempt, not all of it deserved, showered on Newton D. Baker, Wilson's Secretary of War, we had learned something from the Spanish and Civil Wars.

This cannot be a history of the World War, nor yet of the covenant. But these great facts of course had their bearing on the strength of the parties at the opening of the next campaign.

The Republican party was active, had become once more solidified, had won a notable victory in the congressional elections of 1918.

The Democratic party was Woodrow Wilson.

That the Democracy was for the practical purposes of the campaign bounded on all sides by the personality of the President, his visions, his very thoughts and wishes, is indisputable. His policy of surrounding himself with second class and easily dominated men had left the party without reserves to draw upon for the battle of 1920. Responsible leadership, leadership which might have come to Wilson's aid through independent mental processes rather than by adulatory acceptance of the mental processes of the President, leadership which might conceivably have made an impression and a change of procedure, though not of principle, on the President's leadership had, as Secretary Lane expressed it, been completely "drowned out." Wilson was the only party asset. He was proud to walk alone. But in the view of the American people, which he was too self-centered to interpret, although he believed until the final disaster that he did interpret it, there had been a tremendous shrinkage from the high estate of the man who had seemed for his day in Paris the great leader of the world.

The public never loved Wilson. The average voter may not searchingly appraise public issues, but he quickly understands the disposition, frailties and crotchets of a man. And he feels intuitively the scorn of an intellectual aristocrat. The politician who depends upon the suffrage of his fellows will do well always to remember the day described by Tennyson when "no knight of Arthur's table dealt in scorn," and to recollect that Abraham Lincoln never knowingly planted a thorn in any man's bosom. A flash of scorn in a foot to foot forensic battle with an equal does the user little if any harm. But when a man habitually betrays his sense of superiority to men of tested leadership, men who intuitively feel themselves below those leaders in intellectual equipment feel that they are at least equally disdained. And though Wilson might respect the public as an entity, it seems reasonable to believe that there was no individual alive (at least on this side of the Atlantic) to whom he did not feel superior. Perhaps in his secret way he loved his fellows. That is not incompatible with his feeling far above them, and feel above them he did.

Wilson went exactly the right way to work to have this known. He showed it immediately to the press. The description of Wilson's first interview by Edward G. Lowry in "Washington Close-Ups" is significant.

"Mr. Wilson stood behind his desk, his visitors filed in and stood in a thickened crescent before him. There was a pause: a cool silence, and presently some one ventured a tentative question. It was answered crisply, politely, and in the fewest possible words. A pleasant time was not had by all."

This was more than a lack of social instinct, unless social instinct includes making those with whom one comes in contact feel on the same plane with one. Coolidge lacks the social instinct to a very great degree, but he has never been accused of seeming to look down from any lofty eminence upon those with whom he comes in contact. There might be strong editorial support for Wilson in some of the papers represented before him, but the human beings who reported Wilson himself could not disguise his sense of intellectual elevation. It crept out into the public consciousness through a thousand unconscious reportorial touches.

The public will forgive much, but it will not forgive ingratitude. It knew to a man, Wilsonians and anti-Wilsonians alike, that the aloof heroics of the President had no room for gratitude. They had seen him turn away from his most faithful friends once they had served his turn. He might be faithful to principles, he was unfaithful to those who served him, some almost to the point of idolatry. Loyalty to an abstract principle may be inspiring, but not to a public which sees friendship and gratitude abused.

Again, the public loves a magnanimous man. Wilson's treatment of Roosevelt and Wood seemed to them anything but magnanimous. There were good reasons for Wilson's attitude on these men. He did in both cases what he should have done. But before the war, when Wood, the commander of a citizens' training camp, was officially rebuked for what Roosevelt had said in an address at that camp, a rebuke to which, in that "livery of silence," the uniform of the army, he could not reply, the administration showed its feelings toward these men. Wilson's antagonism to Roosevelt was welcomed by the latter, worn as a decoration and enthusiastically reciprocated. But it would have been a political crime for Wilson to have sent either of these men to the front for the sake of an easy gesture of magnanimity. There seems, through recent revelations, to have been an adequate physical reason for keeping Wood at home and great credit is due to Baker and Wilson for not revealing it. As for Roosevelt, his temperament, his record of almost insubordination in the Spanish War, the famous round robin and the like, gave no assurance that, with the prestige of the presidency behind him, he would be a safely subordinate cog in the war machine. And the disciplining of an ex-President of the United States would have been a matter which could hardly be done without great injury to the American *esprit*. But to the public at large it seemed a terribly petty performance and one which showed Wilson's smallness. Wilson was small enough, there is no doubt of that, but in this matter he was right. To say a truly great man cannot be petty is a better aphorism than it is a truth. But a well-rounded man is not petty, a completely great man cannot be petty. For the public the pettiness is far more quickly discerned than the greatness. Wilson's withdrawal from and dislike of men who disagreed with him was distinctly petty and the public sensed it.

Some of his sayings were unfortunate. Only an egotist would not have modified a speech he had written before the sinking of the *Lusitania,* and have delivered it after that outrage, "too proud to fight" and all. In his noble desire to be the peacemaker of the war, his anxiety that we should do nothing to prevent that splendid achievement, he entirely misjudged the effect of his injunction to be neutral in thought as well as act. It was the same way in "peace without victory." Wilson's vision was of a war ending with mutual consent, with no party harboring the grudges of a loser, with a covenant, even then in his mind, to prevent another outbreak. It was honest Utopianism. But practical men saw an inconclusive peace, with festering sores and an armed world sullenly preparing again to fight it out. To the man in the street it meant that some nations (there were then two American opinions as to which those nations were) who well deserved a good licking were to get off scot free. And so such things as these decreased confidence in Wilson.

For a while in April, 1917, Wilson's leadership was unquestioned. Any President who leads into a foreign war is accepted enthusiastically at the outset and ought to be until the end. His war speech and "make the world safe for democracy" were good for much Wilson enthusiasm. But Wilson, much as he had yearned for it, did not know how to safeguard this popularity. It turned out to be temporary and ephemeral. Among the imperialistic functions assumed for the war and in some cases continued into the peace, were censorship and the remarkable antics of that monumental publicity faker, George Creel. A resentful public soon realized that it was being fed with doctored facts. All this resentment fell on Wilson's head. He was, and he intended to be, responsible for the war government.

After war was declared, Wilson issued a statement declaring politics adjourned. The people accepted it with enthusiasm and then gradually lost faith in it. From what they gathered, the adjournment of politics meant not the utilizing the ability and patriotism of Democratic and Republican party leaders jointly, as the English had done between the Conservative and Liberal, but barring practically all the Republicans and most of the Democrats from responsibility and building a purely Wilson machine, almost wholly Democratic, to do what he wanted. The public estimated this truly and Wilson fell another peg in its esteem.

After the summer of 1918, it was seen that we and our allies were winning the war. The opposition was disintegrating. A new Congress would be elected in November. The Republican party had distinguished itself far beyond any of its historic predecessors, the Federalists of 1812, the Whigs of 1840, the Democrats of 1861, as a minority party in war time. Its candidates now showed increasing strength. Then Wilson did a remarkable and foolish thing. Nothing in Teutonic psychology was more blundering. He re-convened politics. He, the war President, in an election where both parties were supporting the war, pleaded for the election of the Democratic ticket all along the line. It was an outrageous example of public ingratitude. He said that the election of a Republican Congress· would be a repudiation of his leadership. The public at large responded to this statement enthusiastically, but not as the President expected. With a bang they repudiated Woodrow Wilson, horse, foot and dragoons. They said to him, "We are for your war, but damn you personally." But Wilson ignored his own words. He had preferred to bring the question of repudiation before the public when he might have left it alone, and he now blandly repudiated the repudiation. He assumed for himself the rôle of peace arbiter. Perhaps he could do nothing else. Already he had "drowned out" leadership and would rely only on himself. But, on the whole, the public didn't like it.

There is no need in this chapter to write of the conference on the treaty and covenant, as we are simply considering the public reaction which led to the débâcle of 1920. There is one thing, however, that concerns this fact. It was his leadership in uniting the League covenant with the treaty of peace. This made it impossible to defeat his League without rejecting a treaty of peace. Wilson thought he had "turned the trick."

Probably the American people were willing to accept the League at that time. I believe that the public opposition was led rather than instinctive. If the leaders had accepted it the people would not have fretted. But it was easy for the people to be led away from the League, because Wilson was its protagonist. When opposition developed, Wilson began his ill-fated propagandist tour. He lost good nature. His temper went down before disagreement. He was laboring under a tremendous strain. The irritation yielded to angry brooding and then to intense fury that so great and noble a thing as he had conceived could meet with such opposition. He tried to make the people see what he saw and, when they closed their eyes, his sense of impotence added to his strain. Not many people believe that his breakdown and subsequent stroke would have occurred had he sent others to Paris and accepted their treaty. He fought with all his nervous drive and power, with his whole heart and life, for his great dream of a world civilized at last. He gave to that dream the last ounce of his strength. He broke his heart for it, and it almost took his life. It may go down as one of the supreme immolations of history. But what the people visioned was an ill-tempered violent man, scolding them roundly and fretting himself into a breakdown. To them it was a petty tragedy and they missed its pathos and, what many of the comparatively small but now increasing number of Wilson admirers believe to be, its grandeur.

After the brief illegal presidency of Edith Bolling Wilson, the President recovered his mental faculties and spirits. He never recovered his physical health.

Then came the struggle with the Senate. Need we consider the reservations and the clauses at which they were aimed? Surely not. There were three senatorial groups, the Presidential covenanters, the reservationists, and the anti-Leaguers. The covenanters could not carry the treaty. The anti-Leaguers could not defeat it if the covenanters and reservationists made common cause. This was as clear as daylight from the start. There was a time when the treaty might have been confined with certain very harmless reservations. Wilson let this opportunity pass by. The President's great antagonist was Henry Cabot Lodge, Senator from Massachusetts, many years before

the first editor who had accepted an article from Wilson's pen.
He was as cold an antagonist as Wilson himself, and cool as
well as cold, which Wilson certainly was not. In my opinion
Lodge believed the League would not be an instrument of
peace but an international irritation. I think also that since
Wilson sponsored it he was glad to believe it. Also, I think
at heart he belonged with the left wing of the Senate, the
anti-Leaguers. But he was a tactician and he knew his Wilson.
He proposed a remarkable list of safeguarding reservations:
The other nations would rather we should come in with those
reservations than stay out. Here was Wilson's great opportunity. He could have gathered Lodge into camp and left that
doughty campaigner hoist with his own petard. But Lodge
counted, and not in vain, on Wilson's egoism and autocratic
ill-temper to play into his hands. Wilson did what Lodge
expected of him. He fought imperiously for every dot of an i.
Lodge got his reservations accepted with the aid of the left
wing, which would not vote for the treaty under any conditions. Then the Wilson forces joined the anti-Leaguers and
killed the treaty. Probably the great mass of our citizenship
was with the reservationists. Certainly the tremendous majority were against any covenant which would embroil us in European politics.

Wilson brought about the total defeat of his own treaty
and then called for "a great and solemn referendum."

He got it.

Whether the League of Nations was the chief cause of the
defeat, or whether Wilson was the chief cause of the overthrow in America of the League of Nations, is a question.
Certainly the League might have fared better if Wilson and
Wilsonism could have been left out of the campaign. But that
was impossible. It was all the Democratic party had left. The
Wilsoniacs were a cause of great antagonism from the average
man. Their adulation, in view of what the public absolutely

knew of the defects of Wilson's qualities, increased the dislike. It might be that these worshipers did not class Wilson with, and generally above, any great and selfless man from Lincoln to St. Paul, but they gave the public that impression. The fact that so many echoed Wilson's phrase about "breaking the heart of the world," and accepted at face value the avowed purpose of the League, took umbrage at the mildest reservationist, and were quite above discussing its potentialities, did the League untold harm. When a public is shortsighted in its view, lacks proportion in its judgment of a character, and bases that judgment on actual defects, it does more harm than good for that character's admirers to be blandly blind to those defects and seek to bedeck the character with a halo.

As the time for the nomination drew near, it was evident that there was no public trend toward any candidate of either party to dictate a nomination. The Republican party was to meet first. Its nomination was sought by General Leonard Wood, the movement for him being in part based on his relations with Roosevelt, now dead and greatly lamented, and in a very great degree upon the feeling that nominating a man to whom Wilson was believed to have behaved unjustly would give point to the public feeling about the President.

Governor Lowden of Illinois, a candid, fair, honest, able man who had gained favor by his excellent state administration, was also in the field.

Another who, if nominated, would have crystallized the old Roosevelt sentiment and the Wilson antipathy, was Senator Hiram Johnson of California, running mate to Roosevelt in 1912, and leader of the bitter-end opponents of the covenant. But the public, mistakenly, as it now seems, blamed the defeat of Hughes and the loss of California to Johnson. He was not a type that a convention could select as a compromise.

Fourth in estimated strength was the amiable and popular

Senator Warren G. Harding of Ohio. For months before the convention the wise ones were saying that it was "all set" for Harding, but they were somewhat disconcerted by the gains of Wood and of Lowden. Before the convention met it seemed likely that the nominee would be one or the other and that Harding and the lesser candidates would disintegrate and go to one of them, rather than break the leaders by holding to their balance of power. The lesser candidates, all hoping for the lucky break, were Governor Sproul of Pennsylvania, President Butler of Columbia, who had the New York delegation, Governor Coolidge of Massachusetts, Senator La Follette and half a dozen lesser lights.

By the time the convention was on the point of assembling, the two leaders had drawn on themselves the disapprobation of the purists. It was clearly evident that their pre-convention campaigns had been waged with prodigality. In Missouri a delegate had been given Lowden money, although the candidate himself was not directly responsible for it. A prominent and wealthy soap manufacturer had gone about cleaning up things for Wood. If it had not been for these facts Wood and Lowden would have fought it out to a finish and one of them would have won by votes transferred from the lesser candidates.

The convention, with no acrimonious disputes over contesting delegations, came together harmoniously in Chicago on June 8. The arch opponent of the President, Senator Lodge, was elected first temporary and then permanent chairman, the very selection being a keynote in itself. Lodge made a biting and sarcastic, rather than a large speech. But neither the convention nor the people it represented, nor the entire public, were in a large frame of mind at the time. In one sentence in particular, criticized though it was, he made articulate the national spirit of the moment. "Mr. Wilson and his dynasty, his heirs and assigns, or anybody that is his, anybody who with bent knee has served his purposes, must be driven from all control."

There was a slight flurry over the platform. The Republican covenanters and mild reservationists sought to control the plank on the League of Nations. A usually shrewd observer, Mark Sullivan, wrote to his papers from the ground: "If there were no politics concerned, no necessity for seeming to differ from the Democrats, Mr. Wilson's League of Nations would probably be adopted without any qualifications, except those unessential ones which would be acceptable to him." Mr. Sullivan ought to have known better than to write this kind of tosh, even to strengthen the President. There was a minority which wanted the League. Ex-Senator Crane of Massachusetts, now at odds with his old colleague Senator Lodge, was the leader of this group. But he was a weak leader. For the first time since 1896 he found his influence had waned. He had no ability to fight on the rostrum. He was entirely the representative of the financial interests. Lodge was bitterly opposed to Crane's interference. According to an observer, Arthur Wallace Dunn, Lodge "knew that Crane knew nothing about the League; he knew that Crane had neither read nor understood the Treaty, and that he was at the convention representing certain elements in the country which were deeply interested in having a League with mild reservations." When Dunn told Lodge that the Senators on the resolutions committee "had been in conversation with Crane and told him in emphatic language that he was not running the convention," Lodge expressed great delight. The plank was said to be a compromise. If that be the case, to avoid a contest between the Crane and the Lodge stand, they compromised on Lodge. No doubt Lodge would have liked a platform that went still further, if such a platform would not have been a repudiation of his strategy in the senatorial battle, for, as I have said, I believe he was an out and out anti-Leaguer at heart. The plank called for an agreement among the nations of the world to preserve peace. It was against involving us in a "multitude of quarrels," and strongly opposed the President's covenant which had "failed in its purpose, was intolerable for an independent people," and "certain to produce the injustice, hostility and controversy among nations which it proposed to prevent."

After the nominating speeches the first ballot disclosed Wood in the lead with two hundred and eighty-seven and a half votes. Lowden was only seventy-six behind. Johnson came third with a hundred and thirty-three. Far below this, but with a good hand to draw to, came Harding with sixty-five and a half, Coolidge was seventh, with thirty-four, behind Sproul and Butler. Coolidge began with twenty-two of his own state against seven for Wood; at the end of the day Wood had sixteen to Coolidge's nineteen. As a matter of fact, when the day ended with the fourth ballot and there was no radical change in the standing, except that Lowden had the best of the gains made by all the leaders from the small fry, it was known by every delegate present that there were but three possible chances. The convention would nominate Wood, Lowden or Harding. Although Johnson held his own he was considered impossible. The last ballot of the day gave Wood 314, Lowden 289, Johnson 140½, and Harding 61½.

But Harding was faced with a problem. He was happy in the Senate. He was reaching for the presidency, but it was by no means certainly within his reach. His senatorial term was expiring. He could beyond all doubt be re-elected. But the day of the balloting was the last day on which he could sign the paper which would put his name on the Ohio ballot as a candidate for the senatorial nomination. If he signed, that act would settle his chance for the presidency. He would be deemed a senatorial candidate and some other dark horse would be brought forward to overtake the leaders. If he did not sign, the senatorship was absolutely lost. Harding was reluctant to give up the surety for the possibility. But his friends urged him to keep in the fight. He did not sign.

Next morning the convention opened with the belief that the end would soon be in sight. It was Saturday and the delegates had had enough of Chicago. They wanted to go home. On the fifth ballot (the first of the day) Lowden passed Wood, but by only four votes. For the next two ballots they were an actual or practical tie, at 311½ each; on the sixth ballot Wood gained half a vote, and Lowden remained stationary on the seventh. Then Lowden again took the lead by 307 to 299. But in the meantime Harding forged forward. On the sixth ballot he had 78, a gain of 16½ over his highest of the day before. Then he went to 89, then to 106, and then to 133½. This had been a steady and consistent gain, while Johnson had dropped steadily, and Harding ousted him from third place on the seventh ballot. On the announcing of the eighth ballot the prospect of a quick close was evident. And it was fulfilled. Lowden, the leader, satisfied that he could not win, permitted a break from him which set things going. Harding went up to 374½. To all intents and purposes he was nominated. The tenth ballot registered the rush to him which was inevitable under the circumstances. He had 692-1/5. Lowden had been the most cordial toward him and nearly his entire vote had gone to Harding, the Governor of Illinois having only 11 "last ditchers," to Johnson 80-4/5 and Wood 165.

After the customary motions to make the choice unanimous, the convention hastened to the choice of the vice-presidential candidate. Johnson, who had been willing, it is said, to accept second place with Knox of Pennsylvania, could the convention have been swung to him, resolutely refused to be Harding's partner when the candidate requested it, and so lost the presidency. The senatorial group had seen one of their number nominated. They sought to finish the job in the same way and they gave Lenroot of Wisconsin their benediction. It would thus be a senatorial ticket, up and down. Medill McCormick of Illinois presented his name. The convention was not enthusiastic. It was bored and lacked order. Then in the hum of conversation it was discovered that Mr. Wallace MacCamant of Oregon was speaking. He is what William Allen White calls a school reader patriot. He has been national president of the Sons of the American Revolution and believes that school histories that admit the existence of any good in a British or American Tory of the eighteenth century should be very carefully scanned. Mr. MacCamant was speaking quite without senatorial permission, but Mr. MacCamant was speaking because he had something to say. The audience, however, heard almost nothing of Mr. MacCamant's speech. In a few moments the gavel of Senator Lodge would command quiet enough so that the Oregonian could shout into every ear in the convention one word. While Mr. MacCamant, apparently in pantomime, is approaching that moment, let us emulate the directors of moving pictures and indulge in a cut back.

CHAPTER SEVENTEEN

"AND SOME HAVE GREATNESS THRUST UPON THEM"

ON the first day of January in 1907 there arrived in Boston, unheralded and unknown, a sandy-complexioned young man of nearly thirty-five who had been something of a local figure in a western Massachusetts city and was to enter the Massachusetts legislature the next day. One of his friends, a judge of the Superior Court, had recommended him to a former colleague as resembling a singed cat and being better than he looked. It was a significant introduction. He was not exactly gawky, he was not exactly angular. But his colleagues, if they pondered it at all, must have realized that he had been gawky once and that a little more height would have emphasized his angularity. He had a straw-like pallor, set off by tawny red hair. His perpetual expression was of smelling something burning on the kitchen stove. He was not quite a typical "up-stater," because he was more "up-state" than the average. There was an urban touch to the genial "Bill" Turtle of Pittsfield, for instance, and Mr. Hobson of Palmer was an exceedingly presentable and citified attorney. But Calvin Coolidge seemed fresh from the hay. There was nothing the matter with his clothes, the fit was impeccable, but they looked as if they were not fond of their wearer and would rather be hanging in the closet. His nasal twang would have delighted an actor of bucolic parts. His reticence was appalling.

He took his luggage to the Adams House. I would like to say "carpet bag" here, but I am convinced they were out of

215

date in 1907, and Calvin was not burlesquing the part. I rather think he may have carried a telescope box, but it was probably, after all, a leather-board suit case. Next day he climbed the hill and was sworn in by Governor Guild, and on the day after he saw the Governor himself take the oath and heard the inaugural. Later, Mr. Speaker Cole appointed him on two committees, Mercantile Affairs and Constitutional Amendments, the first—if not a committee of prime importance—of some consequence. Not many new men got more than one committee, but the representatives, realizing the constituency he represented, immediately understood. He was "one of Uncle Murray's boys."

Senator Crane (he had not then retired), both before and after holding the senatorship, was the undisputed ruler of Republican politics in the western half of Massachusetts and a force in the east as well. And Uncle Murray was always especially interested in the boys from the towns within thirty miles of Dalton. The fact that this particular protégé had no predilection for throat splitting, no doubt endeared him to Crane. He was his kind of a safe representative. Uncle Murray was on the whole an easy boss. Nobody was forced or overurged by the man from Dalton. But you weren't accepted as a candidate by many people out his way unless you "just naturally" thought a certain way and curiously that was also the way Uncle Murray "just naturally" felt too. And so Uncle Murray's boys usually were sound and kind and stood without hitching, nor was our hero different from the rest. He had doubtless set down in his copybooks the maxim, "He who would command must learn to obey," and accepted it in politics as well as in war. And there is a kind of obedience that needs no specific orders.

Calvin Coolidge sat unnoticed in the House for two years. Perhaps now and then he took charge of a measure reported by a committee, very likely he may have explained it to such as would listen during the interminable buzz of conversation which continues during the speaking of any man who cannot give the House sport. Coolidge, with his unemotional periods and nasal voice, explaining the commonplaces of legislation, could not then give anyone sport. He found among his colleagues men who could hold the House, Joseph Walker, dignified, cool and candid; Robert Luce, a vigorous debater and political scholar; Norman White, passionate and vigorous; Grafton Cushing, to a tactical mistake of whom Coolidge was to owe much; and William E. Weeks, a youngster of remarkable oratorical qualities. There were many others, just below them in the second group, but Coolidge never approached the importance of the second group of leaders. He had a certain small importance because Crane wanted him there, and he was advanced to the Judiciary Committee with his second term. But so far as his initial legislation service went, an unconsidered trifle he came, continued and went away, typical of thousands, probably up to the average, who go their way never to return and are quickly forgotten. This is the lot of at least half the men who come to the legislature in Massachusetts. It was not to be Coolidge's fortune. His party ran him for mayor of his city and he got the job. After he served the allotted days of an unobjectionable mayor, he was sent to the senate. It was Northampton's turn in the Berkshire, Hampden, Hampshire district. Here he had a better chance than in the House. Brilliance commands the floor of the Representatives' chamber. Serviceable mediocrity can impress itself on the Senate. Coolidge was by this time forty. As a Senator must, he served on several committees, being in his second term chairman of that on Railroads, a committee practically never chosen within the walls of the State House.

A shrewd, quiet, unemotional statement was of more value in the smaller body than it could ever be in the larger. Cal Coolidge began to feel at home and to gather confidence. He has not been a continuous holder of political office since 1905, as some state. There may have been three or four years since then during which he has not been the recipient of a public salary, small or large. He was one of the hard working Senators. But his tenure was expected to be comparatively brief. Soon it would be the "turn" of some other city or town in the Berkshire, Hampden, Hampshire district to have the Senator. He might then, perhaps, be appointed to an office of some dignity and profit (Uncle Murray always did his best for his boys), but it was uncertain, and here sat Calvin Coolidge, looking at a blank wall and wondering what was behind it. And just here Fate entered and took him by the hand.

It is easy to say that a combination of circumstances was entirely responsible for his rise. It is easy also to say that no career is built without some such fortune and that Coolidge simply has had his share. The truth is between these statements. He is resourceful enough to take advantage of these circumstances, but it is only candid to admit that seldom in a public man's career have there been so many fortunate turns as came to Coolidge. While Coolidge was getting elected for a third term, there was another contest which interested the state. The President of the Senate, Levi Greenwood, was running for re-election. There was in Massachusetts at that time a militant, resourceful band of woman suffragists, who sought to defeat their proven enemies when they came up for new or continued honors. They had already defeated some minor figures, including Roger Wolcott, son of the Spanish War Governor of Massachusetts. The most forceful of the group, Margaret Foley, known all over the state as "Maggie," advised going after big game. Certainly Levi Greenwood, an outspoken opponent of woman suffrage, was that. Miss Foley's colleagues were doubtful of the possibilities, but she took on the effort with scant and dubiously granted assistance. Miss Foley is a big, vital, hard-hitting, good-natured, resourceful woman, who has trained herself to "the game" and after a battle has no bitterness or hatred remaining, as typical an Irish political fighter as any man of the race. She stated that they were going to cook Mr. Greenwood's goose, to which he playfully replied that he did not think she knew how to cook a goose. Miss Foley is a good cook, practically and politically. After she had followed Greenwood through the district, harping on his conservative votes in a day of progressive tendencies, wisely emphasizing this above the suffrage question, aforesaid goose lay steaming in its platter on her table, delicately basted and roasted to a turn. Greenwood's defeat was a surprise. Probably it could have been avoided had it been foreseen. A Democratic governor was re-elected and Greenwood could have saved him some embarrassment, for if bills, too progressive, do not reach the executive desk, even though he mildly advocates them on the stump, he is saved much embarrassment. Little tips to defeat a minor candidate of one's party are not unknown. But Greenwood was left to his fate and went down. Immediately Coolidge got into touch with Crane. The same forces responsible for his appointment to the Railroads Committee were put in motion and within forty-eight hours Coolidge had the presidency of the Massachusetts Senate in cold storage. Crane, as easy and a far better boss than Platt, had delivered.

When Coolidge was formally elected and took the chair, he made what I think was the finest speech of his career. It was short, of course, but even then a portion of it was of little importance and may well be forgotten, even to the quoted epigram, "Men do not make laws; they simply discover them." This paragraph is the real speech and it deserves fame:

"Do the day's work. If it be to protect the rights of the weak, whoever objects, do it. If it be to help a powerful corporation better to serve the people, whatever the opposition, do that. Expect to be called a stand-patter, but don't be a stand-patter. Expect to be called a demagogue, but don't be a demagogue. Don't hesitate to be as revolutionary as science. Don't hesitate to be as reactionary as the multiplication table. Don't expect to build up the weak by pulling down the strong. Don't hurry to legislate. Give administration a chance to catch up with legislation."

In this paragraph Coolidge stands out at his very best. Platitude perhaps. But there are times when platitude hits the mark. Was it not Tom Reed who congratulated Theodore Roosevelt on his discovery of the moral law? Find anywhere if you can as fine and compact a general statement of the duties of legislators. But mark one thing, true so often of Coolidge's speeches even to-day, this is the wisdom of Captain Cuttle, and "the bearings of this observation lays in the application on it."

So Coolidge entered upon a real distinction, his first. Three months before no man could have foreseen it. And curiously enough only one of his advancing steps to the presidency was indicated or could have been foreseen.

In 1914, Samuel W. McCall, the man who shared with Henry Cabot Lodge, though they were far apart personally, the reputation in Massachusetts for scholarly statesmanship, was persuaded to leave Congress and run for the governorship, in hopes of ending the Democratic line which had come in, in Foss and Walsh, as a result of the Progressive split in 1912. On the ticket with him for Lieutenant Governor ran Grafton Dulaney Cushing, Speaker of the House, perfect flower of cold-boiled Boston. McCall reduced Walsh's plurality and his candidacy put things in order for a future victory. Cushing, having a blatherskite to beat, was elected. Now it is generally a foregone conclusion in Massachusetts, in the Republican party at least, that the Lieutenant Governor becomes the nominee for Governor when the Governor retires. Also in 1914 no defeated candidate for Governor had been renominated for many years. But McCall had yielded to the leaders and abandoned Congress, where he was prominent and happy, being assured that a good fight in 1914 would give him the place in 1916. But Cushing, who might have had the lieu-tenant-governorship for four years, and then been elected to the chief office, chose to assume that his office put him in line for it immediately and announced his candidacy for Governor. This left the office of Lieutenant Governor unexpectedly open. A candidate for this position was Guy Ham, a member of the Governor's Council, who had had much experience in the legis-lature, an almost faultless orator, one of the most attractive figures upon the stump that the state has ever seen, and a man who had given himself to party service unstintedly for years. But Guy Ham was a restless Republican. He was not so "reli-able" as he might have been, in the eyes of the leaders. And worst of all, he was a temperance man and would be friendly to restrictive liquor legislation. It was an independent, expe-rienced, capable young man with many warm and faithful supporters against the machine backed by the breweries. And the machine and the leaders decided to oppose him. The speak-ership of the house was supposed to be the best springboard to the lieutenant-governorship, but the speaker was not ready to run just then. So they fell back upon the President of the Senate. He thought it over and then placed a slip saying "I am a candidate for Lieutenant Governor," on the desk of his closest friend, Frank Stearns. It was a hard fight. Coolidge with his voice, appearance and lack of magnetism, made little personal headway against the showy and attractive Ham. But the machine was at work, so were the breweries. By a margin by no means wide Coolidge won. Ham with his usual party loyalty took the stump for the whole ticket. McCall and Coolidge were both elected, but Coolidge's plurality far ex-ceeded that of the head of the ticket. One of his partial biog-raphers, William Allen White, cites it as indication of his personal strength. Mr. White knows nothing about Massachusetts. Time after time he refers to the House of Representatives as the "assembly," and to the "Speaker" of our Senate. McCall was ousting a popular Governor, a resourceful campaigner, a man the Commonwealth respected, as of course it did McCall as well. Coolidge's opponent was the blatherskite already once repudiated, who had in a term just previous disgusted his own party by his conceited contortions in the office. McCall's small plurality was in reality a greater victory than Coolidge's great one.

It was while he was Lieutenant Governor that I first met Coolidge. It was during the campaign of 1916. I was to deliver the dedicatory address at the unveiling of a monument to the pioneer settler of what is now called Germantown, in Quincy. Mr. Coolidge was to represent the Commonwealth. We were to go from the State House together in the car of a lady who was a member of the committee. I had just come back from Maine, where I had been stumping for Hughes. I was full of news, of a minor sort, of the way things were going. I had taken similar rides with Long, Guild, McCall and Foss, all Massachusetts Governors, and had had charming chats. It was a beautiful October day, clear, crisp and invigorating. As we went through the business district flags were flying everywhere—I think the troops were still in Mexico. It was a day to inspire brightness, but we were a silent and funereal party. Every five minutes I would try to start a conversation on some topic. I would get a monosyllabic reply. I would busy my mind for another topic. I would reform my forces and try again. Always the same result. It was my conversational Bunker Hill. Only I made more sallies than ever General Howe attempted and unlike him I never set foot in the redoubt. After the ceremonies, our hostess asked me if the Lieutenant Governor was married, and on my answering in the affirmative, she walked away visibly puzzled as to how he had managed the necessary conversational preliminaries which lead to the happy state.

From the lieutenant-governorship to the governorship is a natural transition. In the Republican party in Massachusetts a nomination for one is practically a nomination to the other. And so in January of 1919 Mr. Coolidge became Governor. This was as far as he was expected to go, although there was the possibility that he might reach the senatorship. I think only one man in the world expected to see him President, but one man did. He once told me so, as I am sure he told many others. That man is Frank Stearns, by vocation (before his retirement) an active and important Boston merchant, by avocation the brusher of cobwebs from the onward path of the President of the United States. He early conceived a strong liking for Coolidge as an Amherst alumnus. In his reticent and undemonstrative way Coolidge has reciprocated it, as he has never reciprocated the feelings of many other admirers. And in this he is right, for Stearns is, I think, the only affectionate supporter that Coolidge has. He has many supporters and they fit into their places, large and small, in the army, by no means mercenaries but with their positions in the ranks, serving Coolidge and serving themselves. But Stearns wants nothing but to see Coolidge successful. He treasures, perhaps, the feeling that he is an important strategist, though as a matter of fact he is as innocent as a lamb. He could now and then go home from Washington and be closeted with the Governor and presumably deliver a message with intelligence. Beyond this he was never personally a factor. But when a Boston merchant, placing almost daily large blocks of advertising matter, lets it be known that his chief foible is the career of a certain office-holder, that particular office-holder is apt to receive some gentle impetus. And not corruptly. Not at all. No Democratic paper was expected to cut its own candidate for Coolidge. But if he made a speech it was apt to get a fuller report, if the paper had the space to spare, than another speech could get. If he was present at a ceremony, it would be his part that would be photographed. If there was an entertaining and creditable anecdote to be told of Coolidge, the papers were glad to print it. They made him a familiar figure before the public, a far more familiar figure than he would have been but for Frank Stearns. He certainly has earned the honor of being the first parlor boarder of the land.

But although Stearns was fond of saying that his friend was a future president, I take no stock in the statement so often printed that on 1916 Stearns went to Chicago and canvassed the delegates for the unknown head of the Massachusetts Senate for the presidency of the United States. There are two insuperable arguments against this. One is Stearns, the other is Coolidge. Both have common sense. Stearns had seen the President of the New Jersey Senate given the vice-presidential nomination in 1896. He may have done some missionary work with this in mind. But my guess is that Stearns went to the convention to talk about his friend, to make his name not entirely unfamiliar, if the time arrived, nay, when the time arrived, for Stearns had absolute faith in Coolidge's star. Perhaps he is an unconscious metaphysician, and has, with that faith within him, given America absent treatment. Who knows?

At any rate, Coolidge had the governorship. It was a high honor and a high responsibility. And then the police strike set him on a pinnacle. That it did not set the right man on the pinnacle I unhesitatingly affirm.

In September of 1919, the Boston Social Club, which was the organization of the police patrolmen in Boston, began to agitate for certain reforms in their conditions. The Boston Police Department is not, except in certain emergencies, a municipal affair. A partnership between the police and almost any municipal administration Boston had had since the adoption of a city charter, which was to work wonders and hasn't, would have been disastrous. The head of the department is a single commissioner. In 1919 it was Edwin Upton Curtis, a keen politician, but a scrupulously honest man, who had been Mayor of Boston for a single term in the early nineties and had given Boston one of the few thoroughly decent administrations she had had in forty years. He was a stiff-necked executive and had a bit of the Roscoe Conkling machine aggressiveness without any of his conceit. He was never a truckler, he was wealthy and was in the public service because he enjoyed it, and doing his plain duty was his greatest pleasure, and his next greatest was helping the Republican party. But Curtis had a real sympathy with the conditions under which the police worked. He began as their friend, in spite of being a good disciplinarian. He sought to get the inequalities of pay and condition ameliorated. But the progress was slow. Too slow for the Boston Social Club. Then they did a foolish thing, a thing which anyone who knew Ned Curtis would not attempt unless he wanted a regular fight: they tried to coerce him. They proposed forming a union with a charter from the American Federation of Labor. Curtis issued orders forbidding it. Of course there is no room for such a union in any military body. A policeman is an enlisted man in the same sense as a soldier. The union was formed in the face of this prohibition. Old Sam Gompers wanted to have it successful and duplicated in every American city, so that disorder during strikes could be unbridled. Curtis had courts of inquiry sit on the ringleaders, and disciplined them as he ought. Then on the night of September 9, 1919, the patrolmen of Boston went out on strike. There were only a pitiful number of loyal men, other than the few near retirement age, who were not expected by the union to hazard their pensions, left in each station house. The possibility that the city might be left unguarded had been apparent for some days. An enlistment office was opened for volunteer officers in case of an emergency. There were some volunteers. On the night of the strike the city, however, was left practically unguarded.

There was a seething riot in the downtown districts, especially around Scollay Square. There were other riots in suburban Boston. Wherever there were shops and congestion of population there was violence and looting. Shopkeepers stood with guns at the closed doors of their shops until the crowd rushed them, seized the weapons and broke in. Citizens were robbed on the sidewalks. Women were assaulted. Boston Common was the gathering spot of thugs. In Scollay Square the few loyal officers and the small but heroic force of volunteers who had been summoned were overwhelmed. The old city was for one night as helpless as Paris in the days of the Commune. Hardly a man or a woman living within a circle of three miles could leave home and go three blocks without finding disorder. The great majority would have reached it more quickly. Nothing but a conflagration could have added to the terror. No one knows what the damage was in dollars, no one knows the number of citizens robbed at the point of the pistol. No one can estimate the number of women who suffered indignities and criminal abuse at the hands of the unbridled ruffians who were let loose on Boston that night. Hell in its literal sense was loose and the strikers were, in effect, the allies of thugs and blacklegs.

It is said that on that night, if at no other time, "the situation got away from Curtis." I am not so sure. Curtis, perhaps, knew that desperate diseases need desperate remedies. Perhaps he foresaw that the Boston public is like the indulgent American public, willing to temporize until it gets its dander up. At any rate the Boston striking officers were outlaws in the public mind from that night. But they did not know it.

The politicians did not know it. The Governor of Massachusetts did not know it. Ned Curtis did know it.

On the next morning I received my orders as a volunteer, previously enlisted, to report to Station 9 in the Roxbury District. As I approached the station I could not see the iron palings of the fence for the crowd of striking policemen in citizens' clothes leaning against it. They were peaceable, but they were there, as was evident from their demeanor, to "keep tabs" on the counter activities. As I approached the steps the insolent "once over" which silently greeted me made me see very clearly what would happen to me if they were reinstated and I happened not to clear my sidewalk at the instant the last snowflake had fallen, or should in a moment of temporary aberration expectorate on the sidewalk, or commit some equally heinous offense. All that day we policed the district in Ford cars, a sergeant, a loyal officer and a volunteer in each. Toward night a few more volunteers had arrived, but although the riots of the night before had given some impetus to the volunteering it was soon certain that the raw, un-uniformed levies of citizens, some very eminent, some humble, some elderly, some hardly more than boys, in spite of the patriotism of their motives could not handle the situation.

Now the single exception of non-municipal police control in Boston is in times of riot. The law does not take heed of the fact that a Fernando Wood during the draft riots of New York may be duplicated in Boston by a man in sympathy with the rioters. The mayor in times of public danger may assume command of the police force. Andrew Peters, a thoroughly respectable man, of excellent social standing among our Brahmins, well-meaning but stupid, was Mayor of the city. He was out of sympathy with Curtis. He was not a partizan of the strikers, but he saw what was happening in the city and realized that the quickest way to restore order would be the quickest compromise that could be reached. I am convinced that he did not see, or at least appreciate, the threat to all America which Boston, at a great cost to herself, was to make impotent.

Mayor Peters took formal command of the police. He had called out Boston units of the State Guard, probably at Curtis's advice before he superseded him. What he meant to do is hard to say. Not even his best friends believed him so good a man for this emergency as Curtis. I know, as one of the men sitting in a station house in Roxbury, not knowing what the morrow held for me, how the *esprit* of such of us as were on the job suffered when we realized that our commander was no longer Curtis but the well-meaning Mayor, some of whose advisers we heartily distrusted and despised.

Such was the situation when Governor Coolidge came into the picture. Now Coolidge is generally believed to be courageous. Perhaps he is. The highest quality of courage is not thoughtless. A timid man is sometimes the most courageous in the world. My judgment of Coolidge is that he is a timid man who will avoid if he possibly can any action requiring bravery, but, when he cannot avoid it, will meet it. He does have a Yankee stability and sense of duty. He hesitated before he took a stand. Most men would. He saw the city in a bad way. Fires which had been banked since that first night were burning underneath, they might break out at any moment. All this might be avoided by letting Peters settle by surrender, for any compromise was surrender. The rights and wrongs were perfectly clear of course, but the crisis might be avoided. Curtis had thought of practically nothing else for a month and his course was charted. Coolidge took, as a cautious and perhaps timid man would, some time to make up his mind. He should not have plunged in at once. Impulsiveness is not and should not be one of his qualities.

I do not pretend to know the truth of the stories which have been rampant before and since. It may be that in a stormy interview between the Mayor and Governor something regrettable happened. It may be that Coolidge hesitated and finally followed the advice of Murray Crane. It may be that Curtis in his plea for support threatened to resign and tell the public why if he did not receive it. It may be that when the Governor signed the proclamation he said, "Well, that's the end of me politically." If that be so at least it shows a spirit of sacrifice worth noting.

Where Coolidge was when the strike broke out is uncertain. On the previous Saturday he went to Northampton for the week-end. On Monday he went to Greenfield and addressed the Massachusetts State Branch of the American Federation of Labor. On that day his secretary summoned him by telephone to Boston. He was at the Union Club on Monday evening at 8 o'clock. It is said that he was not in evidence at the State House the next day. This may be so. He may have been in distant consultation with ex-Senator Crane, a man whom nobody need have been ashamed to consult in a great emergency. He may have believed it wise to keep from the pulling and hauling of the crisis. He showed this distaste of counsel when a reorganization of the state departments placed upon him the duty of simultaneously making a large number of important appointments. It was not until the day after Mayor Peters had called out the Boston State Guard units and superseded Curtis that Governor Coolidge called out outside regiments and made his proclamation calling upon Curtis, "as you are Police Commissioner" to take charge under him. Just as we officers felt our hearts go into our boots with Peters' action, we felt them come back when the Governor took this step. We went forward to we knew not what with our heads in the air. The strike was not over. There was mob resistance and in South Boston a dangerous mob was legitimately fired upon. There was bloodshed and that *was* to all intents and purposes the end of the strike. Nothing more was left but the organization of the new force and the efforts of the striking police and their friends to obtain immunity for their treason. One of the arguments of the leaders to the doubtful men had been that if the strike should fail they would lose nothing but a few days' pay, as the city could not run without them. It could run and did. During the interim before the new police force was organized, Boston was splendidly policed by the State Guard and the lesser body of volunteers. But this success was not entirely, due to them. It was my experience that after the blood-letting in South Boston problems largely disappeared and danger entirely. The criminal element knew just how far they could go with a trained officer who had no stomach for a trial for homicide or assault, and who knew what force was legal. They assumed, and I think mistakenly, that we had no such apprehension and would not be long-suffering. But they made no mistake in believing that in the emergency we would not be held by the judges to as strict an accountability as regular officers in peace times. While we did not deserve the reputation of being trigger nervous it was, for all that, a convenient and helpful reputation to have at just that time.

We have seen that Coolidge's restoration of Curtis was the deciding factor. Now what was Coolidge's attitude to this great fact before and after his exemplary proclamation? I have already placed him on Monday in Greenfield, delivering the greetings of the Commonwealth to organized labor. That night the officers who had defied the Commissioner's necessary ruling were dismissed. The labor convention, with characteristic willingness to substitute its sovereignty for that of orderly rule, demanded that the Governor remove the Commissioner and cause the reinstatement of the officers. The Governor's telegram was read to the convention on Wednesday *after* the strike had broken. It can be found in the proceedings of the convention, page 99. Here is what he sent. The italics are my own.

"The Governor has no authority over the appointment, suspension or removal of the police force of Boston. *I earnestly hope circumstances may arise which will cause the police officers to be reinstated.* In my judgment it would not be wise to remove Commissioner Curtis. I wish to thank you for the hospitality your convention extended to me on Monday.

Calvin Coolidge."

Here we have Coolidge at his calculating, timid worst. There is no touch of the famous Gompers telegram in this unfortunate message. He was walking softly, without a big stick, a stick which Curtis was ready to hand him and which he finally grasped. He avoided saying anything of importance of course. But his unfortunate sentence, however the words "circumstances may arise" may be analyzed, was a pitiful phrase. It was no time for "weasel words" and that sentence was nothing else. Notice also his guarded reference to Curtis. Not a word to convey a trust in his abilities, nothing which would strengthen his hands, except a bare statement he might have made concerning Attorney General Daugherty in 1924. "In my judgment it would not be wise to remove Commissioner Curtis." Curtis never felt, in spite of the legal support of the Governor as an officer, that he had the cordial personal support that he, the indomitable sick man, deserved. He took to heart the Pilatian phrase in the telegram to Gompers, "I did not appoint him and I cannot remove him."

Coolidge has an unexcelled ability to make courageous gestures, tempered with a directness and simplicity which relieves them of grandiloquence. To assert that they are simply political would be a great injustice. But Coolidge has one of the most acute political consciousnesses in the world, although his natural timidity will be seen to have once obscured it. But acute as he is when he has slowly approached a duty, viewing that duty perhaps from the political as well as from other angles, he is unpretentiously firm. So when he took his position in September of 1919, as was to be expected of him, what he said he said simply and with a clarity which is always his gift when he does not choose to be enigmatical.

When Gompers bustled into the situation with the victory of frightfulness and the passage of the Adamson law hanging at his belt, he was simply blown out of the water by a telegram which went all over the country and clarified the situation. The action of Curtis and Coolidge had ruined the strike in Boston. The public reception of Coolidge's famous telegram ended any prospect of the experiments being repeated in any other city. "There is no right to strike against the public safety by anybody, anywhere, any time," was a simple sentence, but all America said Amen!

Circumstances had somewhat cleared Coolidge's vision toward the striking officers. The Greenfield telegram was forgotten. On September 24 the public believed that his boots were nailed to the floor. In a proclamation of that date he characterized the striking officers in measured, just and vigorous words:

"In the deliberate intention to intimidate and coerce the government of this Commonwealth a large body of policemen, urging all others to join them, deserted their posts of duty, letting in the enemy. This act of theirs was voluntary, against the advice of their well wishers, long discussed and premeditated, and with the purpose of obstructing the power of the government to protect its citizens or even to maintain its own existence. Its success meant anarchy. By this act, through the operation of the law they dispossessed themselves. They stand as though they had never been appointed."

This was a stirring passage and the public responded. The last quoted statement gave analysts some anxiety. They thought they saw politics in it. It stopped short of the real truth. The men being placed on the new force stood prior to joining "as though they had never been appointed," as indeed they had not. If that was the status of the deserters they might be recruited. But in the view of the Commissioner they were comparable with soldiers dishonorably discharged and the ranks were closed to them. Coolidge seems to have left that responsibility to Curtis. He was safe in doing so.

There is another phase of the police strike to be considered in its application to Coolidge. A campaign was imminent. Coolidge was renominated. In cold but genuine eloquence he referred at the state convention to the situation. It was a typical Coolidge speech. It seemed like striking sparks from ice. But from that moment he turned away from the police strike. Politically he seemed to fear it. Organized labor has always been a political bugaboo. Politicians vision it from its numbers. They are unconscious of the fact that thousands of men in skilled trades have union cards and for no reason than that their trade is unionized and they detest the petty tyranny of certain leaders. They forget that many others who seek honestly the welfare of their fellow workmen are honest, temperate men. The pistol of the Adamson bill was held at Wilson's head just before the election of 1916 and he threw up his hands. Coolidge had not done that, but if sleeping dogs would lie he was content. It is an open secret that some of his advisers felt the same way. The campaign was soft pedaled. But the chairman of the City Committee of Boston did not agree. He was responsible for the Boston vote. He was convinced that the defeat of the strike ought to be in the campaign. He wrote a letter demanding to know whether the Democratic candidate for Governor would reinstate the strikers. It is said that he was urged, even by Coolidge himself, not to continue his ruinous policy. But he remained recalcitrant. It was a brave thing to do. Had he mistaken the force of the issue he would have been politically ruined. But he believed he was right and he went ahead. He finally smoked the opposing candidate out. Yes, he would reinstate

233

the striking officers. This candidate plunged into the strike as an issue. It was forced on Coolidge. Thus we see two more architects of the Coolidge fortune, Herman Hormel, chairman of the Boston Republican Committee, and Richard C. Long, Democratic candidate for Governor.

Of course Coolidge, faced with the issue, responded with vigor. Once more the eyes of the country were focused on Massachusetts. Thanks to the Democratic candidate, who mistook the value of the issue, the Republican candidate, who had also mistaken it, rode into office on an overwhelming plurality, which was emphasized by the public congratulations of the Democratic President. For once Massachusetts held the center of the American stage at a state election. Coolidge's opponents had not been merely defeated, they had been blown to fragments and the country which had already taken note of Coolidge took note of him again.

In Massachusetts a Coolidge cult arose. It was not altogether opposed to the conservative machine, nor was the machine antagonistic to the circle of especial Coolidge admirers. Still they were distinct. The Coolidge circle believed Coolidge had attained a stature before the United States which might bring him to the Presidency. Most of the "old timers" did not. They liked Coolidge, he was safe, sane and a friend of Crane, but the presidency for a Massachusetts man seemed too much to expect.

Then there was Leonard Wood. He was in common esteem the heir of Roosevelt. His technical domicile was Massachusetts. A few years previously the Progressive candidate for Governor, although defeated, had pushed the Republican vote into third place. That showed what the Roosevelt strength amounted to in Massachusetts. Many of those men would not waver. If there was anything under the surface of the Coolidge movement it was to prevent Wood from having the support of the delegates of the state of his ostensible residence. Doubtless Johnson and Lowden gave their good wishes to Coolidge within the boundaries of his home state. But Frank Stearns believed in the destiny of his protégé. Then a curious political comedy was enacted. It might have been named, "He Would and He Would Not." James B. Reynolds, a notable organizer, known of all men who are familiar with organization politics, was put in charge of the movement. Suddenly the candidate declined to be a candidate and the headquarters were closed. Then the movement went merrily on. Coolidge's name was not on the primary ballots. But Massachusetts had recognized the renunciation as a gesture, purely and entirely, a gesture aimed to help the cause not to end it, a gesture to seem to reveal a man not self-seeking but working only for his state. Certain delegates in Massachusetts, but not all of them, expressed themselves before their selection as Coolidge men. Stearns sent broadcast over the Union and especially to the convention delegates a book of Coolidge's speeches. And when the delegates were in Chicago and a supporter telegraphed to the Governor that his friends sent good wishes and wished to know if he were a candidate, Coolidge replied, "Thank my friends for their good wishes and tell them the truth." This is quoted by one of his most friendly biographers, as if it were a profound, candid, and adequate answer. As a matter of fact, it was as much a piece of shifty political indirection as his verdict on the occasion of the Henry Cabot Lodge–A. Lawrence Lowell debate on the League of Nations, at which he presided,—"They both won!"

But not all Massachusetts was with him. There was absolutely no reason why it should be. There had been no state preference to direct their votes. Wood had many supporters and had a right to be represented in delegates. But ever since the ten ballots which eventuated in the nomination of Harding, the Massachusetts delegates who did their own thinking, who went into the convention free men and went out of the convention free men also, have been treated as if they had stained their honor in not voting as they were in no way bound to vote. Benjamin F. Butler, who went to Charleston under instructions for Douglas and voted steadily for Jefferson Davis, received no more vilification than these honorable men who made their own honorable choice against a man to whom they were nowise pledged. Senator Lodge voted for the devoted friend of his dead friend, Roosevelt. So did Louis A. Coolidge, author and business man, also a warm Roosevelt admirer. So also did the son of Robert Bacon, another inheritor of the tradition, and Lewis Parkhurst, an eminent Boston publisher, whose interest in politics is entirely above reproach. These were fine-fibered and superior men, far more so than a certain political roustabout, a delegate in the convention, now high in the Coolidge councils, who on notification day at Northampton, in conversation with me, referred to Lodge by that epithet so beloved by our literary realists, which Mr. Wister's "Virginian" demanded should be delivered with a smile. The "send 'em to Coventry" wing in the intimate Coolidge circle is rather too large. "Great men gain doubly when they make foes friends."

But now Mr. Wallace MacCament has got his chance. Though he made a speech, as the record shows, the one audible word was "Coolidge."

And the convention was ready for it. It felt like doing as it pleased and if the senatorial group, the fathers in Israel, did not wish them to, no matter. Who was this fellow Lenroot, anyhow? A Senator, yes, but what else? They knew Lodge because he was Lodge, Borah because he was Borah, La Follette because he was La Follette, and so with a half dozen others. The average delegate knew Lenroot because he was a Senator. That was all. To the senatorial machine that ought to have been enough. But it was not enough. Not nearly enough. The finest piece of pre-campaign publicity which they had received was the Coolidge volume with the delegate's name in gold letters on the cover. They could keep that in their bookcase or on the parlor table. It was worth reading, too, and most of them had read it. Here was a chap that had said something. He was a plain speaker and his words sank in. They remembered that the very thing which their own policemen might have done had been crushed in Massachusetts under this man and that the defeat had been so disastrous that there was no chance that any other policemen would try it. This man looked good to them, darned if he didn't. Why should they trail after a lot of Senators? Give the little fellow from Massachusetts a chance. Plainly the convention was out of hand. But the senatorial group persisted. They thought they could pull things together again. Soon the voting commenced and the Senators realized their mistake. Almost from the first state called the votes began to pile up. When Pennsylvania was reached its vote gave Coolidge the desired majority. When the roll was finished Coolidge had 674½, Lenroot 146½, and Governor Allen of Kansas and some others a small scattering endorsement. It was really the exciting hour of the convention, the first real stampede in a Republican convention for forty years.

In an hour or so the delegates were on their way home and the Sunday papers told the nation of the choice of Harding and Coolidge and described their virtues and their careers; and with no tremendous fervency, but with plain intention, the country at large prepared to elect them.

CHAPTER EIGHTEEN

THE REFERENDUM CLOSES

WHEN the Democrats met in convention in San Francisco during the first week of July, they found their problem not unlike that of the Republican convention, except that the Republicans felt the inspiriting blood-quickening of anticipated success, and over the San Francisco convention the clouds hung heavily. There was no outstanding candidate. It was evident that it would take many ballots to select the leader of their forlorn hope. If Wilson was not a candidate himself, and his candidacy would have been as fatal to him as to the party, there was no one to whom the convention could surely turn.

The President held himself as aloof from the other candidates as if he were in the contest himself. Probably only the intimate circle of a few will ever know whether this invalid with an unquenched spirit and an untamable egotism wanted to be the standard bearer. There were, however, signs of "perking up" about the White House as the convention drew near. New and healthier looking photographs were released, newspapers published leading articles on the President's improved condition. That eminent anonymity, "a party leader," was quoted as saying that "Wilson would let his name be used only as a rallying point for friends of the administration and League of Nations." This statement followed an interview with Wilson himself on the League of Nations, in which he said, "This thing is too deep to permit any political sculduggery."

Whether or not these were all gentle hints of the avail-

ability of the only Democrat who had been elected to two
consecutive terms since the days of Andrew Jackson, whether
the presence of Secretaries Colby, Daniels, Burleson, and
ex-Secretary Glass, now Senator, meant an organization to
carry the convention at the right moment, will probably always
be a question. Certainly Wilson himself showed as little consideration for any other candidate, and three of them were
or had been in his cabinet, one being his son-inlaw, as if he
were contesting the place with him. When the convention came
together friends of eleven men were organized to further
their candidates. They were ex-Secretary of the Treasury
McAdoo, Attorney General Palmer, Senator Hitchcock of
Nebraska, Homer S. Cummings of Connecticut, Governor
"Al" Smith of New York, Governor Edwards of New Jersey,
former Minister to Germany Gerard, Governor Cox of Ohio,
former Secretary of Agriculture Meredith, John W. Davis
of New York or West Virginia, and Senator Owen of Oklahoma. There was no administration and no anti-administration candidate. Nor were there any straight administration
or anti-administration delegates, but for all that there were
many shades of opinion represented. There were those who,
worshiping devotedly at the Wilson shrine, dared not advocate him personally, on the one hand, and those who for the
party's sake wished he had never been born but who dared
not oppose him, on the other. But Wilson in the White House
would make no gesture to mark his own passing. It seems
incredible that this physically broken man would for a moment have considered making an attempt to overthrow the
two-term precedent of Washington, with the experiences of
Grant and Roosevelt in the background, yet you will find men
who think they know who will tell of that expectation in the
White House. Organized betting recognized his chance as
better than that of any single announced candidate. But the
convention was not to break to him.

Roughly speaking, the candidates, the nomination of one of whom would have seemed to the especial Wilson admirers an endorsement of their chief, were McAdoo, Hitchcock or Meredith. Prominent among those who, while not exactly off the Wilson reservation, were as near the boundaries as prudence permitted, were Edwards, Smith and Cox, all governors and all "wet." Palmer, who was using his office outrageously to secure the nomination (his appointment of an attorney who had once been suspended from practice by the Massachusetts courts to be United States District Attorney in that district, an act which resulted in certain influential but notorious support for Palmer in that state, is indicative), sought votes from both sides.

Though Wilson was never voted for, his shadow fell upon the convention. The delegates could not avoid what almost seemed his ghostly presence. Their policies had been irrevocably dictated by events and they nearly all saw that these were losing policies, yet inescapable ones. The platform as adopted called for the ratification of the treaty of Versailles and the League of Nations covenant without any reservation "which would impair its integrity," but it did not oppose reservations which made more clear or specific our obligations to the associated nations. The possible ambiguity here was not enough to help it among the foes of the league, but it somewhat chilled its friends. "The old master," William Jennings Bryan, never afraid of being in the minority, never seeking issues merely for the sake of votes, with the courage which had always distinguished him and which was to ennoble him once more in four years, went before the convention in advocacy of a "bone dry" plank. An adoption of such a plank would have removed the three governors from serious consideration by the delegates. He was defeated. But it is possible that Senator Glass, probably unconsciously, gave the *coup de grâce* to the incipient Wilson movement. He wanted the platform adopted as reported, lest there might occur something as disturbing as were the acts of those who "knocked at the door of a sick man's room." The delegates appreciated the meaning of such a reference by the President's spokesman on the adoption of the resolutions. To them it must have sounded like Benedicite and Farewell to Woodrow Wilson.

When the balloting began, McAdoo was in the lead with 266 votes on the first ballot, closely pressed by Palmer only ten below him. Then came Cox, Smith and Edwards, in a "wet" phalanx of 285, Cox leading the allies with 134. All these Cox-Edwards-Smith delegates knew what they wanted. They were the "Taggart-Murphy bunch," with the strength of the New Jersey machine, built on New York lines, thrown in for good measure. Throughout, McAdoo was the strongest of the forces which accepted the administration most completely. Palmer was always a force to be reckoned with, but in spite of his compact strength, generally in the vicinity of two hundred, he was never really dangerous. It was the field against McAdoo from start to finish and the Taggart-Murphy organization was the great nucleus of that opposition. The Democrats have a tenacious way of sticking to their candidates and yielding slowly, if at all. Smith, who was nominated by the veteran war horse Bourke Cockran (now returned from his Progressive excursion) was not an avid candidate. He was in, although not without hope of being "the man," as a refuge for Tammany until the prospects became clear. With ninety-eight on the sixth ballot, he practically disappeared on the seventh. Meanwhile Cox was rising. On the twelfth ballot he passed McAdoo, going from 382 to 404, while McAdoo dropped from 380 to 375½. But he had a long road to go. There was a diversion in favor of Davis on the seventeenth ballot, when he rose to 57, but he soon fell back. Cox mounted to his mid-convention peak with 456½ on the twentieth. But the McAdoo forces were not done fighting. There were realignments and McAdoo regained the lead on the thirtieth with 403½ to 400½ for Cox. Not until Palmer released his delegates did Cox's lead return. On the thirty-eighth ballot McAdoo led with 405½, Palmer's score was 211 and Cox's total was 383½. Then Palmer quit. The disposition of his vote is to be seen in the totals of the next ballot—McAdoo 440; Cox 468½; Palmer 74. Palmer nominated Cox. But the final two-thirds was not reached until after the forty-fourth ballot, on which Cox with 702 was only 27 short of the goal. Before the next ballot was reached the McAdoo forces bowed to the inevitable and saved the convention's time by moving Cox's nomination by acclamation. Of course the motion prevailed and there was nothing left to do but to present the vice-presidential choice.

Several nominations were made, including that of the now famous Mr. Doheny of California, who might have poured soothing financial oil upon the troubled waters of the Cox campaign. But Franklin Roosevelt's personality had attracted the delegates and when he was presented by the redoubtable "Al" Smith, the other candidates withdrew and the nomination was unanimous. Although Roosevelt was a good man, his nomination was typical of the attitude on the vice-presidency after a strenuous presidential battle. "Let's finish up the damned thing and go home," is the almost invariable attitude of the delegates, and though there may be only one life between their nominee and the greatest political office in the world, who can blame them? Eagerly the delegates seek credentials for the big show. Except those elected at large there are few real party leaders among them. They are elected as a reward for being good soldiers, and after the big battle they have had enough.

When the convention adjourned, Bryan, who had stopped Tammany in 1912, refused an interview with the word, "My heart is in the grave with my cause and I must wait until it comes back to me."

Certainly the San Francisco convention was a Tammany victory. Murphy had helped secure the nomination of the man he really wanted. His "hail fellow well met" Governor of New York had made a favorable impression and would live to fight another day, and a New York man, not allied with Tammany but respectable, who could be depended upon, had been placed upon the ticket. These successes meant more than a final victory, which he was too shrewd a man to hope for.

But Cox, immediately congratulated by Harding, his fellow Ohio editor, walked under the Caudine forks and called at the White House. He was quickly transformed from a half-hearted Leaguer to an enthusiast. His campaign speeches were largely devoted to adulation of the President, with bitter and violent attacks on his opponents, especially Senator Lodge. Though he was riding for a fall his equestrianism was spectacular.

Among the drawbacks of American politics is the lack of concentration upon a single issue. When the government goes to the people in England that appeal is upon some immediate question which has become acute and which in itself has caused the election. The four years' accumulation of disagreements between the parties or factions upon legislative and executive matters complicates our decisions and obscures our mandates. But there can be little doubt that what may be generally called "Wilsonism" and the League of Nations made the transcendent issue of 1920 and that the election turned upon it.

The day of decision relentlessly advanced and Cox grew steadily weaker as it advanced. Although Wilson had taken Cox into camp, there was no activity which the public could discern as traceable to the White House. Cox did all he could for Wilson. Wilson did nothing for Cox. The defeat was

243

more than decisive. The popular vote was almost two to one. Harding had something over sixteen millions, Cox just above nine millions. Harding had 404 electoral votes, Cox, 127. Among the states that had occasionally gone Republican, Cox had only Kentucky. All the rest of his electoral votes came from states in which their chief issue is never put in the platform, and which had never cast a Republican electoral vote since the withdrawal of the Federal troops from the South. Harding's victory was complete.

CHAPTER NINETEEN

COOLIDGE "IN HIS OWN RIGHT"

ONCE more the fourth of March saw great rejoicings in Washington, as is always the case when the "outs" again become the "ins". But there were some wise men and women among those who had voted for Harding who looked upon his tremendous victory somewhat dubiously. His truly sweeping partizan majority in Congress was too great. They felt that there might be room for much shrinkage among independent and patriotic congressmen and yet an opportunity still remain to put through a party program based more on selfish policy than would be good for the country. These citizens looked on Harding as an amiable man of moderate talents who would, they hoped, cut loose from his Ohio machine affiliations and make himself and his administration a register of the highest party thought and leadership, a sort of impersonal center of the best his party had to offer through its ablest and most unselfish public servants. They neither wanted, nor expected, an inflexible executive to whom party leaders must be an echo or else be anathema in the White House. Cleveland, Roosevelt and Wilson, who were representatives of this type of President, had all been party wreckers. When Harding appointed his cabinet these well-wishers were pleased. So also were those whom he believed to be his well-wishers. The first group were heartened by the presence of Hughes, *sans peur et sans reproche,* Mellon, a wealthy Pennsylvanian, long eminent as a financier and, so far as the public outside of Pennsylvania knew, without any strong political affiliations, and Hoover, a remarkable administrator, who, up to that time, was no great partizan. They also believed in John W. Weeks of Massachusetts, good party man but an honest and able official. The second group was equally pleased because they had Fall and Daugherty. And there was Denby, who drew from them a smile of satisfaction, a man who in a pinch the public would acquit of anything, including intelligence, as indeed it afterwards did. Then there was the beamingly complacent Will Hays, soon to sell his placid smile as a trade mark and guaranty of high purpose to the movies.

As Harding's term progressed, there was a vague uneasiness among patriotic men. Although the sincerity of his cry at Hoboken over the bodies of dead soldiers, "It must never happen again," seemed to be bearing fruit in his invitation to the powers to join in a disarmament conference, he did not seem to be a vital leader, and they began to suspect that the wrong elements were molding the party policies both in the White House and in Congress.

Harding was exceedingly good-natured and tolerant in his personal observance of the Volstead Act, which did not seem a pretty thing in a President, even to the wringing "wets." The law which forbids the transporation of films of prize fights, a foolish law perhaps, but still a law, was broken under his dispensation, and at the White House a party, including not only the President but the stately and supposedly meticulous Secretary Hughes, saw that gallant bantam Georges Carpentier go down under the sledge-like batterings of a shipyard slacker. Delectable, no doubt, but quite illegal. A small thing perhaps, but, as we look back at it, typical of Harding and his administration in greater things.

Long before the Alaskan trip and the scandalous oil revelations, Harding was reluctantly slated, Taft fashion, for renomination, and the party managers looked resignedly to the day when the Grand Old Party should once more be in opposition. It is said that the same managers who expected to renominate the President had it in mind to "strengthen the ticket" by giving him a different running mate.

There is nothing to be gained by injecting into our story the sad revelations concerning the Teapot Dome, nor in analyzing the Veterans' Bureau scandal. The first was not exposed during Harding's life. Whether or not its revelation was foreseen by the harassed President will always be a matter of conjecture. At any rate, he went to Alaska a heavily burdened man, one who realized what civic complacency and good-fellowship had, and might, cost him in fair fame. He knew that in the estimate of strong and thinking men the party stood at its lowest ebb since the days of Grant. Defeat at the polls in something over a year's time stared him in the face. With these matters on his mind and perhaps upon his conscience, he was taken suddenly ill in California and at last turned his face to the wall and died.

Thus Calvin Coolidge came to the presidency. There was sincere grief for Harding, a very real sorrow that took note of his lovable humanness and his weaknesses, a sorrow observed none the less sincerely because so many felt in their hearts that, after all, it was for the best. After the President's funeral the country turned to Coolidge with relief and confidence.

The two great enigmas of the first third of the Twentieth Century are the success of "Abie's Irish Rose" and the political career of Calvin Coolidge. If before he had become prominent in the public eye, the portrait of a man with the attributes of Coolidge had been sketched to any political leader and that leader had been asked what such a man's availability was, the answer would invariably have been, "A political impossibility." Coolidge's unimpressive physique, his reticence, his lack of florid speech, his utter want of social attributes, his entire aloofness, are proverbial. How could such a man ever be elected to a municipal council? And yet he has been elected President of the United States. I have shown how he mounted. I have not undertaken to show why, nor can I. Calvin Coolidge's attributes and his successes taken together are probably the greatest paradox of American politics.

But with Coolidge once on the threshold of the presidency, the confidence which he gained on his accession is not mysterious. It is a terrible commentary on the practical leaders of the Harding administration that straightforward Yankee dependableness and simple honesty were qualities that seemed of tremendous worth, yet such was the case. And the very qualities which seemed a bar to popular success now seemed worth their weight in gold. This could be no back-slapping administration. Tom, Dick and Harry could not be cheek by jowl with this reticent and almost forbidding personality. Here was a man of cold exterior, with few real friendships. So much the better; friendship is apt to be a poor rudder for the ship of state. The President might be cold and calculating. Coldness and calculation combined with honesty never yet wrecked a government. And despite all his lack of warmth, no one has yet had the temerity to suggest that Coolidge is not personally an absolutely honest man.

That Coolidge is in all but one respect a very astute politician is known to those who have a reasonable measure of familiarity with him, but he has a wonderful ability for making gestures which seem non-political and careless of his own fortune. Not one of these gestures has injured him yet. In his want of magnanimity only is Coolidge lacking in the quality of political astuteness. He seems to me totally disregardful of Richelieu's maxim, as Bulwer records it: "Great men gain doubly when they make foes friends." From the time that Henry Cabot Lodge refrained from assisting in the

Coolidge presidential candidacy at the convention in 1920, he became anathema with the entire Coolidge machine in his home state. This took form twice in an opposition which was stubborn and vindictive. After Lodge voted to pass the bonus over Coolidge's veto the antagonism toward him was tremendous. In the convention of 1924 which renominated the President, Lodge, though he could not be kept from membership in the Massachusetts delegation, was sent to Coventry so emphatically that it aroused comment all over the country. He was even assigned so poor a room in the hotel where the delegation was quartered, that his former secretary, Louis A. Coolidge, who had secured excellent accommodation as a spectator, gave up his room to the Senator.

Louis Coolidge himself, then a business man of great importance and a former assistant Secretary of the Treasury, became a candidate for nomination as Senator in that year. He had voted for Wood in the convention four years before. Although the aspirant who was closest to the President, National Chairman William M. Butler, withdrew in a panic, and although Louis Coolidge's rigid constitutionalism would have made him a valuable ally to the administration, the Calvin Coolidge forces put into the field the venerable and colorless Speaker of the House of Representatives and forced his nomination. Any Massachusetts man who has refused to make mental genuflections in the direction of the ex-President, no matter how near he has been to his policies, was distrusted and cold-shouldered from the time of his accession.

The ex-President has not been personally responsible for all these acts. But if his attitude to his late opponents within the party had been conciliatory or even not forbidding, his henchmen would not have inaugurated them. Lodge had voted against Harding's veto of the bonus and it had not raised any storm. It was because he was *persona non grata* with Coolidge that the tempest broke. When, for the papers of the day

249

before the primary, National Chairman Butler and Governor Cox came out in statements urging the nomination of Speaker Gillett for the Senate, it was accepted as an administration bugle call. In fact the Governor put into his statement the words, "We all know how the President feels." These pleas and these alone upset the situation over night and put the man whom experts rated as the weakest of three candidates at the top of the poll. It has been a hard six years in Massachusetts for Republicans who have not abrogated their intellectual sovereignty for that of the President of the United States and his special followers.

Coolidge is considered a man of dignity. So far as reticence and impassiveness make for dignity he has it. In the larger sense I am not so sure. Perhaps he believes that a certain amount of foolish publicity is the price which any man must pay for position since the advent of the movies. Certainly no President has ever been willing to submit to such nauseating exhibitions in the news reels as has Coolidge. Cultured Americans wince at the thought of their President putting on a smock frock to pose as pitching hay and milking a bossy, or cavorting with a sickly grin in "chaps", like a Wild West supernumerary. Certainly Coolidge's pictures do not look as if he enjoyed it. But he does it. His predecessors never went further than being taken in the red fez of the playboys of the Masonic world.

And yet Coolidge is sensitive of his position almost to the extent of having a complex. His first biography was written by Robert M. Washburn, at one time his legislative associate. It was a readable glorification of his friend, a little gushing perhaps, but a delightful bit of writing. In some ways it is the best literature of the Coolidge books, certainly partial enough to suit any man who does not desire a recrudescence of Parson Weems. During the campaign it was republished in popular form and distributed as a political document. The

President Coolidge in the West

changes made in it for partizan publication by the representative of the National Committee, presumably understanding the President's wishes, are illuminating. Here are some of the phrases in the original which were deleted in the political edition. "A great Police Commissioner gave wings to his feet." "Even Death rode on before him and cleared the way." "When asked if he has participated in college athletics, he replied, 'Yes, some,' adding, 'I held the stakes.'" [The new police force] "which remains non-unionized," "He now holds the highest office on earth by virtue of a title greater than that of any electorate. God made him President," "When he was a senior at college and a grown man, and a class of one hundred voted on that man who promised most success in life, he received but one vote, the vote of Dwight W. Morrow." "Then" [at the time of the Police Strike] "Mr. Lodge, a master of diction unexcelled, said of him: 'Here's to the pilot who weathered the storm.'" In reference to the sturdy industry of John Coolidge, the President's son, the word farm is substituted for "tobacco plantation."

Not one of these references was critical. They furnished excellent literary contrast and strengthened the book, but they had to go. God's help was not to be spoken of and as for Senator Lodge,—away with him, as a matter of course.

That the ex-President is ruthless to all who stand in his path cannot be denied. It is the custom for a retiring Governor of Massachusetts to leave his secretary safely ensconced in some good political berth. As Coolidge's governorship drew to an end, his secretary cast his eyes on the commissionership of Corporations and Taxation. The time of the Commissioner was expiring. He was an elderly man who in 1890 had been elected State Auditor on the Democratic ticket. When the next year he was defeated as the majority party regained power, he was appointed Commissioner of Corporations. He had been reappointed by a long series of Republican governors. He was a competent man and his age had not slowed him up. He was approaching a time when he might expect to retire on a pension. He was attending a convention of taxation commissioners in a neighboring state when a friend telephoned to him that Governor Coolidge had appointed his secretary to his position. He had received no intimation of this until the fact was accomplished. He returned home broken-hearted, and soon after took his own life.

Another evidence of this ruthlessness also illustrates the complete absence from his make-up of anything which may be termed, in the highest current sense of the adjective, as social intelligence. Coolidge's old Massachusetts friend, Washburn, by the untrammelled act of one of the few untrammelled speakers, Joseph Walker, had been chairman of the joint committee on Railroads on the part of the House of Representatives while Coolidge was chairman on the part of the Senate. Washburn had always been an indefatigable supporter. He had written a book which had been so interesting and at the same time so partial that it made votes for the President at the election and was probably the best piece of propaganda which the Republican Committee used during that campaign. Coolidge had been Washburn's guest in his home in Worcester. Washburn is a man of distinct social gifts. As a conversationalist he scintillates. There are moments when his companion becomes perforce a listener, but that would never trouble the ex-President. Listening is his one social accomplishment. During the administration Washburn went to Washington as a journalist. He sought out the President's secretary and said plainly that it was not his intent to besiege his friend and that at any time Mr. Coolidge was in need of him he would respond. He saw Coolidge every week at his meeting with the journalists. Once when he sat in the front row Coolidge said, "How are you, Robert?" That was the extent of their intercourse until one day after some months had elapsed Washburn was sent for to come to the White House. The President asked him if his brother (former Congressman Charles Washburn) was in town. On receiving a reply in the negative, Coolidge informed Robert Washburn that his secretaries had confused him with his brother, who had been in Washington shortly before. Said the President, "I wanted him to take lunch with me." Robert Washburn rose and repeated the substance of his statement to the secretary when he first came to Washington.

Said the President, "Were you invited to a presidential reception?"

Washburn admitted the soft impeachment. In common with some thousands he had received such an invitation.

"Then," pronounced the President, "my social obligations to you are canceled."

That was all.

But Coolidge was greatly fortunate in having in the White House Grace Coolidge, the most gracious, discerning and intelligent woman who has held that position since the days of Frances Cleveland.

Coolidge has had great good fortune in his career. He has had one bit of singularly bad fortune. He has been so tremendously overpraised by his partial supporters that it has raised up against him a large element of opposition which does him much less than justice. Whatever he may have seemed early in his career, he is no mere small town politician. He is not too little a man to be President. But when among his coterie of worshipers it is almost sacrilege to disagree with him and lese-majesty to point to others who will completely over-top him in history, such an attitude must, especially in these days of unrelenting modern biography, inevitably turn upon his head the vials of iconoclastic disdain. Much of this is undeserved. He is a plain, competent man of more than average parts. He knows far more of the history of his country than most recent executives, Wilson and Roosevelt excepted. He has at least a good working knowledge of law. He is temperate, not alone in habit but in thought and act. He may have his secret animosities, but he never rages. His English is trenchant, ample, and admirably simple and direct. He is a skillful politician, a quality which we do not disdain in Lincoln. Like Lincoln he practices politics within reasonable limits and the game of politics of the administration is not played for him by others. It is a pity that those who see so much more in him have blinded others to these moderate excellencies.

Coolidge is not among the great American Presidents. Neither is he among the presidential failures. You may put a few, three or four, into the first class. You may put Grant, Harding, Buchanan, Tyler and Pierce into the third class. Between these two groups stand the great bulk of our Presidents, leaving out of the reckoning the first Harrison, Taylor and Garfield, who died too soon for estimate. This long line were able, honorable, generally useful men. The serviceable Coolidge does not lead the group. He has neither the great qualities of a Hayes, the deep intellect of a Harrison, nor the tact of a Van Buren. On the other hand, both in purpose and ability, he transcends a Polk and a Fillmore.

One thing he has, perhaps, in a greater degree than any of his predecessors, the presidential temperament. He does the day's work as it comes to him, calmly, quietly. He has no nerves. The racking years of responsibility which have burdened his predecessors sit lightly upon him. The words, "Why should any man covet this place?" have never risen unbidden in agony to his lips. The steely coldness which the heat of partisan contention and the pleading of sympathy can never touch, may not be enviable in an individual, but it is the best temperamental equipment a President can hope to have.

It is something to be President of the United States and

not be below the average. That much must be said for Calvin Coolidge. I doubt if a better fitted man for the task could have been produced at the end of the Harding administration. He was the antithesis of his predecessor and an antithesis was needed. And if I have borne too strongly on what seem to me his weaknesses, I cannot forget that men who have left highly honored names bore as hardly on Abraham Lincoln when he was a living man. Richard H. Dana estimated Lincoln as a man of "no admirers," "fonder of details than of principles," as one who loved "to tell stories to all sorts of persons," who let this proclivity take his mind away from "the noble and manly duties of his great post," and saw in him "a kind of shrewdness and common sense, mother wit, and slipshod, low-leveled honesty that made him a good Western jury lawyer," and concluded with the statement, "He is an unutterable calamity to us where he is."

Facts are material; Truth is spiritual.

Perhaps in our closeness to Coolidge and his time I am finding facts and letting truths go. I cannot tell. But the facts are facts and truth will finally be found, but only from weighing all the facts, of which I have honestly sought to set down a few.

With the tip of its southwestern corner touching Madison Square, its graceful Huntress swinging to and fro upon its beautiful tower, once stood New York's great auditorium. Less than four years ago, for what seemed an almost interminable period, it was the center of American politics. Today it is as if it had never been. A business building is on its almost forgotten site. A new Arena, well above Times Square, carries on under its name. The old garden is now a memory to antiquarians, for four years makes a perfectly good antiquarian in New York City. Many memorable events have taken place under its roof. Barnum has presented his circus for the delectation of the proletariat. Giants of a former day have exchanged fisticuffs to the delight of the "Fancy." Society has looked down affably from the boxes upon beautiful horses. An old waster, who had done important things, has been killed upon its roof by a young waster of no importance whatever. These are memories indeed. "You may break, you may shatter the jar if you will, but the scent of the roses will cling to it still." The zephyrs which play around Madison Avenue and East Twenty-sixth Street must even now sing gently, "Alabama: twenty-four votes for Oscar Underwood."

This futile and monotonous battle cry, heard at least once by practically every man and woman living in any city or town in America which has a radio shop with the inevitable loud speaker for publicity's sweet sake, is excellently representative of the Democratic national convention held there. It went on and on, it got nowhere, and its end was defeat.

Before Harding's death the Democratic party seemed to have a political certainty at the next election.

Then Harding died. Coolidge succeeded to the office, and he had the confidence of the people. True he had sat in the Harding cabinet by courtesy, but he had played only a "thinking part." The oil scandals were uncovered after he became President, but they did not touch him and, although he kept Daugherty in his cabinet for what seemed an unconscionable time, the people were inclined to realize his difficulties and the need of temporizing on his part. Still it was certain that the oil scandal had done the party great harm and that, although its campaign would be no sinecure, the Democratic party had a show.

After the Republicans met at Cleveland and placidly nominated the President as a candidate in his own right, and joined with him first Lowden and then, on his refusal to accept the nomination, Dawes, the chances were in favor of the Republicans, but the campaign might be close and exciting and the first contender to make a tactical mistake be permanently crippled.

This was the case when, in the latter part of June, the Democracy came to its own city for the first national convention to be held there since that in 1868 at Tammany Hall.

When, on July 9, this convention adjourned, the election was practically accomplished. November 4 merely registered the long accepted result.

The tactical mistake had not awaited a candidate. The party itself had made it. The Madison Square convention was one gigantic mistake from start to finish. That another national convention of this party followed the New York fiasco proves the durability of partizanship. For if any one thing was proved to the American public by the Madison Square convention, it was that the Democratic party is composed of two totally different and really antagonistic elements, as falsely joined as it is possible for two factions to be. The Democracy of the North and West has its foundations in the cities. Of course you can point out, if you will, Philadelphia and certain other cities that are under Republican rule, but the great bulk of our cities are carried on by Democratic leadership and, although there is a comfortable Democratic minority in towns and villages, it is the city Democracy which controls the party in almost every Northern state. The basis of the political desires of this city-ruled section of the party is the enlargement of the common man, although sometimes this is greatly tinged with the question of loaves and fishes and the local machine which provides them.

This militant metropolitan Democracy is largely of foreign antecedents. While the Republican party has sought to encourage naturalized citizens and their descendants, it can be conservatively said that if the franchise in the North and West were to rest only in those who were grandchildren of those born in America, the Republican party would hardly

257

need to campaign, so overwhelmingly would be its advantage.

A large number of these city Democrats of foreign antecedents are Roman Catholic in their religion. Proscriptive organizations have always been in bad odor among the Northern Democrats.

To the aid of these Northerners has come the Solid South. Heretofore an irreducible minimum of ten states, from Virginia to Texas, from Florida to Arkansas, has been a sure nucleus for any Democratic candidate. Yet there has been no sympathy between Northern and Southern Democrats. Actually these elements are antagonistic. Although the Tillmans and Overmans have shown a coming into his own of the Southern commoner, the basis of the Southern Democracy is aristocratic. Its foundations lie in the country, not in the city. The basis of its political aims is anti-Negro. It looks backward at Reconstruction and forward at the possibilities of assimilation. The great Negro population is its constant specter. Heretofore whatever the platforms have enunciated, there has been no question but paled into insignificance before this one. The Southern Democracy is native and proudly Nordic. It is aggressively Protestant. Proscriptive organizations have always been strong in the Solid South.

The party has rubbed along with these ill-assorted factions for many years. Neither faction likes the other, but neither has been able to get along without the other. Never had this smoldering feeling been fanned into such flame as in New York in 1924.

To be frank and explicit this convention became a little religious war. The Ku Klux Klan had infuriated the members of the Catholic Church and no one knew how many Klansmen had seats in the convention, though it was deemed to be a substantial number. On the other hand, the strongest man among the bulk of Northern delegates was "Al" Smith of

New York, a governor of whom his machine had asked no act damaging to his reputation as an administrator, a lower East Side boy, carried through his career by Tammany Hall, and a Roman Catholic in religion. The Smith men not only wanted to beat the Klansmen, but they wanted to win a triumph as irritating to an important part of the party as a straightout Klan victory would have been to them. In a short time after the balloting began, the contest was waged for a convention victory, a national victory having been already lost. But still both sides fought doggedly on. From the earliest moment it was evident that neither of the leaders, McAdoo nor Smith, would permit the nomination of the other, and yet it took nearly two weeks of continuous attempts at party suicide before a compromise could be reached. When it was reached, it was too late, a condition which these bitter-enders might have seen, had they not been blinded by their antagonisms. The whole thing was a nightmare in politics and the people, who had never had the opportunity before, were standing, thanks to the radio, just outside the door and catching a real view of the futility and bad feeling of the whole convention. It was an unfortunate affair, but what is likely to happen in any body without homogeneity and with such falsely joined elements as the present day Democracy presents.

But when the convention opened there seemed little of this antagonism on the surface. The ample floor space in the Garden, filled with orderly delegates, was surrounded by the boxes, some of them apportioned to the families of the chief candidates, others to the large contributors to the convention fund.

Pat Harrison of Mississippi was the keynote speaker. Wilson was dead, but his death while clinging to his ideals gave his name a greater potency than ever. "What America needs now," cried Harrison, referring to Coolidge's reticence, "is not a Sphinx, but a Paul Revere to awaken it and call it back to duty and high resolve. Oh, for one in the White House whose heart might be melted and courage aroused to sympathize and to fight. Would we might see in that exalted position one with the courage of a Jackson, the militant honesty of a Cleveland, the matchless statesmanship, far flung vision and the fine fighting qualities of a Woodrow Wilson." The convention responded. Forgotten was the rout of four years before, the narrowness, the self-sufficiency, the disdain. Forgotten likewise was scrutiny of the practicability of his great dream. Before the convention for a moment a shining sword was waving and before the delegates stood the well remembered figure of a man indomitable in the shining armor of an ideal that in itself was one of the greatest for which men have ever stood. At that moment the Crypt spoke more loudly than the Capitol. Woodrow Wilson had come back.

But if the convention began as a memorial to Wilson, it was destined to progress as a tribute to Kilkenny.

There was no lack of candidates, but the battle which was to wreck the chances of the Democratic party beyond hope of recovery was waged between McAdoo and Smith along racial and religious lines. Not all the Catholic delegates cast votes for Smith. There were those who believed that to precipitate such a battle as would eventuate with his nomination would be to inaugurate a struggle in which two bodies of bigots would abuse each other to their heart's content, which would arouse more bitterness than any presidential election has ever seen, and which would leave an abyss which it would take generations to bridge. It seemed to them too great a price for the Church to pay for an ephemeral victory. On the other hand, there were non-Catholics who voted for Smith in a sincere protest against the activities of the Ku Klux Klan. But for the most part the Madison Square convention was a fight on race and religious lines. What was said from the platform was of little importance for the most part. What the delegates said and whispered to each other was the real basis of its deliberations. This was emphasized by the fact that the convention was being held in the Smith territory. The local crowds in Chicago in 1860 may or not have had an effect on the nomination of Lincoln. There is no doubt that the galleries and all official New York were bent upon forcing the nomination of the Governor, if noise and enthusiasm would do it. The police and local door-keepers were flagrant in letting Tammany satellites occupy seats for which others held tickets, turning away the legitimate occupants. During the early stages of the convention, the Police Commissioner of New York City was introduced to make a routine announcement to the delegates and had the execrable taste to conclude his speech by expressing the "hope that you will name in this convention a standard bearer who will carry the state of New York," a clear hint for Smith.

Before the convention was given the report of the Committee on Resolutions, which was having a hard time to reach even an outwardly amicable report, the various candidates were put in nomination. It was ten minutes past three in the afternoon when ex-Senator James H. Phelan of California concluded his nomination of McAdoo. Then began the usual demonstration, like all such affairs cordial and spontaneous at first, artificial and fictitious at last. It lasted seventy-three minutes. It was late at night when Smith's turn came. When Franklin Roosevelt put him in nomination the scene was repeated, and after the real enthusiasm disappeared, as it always does on such occasions, the delegates—watches in the hands of some, kept on until the McAdoo spasm had been slightly exceeded. Thus do American party delegates enforce their appeal to reason.

With the simmering passions it was easy to see that Senator Walsh of Montana would have no easy task as permanent president. In one of the earlier sessions, when one of the periodical disturbances and evidences of ill feeling burst out, the proceedings quote him as saying, "If this convention cannot come back to its business in this city, the chair will entertain a motion to go somewhere else." This was the typical attitude of Walsh, a fair and honest man, and shows how East Side and West Side in militant combination were trying to overwhelm regularly elected and accredited delegates with crowd psychology.

At last the platform committee was ready to report. It had avoided a deadlock, but at one time it seemed so inevitable that Bryan prevailed on the members to pause in their stormy deliberations and pray for guidance. This very act served as a gentle sedative and perhaps prevented a report of inability to agree.

On the old League issue the report advocated in effect a "great and solemn referendum" on the adoption of the principle "with such reservations or amendments to the covenant of the League as the President and Senate shall agree upon."

This was displeasing to Newton D. Baker and he offered in amendment a straightout plank for membership in the League "upon conditions which make it clear that we are not committed to use force."

On the vitally moving issue of the convention the platform reaffirmed its devotion to the "cardinal principles of freedom of press, speech and religion."

This was not enough for the enthusiastic delegate from Maine, Mr. Pattangall, and he presented an amendment specifically condemning by name the Ku Klux Klan, of which the strong Southern contingent was almost wholly Democratic.

The debate was first held upon the Baker amendment to the League of Nations plank. Baker was a little handicapped by having in the process of time been turned somewhat from the stern inflexibility of his late chief. For the thundered "No change whatever," was substituted the "conditions which will make it clear that we are not committed to use force," which in effect meant "mild reservations," though Baker was careful not to use the word. Baker made easily the noblest speech of the convention. He pled with eloquence, he had pathos, and once or twice he was magnificent. He touched the hearts of the delegates as far as they could have been touched. If some wise man could have prevailed upon the Democratic convention to turn to that plank as the chief plea of its platform and nominate Newton D. Baker for President, they would have gone out, not with victory in their grasp, but with a campaign worth fighting. But there seems to have been no opportunity-discerning genius to save the day. Impressed as the delegates were with Mr. Baker, they repudiated his plank with their blessing by a vote of 353 as against 742½, and turned to the bitter battle which awaited the consideration of Mr. Pattangall's amendment to the Freedom of Religion resolution. If Pattangall had not thrown this amendment into the convention, an amicable convention and a workable compromise might have been possible. After this debate and the vote upon the question, that possibility was gone. Senator Owen of Oklahoma, of the committee, disclaimed any favoritism for the Klan. Said he, "My people were Episcopalian, I married a daughter of a notable Methodist family, and my father died attended by Catholic sisters and received the last sacrament of the Catholic Church." But he was against condemning by sweeping resolution an organization that had no opportunity to be heard in its own defence.

Finally, at the end of the debate, William Jennings Bryan comes forward to defend the majority report. Facing an angry gallery, he accuses the minority of elevating three words above all else. He is confronted with boos, jeers and hisses from the New York delegation and the galleries. He stands unmoved, and facing down the gallery he says in a deep and resonant voice, "Citizens of New York, you show your appreciation of the honor we did you in holding our convention here." This scorn meant nothing to the New York mob bent on having its way. It showed this spirit down to the final day. Bryan pays a compliment to the Catholic Church, "my mother church as well as yours." He acknowledges its services in the preservation of Christianity for him and for every Protestant in the world. He has a word of praise for the Jew as well. "Both the Catholic Church and the Jewish Faith," he says, "have their great characters today to plead for them and whose pleading is not in vain. It is not necessary, and, my friends, the Ku Klux Klan does not deserve the advertisement that you give them." The minority would raise the Klan to "a higher altitude than the Ku Klux ever raised their fiery cross." The great commoner sits down. He has made his last stand on a question of party principle. He is no longer the buoyant crusader who brought a whole convention to its feet over a quarter of a century ago. It is a tired man who takes his seat. What has been the effect of his speech? We shall see.

The roll call progresses. It is significantly close, so close that at its end some who have kept a running tabulation say one side has won, some the other. There is a long pause at the clerk's table. Several additions are made. At last comes the announcement; for the adoption of the amendment 542 $\frac{7}{20}$; against the adoption (for the report of the committee) 542 $\frac{3}{20}$. The original resolution is carried by a fraction of a single vote. A later tabulation is said to have made the majority slightly larger, but authorities differ on this allegation. Bryan has won his victory. His first victory was for himself. The platform of 1896 would have been the same had he kept silence. He but articulated the beliefs of the convention and that speech made him the candidate. Twenty-eight years later he did a greater thing. He did not move the entire audience, but it is idle to say that he did not bring over a single man. And when he brought over that single man he won the battle, on so slight a thread did victory hang.

But a great price was paid for victory. Had the other side won, their victory would have been quite as costly. The nearly equal forces were now beyond any profitable compromise. To nominate Smith would be an affront to about half the convention. To nominate any Protestant, whoever he might be, would be a bitter pill to Smith's supporters and one which they would very largely refuse to swallow.

But the convention went on. It was not till the sixth day, after a period long enough for a closely contested Democratic convention to finish its work in, that a vote was reached. The first ballot showed that McAdoo had 432½, Smith 241, Cox 59, Underwood 42½, John W. Davis 31. Other candidates receiving scattering votes were Ralston, Robinson, Ritchie, Glass and Jonathan Davis. At the end of the day, after fifteen ballots, McAdoo had advanced to 479 and Smith to 305, while Davis had almost doubled his original total, having 61. Next day McAdoo began with 478 but slipped to 415½ as the day closed. Smith opened at 305 and made a slight gain on closing, having 323½. This was the thirtieth ballot on the seventh day of the convention. Davis now had 126½. These thirty ballots had proved to every member of the convention that neither Smith nor McAdoo would allow the other to be nominated. It also forecast that the ultimate choice must be Davis, but the partizans of neither of the leading candidates would admit it. And so the battle went on. Already the ultimate choice was being weakened by the strength of the ill-feeling of the convention, but the delegates went on piling Ossa on Pelion.

On the following day, after a ballot which had showed no practical change, Bryan rose and using the same parliamentary expedient which he has used in Wilson's behalf in 1912, the explanation of his vote, tried to bring the convention into harmony. Bryan was clearly a tired and overwrought man. He was heavy of face and figure. Little of the old fire played about him. He looked as if he were the venerable father of the young enthusiast of 1896. He did not realize that just as he and his fellow free-silverites took the party away from the sober elders in that day, so the new forces of the metropolis were ready to turn from him. He had kept the words Ku Klux Klan out of the resolutions, but he had infuriated a minority which now detested him.

He spoke, urging name after name, as being worthy of Democratic support. First there was Murphree of Florida, the head of the State University, probably unheard of by nine-tenths of the convention. "He is a scholarly Democrat," explains Bryan. "Never heard of one," is shouted in reply. And if one judged by the actions of that convention, the speaker told the truth. As Bryan goes on the insistent cries "We want Smith" rise almost to a chant. "What's the matter with Smith!" again punctuates the noise. Bryan is drowned out, but he holds on with the tenacity of a Henry Ward Beecher in Liverpool in the sixties. As the confusion recedes he says that this is probably his last convention. An insulting round of wild applause follows this statement. "Don't applaud," he retorts. "I may change my mind." Three times, he states, he has received the Democratic nomination. "Never again," comes the cry. It is a contest between rowdy baiters and an old man who has lingered over-long on the political stage, who cannot understand that he has lost his leadership, a puzzled veteran, but one who faces the fire and never flinches. Finally he names McAdoo. It is the signal for loosing pandemonium. The McAdoo applause is blended with the Smith boos. "Oil, oil, oil!" resounds from the galleries, a reference to the fact that McAdoo had been at one time counsel for Doheny. Fitzpatrick of New Jersey questions the speaker. As a preliminary he says, "I voted for you every time you ran for President." "I am very much obliged to you," replies the speaker. "I am sorry," shouts his heckler, and the Smith cohorts yell delight. Efforts are made to deprive him of the floor. Had he been talking continuously his time would have expired, but Chairman Walsh takes out the interruptions. He goes on. He beats upon a stone wall. There are cries, "Who is paying you for this?" and "One thousand dollars a minute!" At last his time expires and defeated, his leadership overwhelmed, he walks, head in air, back to his seat while one Charles Francis Xavier O'Brien delights his cohorts with the words, "The same old Dollar Bill, the same old Dollar Bill."

Bryan deserves a word at parting. His mind was not analytic. He brought old theories to face new problems with. There was an unction about him that almost equalled that of Dr. Munyon. He turned and rent Champ Clark, perhaps because he felt it his duty, although it is the one thing in his career which it is hardest to forgive. But Bryan kept faith with himself. He followed his political theories without deviation. He might be defeated, yes, but he would keep his flag flying. It has been written by an enthusiastic follower of Roosevelt (Henry L. Stoddard) that Mr. Bryan went "shopping for issues." Mr. Bryan's issues were all akin, one grew out of the other. He was incapable of making certain principles the features of his platform in one year and forgetting them in the next. Gold production settled the silver issue. Bryan never abandoned another. Far above most men of his time Bryan kept the faith. Disagree with Bryan as we must and will, yet we know that no cleaner, finer citizen has ever lived and no nobler influence on party politics has ever been exerted than was exerted by him. But when Bryan resumed his seat he was an historic relic. He could not, later in the session, even second a prevailing motion without cries of "Sit down!" Although he was present the convention went on without him.

And it went on interminably. Davis would rise and fall. An occasional sortie would be made for some other candidate like Baker, who was given 56 on the seventieth ballot and dropped to one on the seventy-seventh. Ralston who, earlier in the convention, had withdrawn in the interest of harmony was trotted out again on the 87th and got 93, while Glass on this roll call got 71. It was useless, although he passed the hundred mark before he was dropped. But Smith and McAdoo were at death grips at each other's throats. McAdoo had until near the end a substantial lead on the New Yorker, but Smith's supporters had the veto power and doggedly they blocked the way.

Various motions were made seeking to break the deadlock. One delegate hoping for wisdom and guidance moved to invite all candidates (and most of them were in New York) to address the convention. Franklin Roosevelt moved to invite the Governor of New York to address the convention in his official capacity. After a tremendous voice vote in favor, which showed how little consideration the friends of outside delegates were getting in the way of gallery tickets, this was foiled by a vote of 604½ in favor to 443 against, 718 being necessary to suspend the rules. McAdoo utilized this for a magnanimous gesture, sending the convention a letter asking that Smith be given the courtesy, but he must have known that the unanimous consent, then necessary, could not be secured.

Then there was an attempt to pass a rule dropping the lowest candidate on each succeeding ballot until only two survived. This would have left two contenders, neither with the necessary two-thirds and a worse deadlock than ever. Another similar scheme was to eliminate, one at a time, all but the leading five. Another panacea was a motion to adjourn after the 75th ballot to meet again in Kansas City, on July 21. Another motion embraced gradual elimination to two and abandonment of two-thirds rule after five subsequent roll calls. On the motion of Tom Taggart, the Chairman of the Convention, Walsh, and the Chairman of the National Committee, Hull, were asked to call a conference of the candidates or their representatives. At this conference all the candidates offered to release their delegates, McAdoo making his offer conditional on the breaking of the two-thirds rule. This of course upset the plans. Hull and Walsh reported an abortive resolution releasing delegates from their allegiance and from the unit rule.

Finally on the twelfth day the McAdoo forces broke. But this break, though it put Smith slightly in the lead, was as much a deathblow to his candidacy as to McAdoo's. The day opened with the 78th ballot, showing 511 for McAdoo, 363½ for Smith and 73½ for Davis. By the time the 87th ballot was reached McAdoo had fallen to 336½ and into second place; but not one of these ballots seems to have gone to Smith or Davis, each of whom had a little less than he had on the first ballot of the day. The diversions toward Ralston and Glass were being tried out. The break from McAdoo was strongly anti-Smith. On the thirteenth day the hundredth ballot was reached. Smith was still practically stationary, with 351½, though McAdoo was only 190. Davis was now forging ahead with 203½. The contest was near an end.

On the fourteenth day three ballots were taken. On the 101st McAdoo had sunk to 52 and Smith at 151 had lost 200 over night. Each man's goose was cooked. But many Smith men felt that Underwood had been their quasi-ally and by keeping his name before the convention kept votes from McAdoo, and the gentleman from Alabama got his reward by jumping up to 229½. But it was not enough. Davis with 316 was in first place. On the next two ballots McAdoo and Smith virtually disappeared and the effort to make Underwood the convention's choice went to pieces when the nomination of

Davis was accomplished on the 103rd ballot, with his 844 to Underwood's 102½.

What for days had been a futility, a mere contest for leadership, with chances for winning the campaign out of the question, came quickly to an end. Mr. Davis, one of those "Wall Street fellers" of whom Mr. Bryan did not approve, sought to conciliate that worthy by suggesting the nomination of his brother Charles, Governor of Nebraska, one of the minor Presidential candidates, as Vice President, which nomination was obediently made. It was the final piece of folly of a convention replete with blunders. Much as they personally respected the elder Bryan, thousands of men though they compared the legal eminence of the Democratic candidate with the small country political lawyer on the Republican ticket, still refused to put the "little" Bryan where Coolidge had been placed four years before, with the possibility of a similar eventuality.

The campaign of 1924 is of no importance. Committees went through motions. There was plenty of shouting. A third ticket endorsed by a "Progressive" Conference and the Socialist parties, consisting of two insurgent senators, the Republican La Follette and the Democratic Wheeler, made its appearance, attracted many who were unfriendly to the chief nominations, and carried one state. But the Madison Square Convention had settled matters. The split was made. The defection from the party which had refused to nominate Smith was very great. Davis was a nominee; he was hardly a candidate. So entirely was his defeat forecasted that the opposition put in no such intensive campaign as it did against Cox and he made on that account a little better showing, but not much. Coolidge had fifteen million seven hundred thousand of the popular vote, while Davis had not quite eight million four hundred thousand. La Follette had a little more than half what Davis received. The electoral vote was Coolidge 382, Davis

136, LaFollette 13. Among the thirty-six states which Coolidge had carried was every state which had ever been doubtful, except three, Oklahoma and Tennessee which went to Davis, and Wisconsin which gave its vote to its own "Fighting Bob." LaFollette crowded Davis into third place in seven western states. For the first time in nearly three-quarters of a century a New Englander entered the presidency in his own right.

CHAPTER TWENTY

MAIN STREET VERSUS BROADWAY

IT IS NOT always the winner of the political battle who most impresses himself upon public memory of that particular contest. If a single name is used to denote the election of 1884 we speak of it as the Blaine campaign. It is safe to hazard that the campaign which in 1928 ended in the vanquished candidate carrying only eight states, will nevertheless be remembered as the Smith campaign. There is good reason for this. In 1884 the tariff and other platform planks might go hang. Blaine himself was the real issue and the campaign was waged around the question of his fitness to be President.

It was so in 1928. Hoover was able, honest, experienced and wholly what a meticulous voter should wish his candidate to be. Any attacks on him only weakened those who made them. But the man we could all fight over, and did, was Alfred Emanuel Smith, the Governor of New York. In the background was a somewhat shadowy Jupiter ready to leave a shadowy Olympus and descend upon the White House if the public called him. But vivid and palpitating in the center of the stage was a very human figure about whom people could differ quite to their hearts' content. Hence it was the Smith campaign which was fought in 1928,—and an exciting campaign it was. There are those, forgetting 1877, who say it was the hardest fought, most exciting and altogether spectacular presidential election since the Civil War. It may be so,—perhaps a boy's vision gives a glamour and the retrospection of more than forty years may have added an artificial color to

272

Blaine's battles, but that still seems to me the liveliest, the hottest, the most vicious campaign which I ever witnessed. Certainly in one way it gave us finer sport than we got in 1928. There were no elaborate systems of discounting the result. If there were any attempts at those diabolical kill-joys and spoil-sports known as "straw-ballots" they were mere guess-work in an election so close that one guess was as good as another. Although the Democratic party in 1928 showed stamina and courage under a difficult situation, the result was discounted and every skillful and intelligent test showed that Hoover was to be elected. In the name of those who enjoy our great American sport, I protest against this, as dulling the edge of our President-making.

When the year opened the two interesting questions concerned Coolidge and Smith. Did Coolidge mean what he had seemed to say in the previous summer when he handed the newspaper men those slips of paper containing the words, "I do not choose to run"? Could Smith wear down the rural opposition which had stopped his nomination in 1924? Events were to answer the second question but the first remains a mystery. Although Coolidge made another statement it was no more definite. Whether he meant it or not, he held the door an inch or so ajar and it was Mr. Vare of Pennsylvania who finally pushed it to. To some of those who have studied Coolidge, this vagueness, which he would never correct, was significant. It made them think of the situation eight years before, when as Governor of Massachusetts he retired as a presidential candidate and yet tried to be one at the same time. That attitude is an historic fact and in so far as the Coolidge attitude of 1927 and 1928 is of historic interest, it must be studied in the light of 1920, whatever conclusion may finally be reached.

No two nominations in the history of the presidency contrast more clearly in one respect at least. In each convention a minority were opposed to the nominee. In the Republican convention the majority were dominated by an inarticulate popular dictation within the party. The minority was composed of the practical politicians, the machine men trying to keep out a candidate they did not want. In the Democratic convention it was just the other way. A clever, active, sometimes ruthless campaign had been carried on throughout the country, tactics of exceeding subtlety had been used and the election of Smith delegates over those for Walsh of Montana, Reed of Missouri and others had been emphatically a politician's victory. After the nomination of Smith, the *Raleigh News and Observer,* edited by Josephus Daniels, contained an article on the editorial page over the initials of the eminent editor, coldly stating that, of the number of Southern delegates who voted for Smith, not one represented the untrammelled wishes of his constituents; and Mr. Daniels after the nomination was a genuine supporter of Smith. It was the minority of the Democratic convention which represented an unorganized public opinion, though no man can say with any degree of surety that, within the party, it was the prevailing public opinion. Certainly the Democratic party wanted to win. No matter how difficult the election of Smith might be, the inarticulate threat, seen in the treatment of Davis four years before, that no man could beat Smith and be elected at the polls, was ever present and ever potent. Therefore it was perfectly evident at the time that the leaders of the anti-Smith movement, honest men they were too, believed that the party would be eventually stronger to lose with another candidate than to take the Smith possibility, with the odds against his election.

It was evident some months before the conventions that, if the Coolidge statement was to be accepted at face value, the strongest candidates before the assemblages would be Hoover and Smith. In California, where the McAdoo strength, supposed to be potent, was for Walsh of Montana, although some of his distinguished supporters had gone over to Smith, there was a lively and picturesque contest in which two eminent women authors bore a part, Gertrude Atherton for Smith and Kathleen Norris for Walsh. The Governor of New York won handily and this seemed to experts to be the most significant of the local contests and to leave only the forlornest of forlorn hopes to any anti-Smith coalition which could be accomplished to take advantage of the two-thirds rule.

In the Republican primary contests the flies in the Hoover ointment, aside from the Coolidge enigma, were the extreme radical bloc from the farm states and the hostility of the practical politicians, some, as usual, in the United States Senate, who always antagonize, as far as it is safe, the Hoover type. His greatest hope came from the lesson of the Harding days, and the public distrust of these same politicians whom so many thousands believed to be cut from the same piece of cloth as the "Ohio gang."

The Republican convention met first. It assembled at Kansas City on June 12. Of course there were the usual guesses in the press of the country preceding its organization. For instance, there were said to be sixty-three votes in the New York delegation which were going to lead a stampede to Coolidge. Coolidge was not especially popular with the "practical" men, but they were still practical enough to think it better to bear the ills they had than to fly to Hoover; and Coolidge finally might stampede the convention. On the other hand we were told that the administration would be solidly behind Hoover if . . . but there always is an "if" in convention prognostications. Secretary Mellon was announced to have said that Hoover was the closest to the presidential standard of any of the candidates. But there seemed a greater significance in his statement that the Pennsylvania delegation would be unpledged. According to the reports in the papers of the Sunday

previous to the convention, Coolidge was the lone obstacle in
Hoover's path. Then the delegates began to gather. With
bated breath and awed mien they awaited the arrival of that
financial superman, Andrew William Mellon, who was apparently to be the oracle whose pronouncement was to be
obeyed. And just then William Scott Vare of Philadelphia
arrived on the ground with most of the Pennsylvania delegates. Now Mr. Vare is said to be the Senator-elect from
Pennsylvania, although some people question that fact. He has
never been quite cheek by jowl with the demure Secretary
of the Treasury from Pittsburgh, who vainly supported that
other Philadelphian, George Wharton Pepper, whom Mr.
Vare ousted, whether or not he succeeded in bringing himself
in in his place. And while people were wondering what Mellon
would do when he arrived, Vare knew exactly what he was
going to do, and he had arrived. It may be truthfully said that
Mr. Vare is a persuasive gentleman. He had been foregather-
ing with members of the delegation all the way along, while
Mr. Mellon was in Washington. Now Mr. Vare, without waiting for Mr. Mellon, announced that the Pennsylvania delegation was for Hoover. Mr. Mellon was not in Kansas City
and Mr. Vare was. Mr. Mellon could not contradict Mr. Vare
over the wire, and for "Cal" to be brought forward as an
active nomination seeker would only make him ridiculous. At
that moment William Scott Vare spilled all the Coolidge beans
in the political pot, that is, if there were any in it. Next day
Mr. Butler of Massachusetts, Mr. Coolidge's very particular
representative and Chairman of the National Committee, was
announcing that the President was absolutely not a candidate
in any sense and had said almost indignantly, "I do not want
to have to issue another statement," which was making a noise
as if he had issued an unmistakable statement previously. The
one point around which the opposition to Hoover could rally
with even the slightest hope was now removed.

When the convention assembled it was to listen to one of the most commonplace "keynoters" in history, Senator Simeon D. Fess of Ohio, an amiable political journeyman. His coin comes from the mint of the spellbinder and, true to tradition, he said nothing original or pause compelling. His omissions were more important than his commitments. He laid a somewhat shopworn laurel at the feet of all the Republican Presidents except Roosevelt. But alas for Simeon, the militant Mrs. Longworth was right on the spot. Between sessions the matter was presented to the unfortunate Chairman Fess in the right light and next morning he publicly apologized for his lamentable forgetfulness so that the Convention might go on and elect Senator Moses for permanent Chairman.

The platform, when presented, contained a law enforcement plank that showed traces of the influence of honest enforcement advocates. Another pledge was of reorganization of the marketing system on a sounder and more economical basis. It glorified the Republican tariff policy and stood by Coolidge's policies in Central America. This platform was objectionable to the farmers and the "wets."

Feeling that their delegates might not get what they were insistent upon, the western farmers organized a pilgrimage to Kansas City, held meetings, paraded the streets and buttonholed delegates. But although the demonstration was noisy, it had been too much press agented. The delegates, who, if it had come upon them by surprise, might well have been impressed, had heard all about it and anticipated too much, therefore it fell flat. In the convention young LaFollette presented the plank of the farm bloc. It declared for the equalization fee without naming it. There was plenty of discussion. These men were in earnest. Their foodstuffs were the mainstay of the country and they did not think they were fairly sharing in the prosperity they produced. They had heard vague promises before and nothing had come out of them. They had their own panacea and wished for none other. A delegate from Minnesota named Murphy referred to this in a blunt, vigorous and defiant speech in which he informed the delegates that the farmers had ceased to believe in Santa Claus. But Mr. Murphy was a paid attorney and lobbyist and his defiance fell on indifferent ears. At the end of the debate Senator Borah, who had emerged as the big man of the convention, took the platform for the majority and led the convention in the direction in which they would have gone without him.

Then Nicholas Murray Butler had his turn. He was for throwing out the enforcement plank. He pled earnestly, but the Convention was not to be upset. No one even took the trouble to answer him. Quickly the aged son of Neal Dow, "the father of Maine prohibition," moved to lay Dr. Butler's motion on the table. Without demur the convention voted aye so strongly that they laid Dr. Butler on the table along with his motion and he stayed there during the entire campaign. The campaign was the most eloquently silent period of the amiable Doctor's life.

After the platform was out of the way, the convention proceeded to nominate Hoover. There were the regular oratorical preliminaries. None of the speeches rose to anything worthy of record. Besides Hoover, the forlorn favorite sons were put in nomination. A single ballot was enough. The majority needed was 545. Lowden of Illinois had 74; Senator Curtis of Kansas had 64; Senator Watson of Indiana had 45 and Senator Norris of Nebraska, the demon of discontent, as one of the characters of Pinero was called, had 24. There were eighteen for Coolidge, in spite of everything, and Vice President Dawes, believed to have the strongest potentialities of any of the field could a promising move have been gotten under way, had 4. There were some scattering votes for others. Hoover had 837 and, with the announcement, it was all over. With the exception of Lowden, who maintained silence, the other candidates were gracious and the apparent feeling at the end showed how last ditchers sometimes show animosity when they have it not. Under Borah's leadership Curtis was quickly chosen as the vice-presidential candidate to placate the farm bloc, the convention adjourned and the delegates went home.

Now eyes and ears turned to Houston, Texas, where in sweltering heat, the Democratic legions were soon to assemble. The Smith delegates had been piling up but there was still the hope that a desperate team might hold the Smith ball on the five yard line and prevent a score, especially under the two-thirds rule. The friends of Reed of Missouri, Pomerene of Ohio, Senator George of Georgia, Cordell Hull of Tennessee, Hitchcock of Nebraska and of a wealthy gentleman, politically unknown, Evans Woollen of Indiana, all had hope, albeit they were dubious.

One of the high lights of the convention was to be the keynote speech. The orator chosen was such as gave the country notice of an unusual and worthy oration. Claude G. Bowers is a brilliant editorial writer, vigorous, ruthless, bitter, who is apt violently to maltreat anybody he is against but who draws a shining blade for anyone whom he supports. He epitomizes the editorial policy of the *New York World*. He is an historian of real talents. But alas, he comes from Indiana and likes the "vine clad cottage" brand of oratory. But the public was unaware of this last fact and expected a durable speech. I hope that Mr. Bowers has forgotten this adventure and I sincerely trust that he never will read this speech now that it has grown cold. Of course it was far more entertaining, able and inspiring than Fess's effort. It would have been a triumph for a Bourke Cockran. But to those who expected something deeper than a lively, slack-reasoned, cheer-provoking stump speech, it was a disappointment. Such a piece of mere oratorical invective would give renown to a political war-horse, but it qualifies the prestige of an historian. Mr. Bowers showed a vehemence that was unbecoming in an historian and a taste for sensational phrases that was damnable in a stylist. He had an especial fondness for the sixteenth letter of the alphabet. He found something in the Republican Administration "putrid beyond precedent", he declared a "war of extermination against privilege." He cried, "Privilege and Pillage are the Gold Dust Twins of Normalcy." Again "the predatory forces before us seek a triumph for the sake of the sacking"; "in the presence of such a foe 'he who dallies is a dastard and he who doubts is damned' "; and at last the peroration: "the time has come, the battle hour has struck, then to your tents, O Israel." Within hardly more than forty-eight hours of this pronouncement, a large section of Israel's Southern wing had taken to its tents in the spirit of Achilles and the death of no Patroclus could ever draw them forth.

Then Senator Robinson of Arkansas had his innings as permanent chairman. He is a deep-chested and old-fashioned type upon the hustings,—Joe to all his acquaintances and fellow citizens. He was a magniloquent permanent president and he did what George Moses of New Hampshire failed to do at Kansas City, he snatched a nomination out of the body over which he presided. Still it is only fair to Moses to say that Robinson's coup had been carefully planned and its success freely predicted before he took the chair, whereas Moses had no such assistance, and though he was a candidate he never had any real prospects. Sensibly the convention sought to get all the ornamental oratory out of the way at once and ordered the nominating speeches before taking up the report of the platform committees. During these speeches the speakers were interrupted by that silliest of all convention devices, the timed and forced ovation. Delegations with banners filled the aisles. The Northern delegates, realizing that victory could not be achieved in such a rowdy manner as that in which it had been sought four years before, had made preparation with lessons in quietness and restraint. But there were occasional fisticuffs. Certain of the Smith Southern delegates sought to tear the North Carolina banner from its anti-Smith delegation and found an opposition which surprised them.

Among the nominating speeches two took high rank. One of these was Judge Crisp's nomination of Senator George. It was not a popular speech. It takes courage in a party convention when all is praise and acclaim, to refer to party mistakes as such and seek to guide the party steps by lessons learned from them. Judge Crisp told the delegates that on a moral issue, that of slavery, the Republican party first succeeded and on the tide of that moral issue had won without defeat for twenty years. He urged the convention to recognize temperance as a moral issue and not to make a nomination which would weaken that issue. Granted that prohibition is such an issue, this was a rare speech.

Franklin D. Roosevelt for a second time mounted the platform to present Smith. He has a fine personality and a disarming presence. His speech was a pure convention speech, not in the least like Crisp's, but it was one of the finest of its kind. He said no antagonistic word, descended to no cheap vernacular. It was a speech which could appeal to the highest intellect there and be absolutely intelligible to the roughest hanger-on at the heels of a New York City or Boston delegation. It may not be so striking as Conkling's nomination of Grant or Ingersoll's presentation of Blaine, but it was in some ways the finest bit of pure convention oratory which has been heard in recent years. Catching a phrase from Wordsworth, he concluded by calling Smith "the happy warrior," a charming designation which stuck throughout the campaign.

Before the balloting the platform came in. The plank on prohibition had been difficult to draw. But as it was reported, with the acquiescence of Smith's supporters, it was quite as dry as that of the Republican party. So far as platforms went, the prohibitionists had won a victory in each convention. Further, the platform in effect told the people that the convention did not think any more of the Republicans than the Republicans did of the Democrats, which was not saying much. It patted the farmer on the back, went much farther in his direction politically than the other party had and did the best it could to attract votes in all the other ways. It specifically disapproved Coolidgism in Nicaragua and there I think it had the best of the discussion. The platform adopted and the delegates all comfortable, they returned, after an adjournment, for the great test. Assembled, the convention was a wonderful sight. Houston, in the last days of June is sultry and the heat was hard for some of the visitors to endure. The men wore white linen and the women all sorts of gay light fabrics and there were flowers galore. While the delegates were assembling, bands stationed at distant parts of the hall sent melody billowing back and forth. Even the membership was not too limp to respond in cheers and song. Then came the roll call. As the states responded and Smith mounted it became more and more evident that he would be almost over the goal line on the first down. As the roll call ended those who had kept tally knew that he was only the fewest possible votes short of two thirds and the nomination. The game was up. He could not be beaten. The necessary votes were transferred to him. He was nominated with 849⅔ as against the 52½ of his nearest competitor, George, with whom Reed and Hull were practically tied with 52 and 50⅚. Jones of Houston, hoping to get second place, had 43 and there were forty-three votes distributed between nine other candidates. It was over. Eight years of struggle had given the presidential nomination to the sidewalks of New York. The exhausted delegates put Joe Robinson on the ticket to give it picturesqueness and Southern flavor and speedily sought cooler climes.

Thus two candidates stood out, entered for the race. Surely here was an inspiration for the youth who has been told by parents and teachers, and has had quoted to him the words of Lincoln, that the greatest place in the land is not out of reach of the poorest boy. Hoover, poor as a church mouse, an orphan and as a child a wanderer from relative to relative; Smith born amidst din and squalor, fatherless at twelve. Hoover early a worker for his bread: Smith the best support of his mother. Hoover in his fifty-fifth year an eminent cabinet minister with years of successful business and humanitarian accomplishments behind him! Smith also in his fifty-fifth year, Governor of the most important state in the Union, with a record of clear-seeing, highly successful and unbesmirched administration behind him. Neither of them lawyers. Each of them with records and achievements which clearly gave him the right to ask for the consideration of their fellow Americans for the greatest honor those Americans can bestow.

There was never any serious effort to belittle Hoover's right to this consideration. There was however an effort to show Smith as a man of local achievement, not great enough to entitle him to seek the presidency. Hoover supporter though I was, I must put this down as unfair. No administration of New York affairs will go down in the history of that state as being better. Smith had behind him what Conkling called "the arduous greatness of things done". No one, friend or foe, thought the nomination of Cleveland a mistake on the ground that his experience as Governor of New York was not enough to justify his nomination. And yet Cleveland had in that office, which he held but a comparatively short time, no opportunity to make the permanent and admirable record which Smith had made. Hayes, another excellent executive and one whose excellence has become acknowledged, now that partizan rancour has ceased to obscure it, although he served, rather inconspicuously, two terms in Congress, had his real training as an admirable Governor of Ohio. Wilson does not properly come into this comparison for, though at the time of his election he had never served in Congress or national office and was Governor of New Jersey, he was nationally known as one of the most eminent of theoretic students of American Government. On the other hand Johnson, who failed because he could not handle men, had not only been a governor but had had ample national legislative experience, and Garfield, who did not live to face the results of his early Presidential mistakes, had attained a congressional leadership which should have trained him amply for his exalted place if it were not that legislators and executives are not necessarily of the same fibre. The fact is that in 1928 both parties presented men who are remarkable executives, trained and proved.

Immediately after the nomination Smith, whose followers in that body had accepted the conventional law enforcement plank, enunciated his views on prohibition. In brief they were a declaration which, while being opposed to the open saloon, said in effect that prohibition was a failure and that the states could do better in their own way. It was candidly a "wet" pronouncement.

This attitude of the candidate had the effect of abrogating the party platform on this subject. These were Smith's convictions. Even as a political move this was a wise one though its results were not what had been hoped by Smith's intimates. If Smith could carry the hitherto solid South, which had always been immovable no matter what the provocation; hold the votes of the Democrats who had voted for Davis and those who had voted against him, the latter as a protest at Smith's defeat in Madison Square, and add to this the bulk of the votes of the anti-prohibition Republicans, he might be elected. It seemed he could be elected in no other way. A plausible campaign on the old issues might be dignified and spectacularly effective; it could not be successful. The country is strongly for the prohibition amendment but if in some states, supposedly Democratic, partizanship transcended issues and in other states this issue transcended partizanship, a Democratic victory might be snatched out of the fire. It would be a close thing at best but it was possible.

There were other issues. There was farm relief, which was expected to be extraordinarily important. It was spoken of frequently, and several locally prominent Republicans, Senator Norris of Nebraska (who calls himself one), Senator Blaine of Wisconsin, and the lively Mr. Murphy among them went to Smith on the issue. But though we heard farm relief noise the issue was really lost. It hardly cut more of a figure than water power.

Smith's Tammany relations were not forgotten. Some eminent citizens, reformers at that, believed that a man born in Tammany surroundings and receiving its support, who in spite of such surroundings had done so well, was especially worthy of their support. Others remembered that his environment in his most impressionable youth had been under the leadership of Tom Foley, a genial Tammany roustabout; remembered the Lexow and Mozet investigations in Smith's younger days; remembered the statements in justification of their acts which Croker and the other Tammany leaders had given at these hearings, statements which were impudent and yet subtle, made to satisfy their followers who did not happen to be entirely ruthless, such followers as young Smith; remembered his constant regularity as an assemblyman. They knew that if he had made certain betterment in state government it was with the acquiescence of Tammany, that he had never opposed it or been opposed by it. They did not believe that the leopard had changed his spots nor that it had had sufficient time to bring forth fruits meet for repentance. Nor was this feeling reduced by the frequency with which Mayor "Jimmie"

Walker, slick and suave, looking like a vaudeville performer off stage, appeared in the news reels in all the country picture houses. While showing no such executive genius as Smith, Walker is undoubtedly a better official than Hylan, but the latter's commonplace solidity would have done Smith better service on the screen than the inconsequential gayety of Walker.

Tammany was an issue but, like the religious question, it was more a word of mouth issue than an editorial or platform one. Although Tammany's sins, and in the past they were scarlet, were those of a dominating organization which amounted to a municipal party and those of Daugherty and Fall were individual, the distinction was not likely to be so clear in the popular mind, and officially the Republicans let St. Tammany alone lest the Teapot Dome become again malodorous.

The only other issue of real importance, and the one which I believe had the greatest influence of any, was the religious issue. To thousands of upright honest and thinking men and women, it had no place in the campaign. To tens of thousands of others, not all of them illiterate, not all of them inspired by ill-will, Smith's Catholicism was a very real bar to his obtaining the presidency. In response to this the cry of bigotry was lustily raised.

In many noble minds bigotry is a bugaboo and tolerance a fetish. Bigotry as I envisage it is an antagonism in which hatred, fear, or stubborn ignorance have a part. Opposition on merely mistaken premises which does not have either of these three qualities is not bigotry. Enlightened men would not call it bigotry to have opposed a Mormon for office in the days when polygamy was one of the tenets of that church. Therefore it is not bigotry *per se* to find something in church doctrines which prevents one from believing it wise to intrust governmental powers to a mentality which embraces it. There were doubtless plenty of bigots against Smith. Among them

286

"TAMMANY!"

Courtesy of Rollin Kirby and
The New York World.

WELL, THEY'RE OFF!

Courtesy of Chas. H. Sykes and
*The Philadelphia Evening
Ledger.*

Cartoons of the 1928 Campaign

were those who think that the Pope has a longing eye on the
flesh-pots of this country, that the Knights of Columbus take
a treasonable oath, that the cellars of "Roman" churches are
filled with arms for a Catholic conquest (what trouble it must
be to keep these weapons from becoming obsolete!), and that
the countless boys' military companies of the Catholic schools
are being made into minute-men for that event, at which time
an inquisition shall be set up under the dome of the Capitol.
These were the comic buffos of the opera. On the other hand
there were men of intelligence who doubted honestly and with
no animosity in their hearts, the wisdom of electing a member
of Smith's church to the presidency, although two Presidents
of widely differing temperament, Jackson and Taft, had appointed Catholic Chief Justices. I think I can epitomize the
reasons of these men in a few words. I am not a theologic historian and I do not pretend to say that these views were true
views or mistaken ones, but they were honestly and temperately held. Briefly their opinions were these: "For centuries,
until the Reformation, the church was the power, temporal
and religious, above kings. This power was never voluntarily
relinquished. Today the Pope remains a voluntary prisoner in
the Vatican as a protest against the loss of his temporal power.
We know," these voters admitted, "that a great majority of
American Catholics accept the separation of church and state,
but the church, as far as we know, has never put on record
any official acceptance of that doctrine, therefore we feel that
Mr. Smith, whatever his own opinions, represents a church
with a different civic point of view from any church in which
other Americans claim membership, and so, with no unkind
feeling toward the candidate, we intend to give the country
the benefit of the doubt."

During the campaign Jefferson's Virginia statute of religious tolerance was made prominent. No reasonable and sane
citizen has anything to say against that great state paper, but

it is, in effect, no more than was the removal of Catholic disabilities in England, being a statute to prevent such disabilities being raised. Not one true American citizen would wish to prevent a candidate from running for office because of his religion. On the other hand, Jefferson never wished to prevent any man from giving his vote according to any reason that the voter considered potent. If all other things were equal can any one doubt that as between a candidate embracing a dogmatic religion and a religious liberal, Jefferson would vote for the candidate whose mind, to use a Wilsonian phrase, gave best evidence of going along with his?

Of course this opposition to Smith tended to solidify the members of his church in his favor. Already, and quite naturally, a very large number of these, thrilled by the opportunity of seeing one of their fellows in the presidency, were for him, irrespective of their former affiliations. As the evidences of antagonism arose this feeling, with certain honorable exceptions, became intensified.

During the campaign both candidates declared that they desired no man's vote because of their religion. I do not question the sincerity either of Mr. Hoover or Mr. Smith. They said it because they meant it. But, meaning it, they said it for the record. Each man must have known, however, much he might wish his injunction observed, that it was only a gesture. On the religious question the voters were immovable.

For centuries the antagonisms between religious forces have been fomented. We think that we have reached a more happy time. We have begun to reach it. But old suspicions die hard. Old theories persist. So archaic a belief as that in witchcraft was recognized in English law until about the opening of the nineteenth century. Green fields may change into closely built cities but thought is the last thing in this world to yield place. Leaders of thought may cry out and forward-looking men accept their teachings and think the matter settled, but the

composite mind moves more slowly than the alert mind real-
izes. Years ago I asked a Catholic priest of my acquaintance
what he considered would bring the solution of this problem.
A shadowy smile flitted across his face and gently placing his
hand upon my arm he said: "Infinite patience and kindliness."
I think, Catholic and Protestant alike, we all ought to add to
that an effort to see the other's point of view and then try to
forget the religious antagonisms of 1928.

Smith's campaign typified the yearning of the urban man for
more power and recognition. He was bone of his bone, flesh
of his flesh. This yearning was recognized and catered to in
the very title of Smith's campaign life, "Up from the City
Streets." On the first page we read: "It is possible that their
[the cities'] evils may be reduced, and that their sons may
show not less energy, persistence and initiative than have come
heretofore from the silences and the long labor of the ox
and plow." Smith was the first urban candidate raised in the
localities which furnish urban rule. Arthur and Roosevelt were
not New Yorkers in the same sense. Three times has the struggle been made for Smith, twice within the party and once
before the nation. In the sense of being the incarnation of his
cause, Smith is the Andrew Jackson of the slums or, if that
word offends, let us submit the words of his biographers, Hapgood and Moskowitz, the localities of "din and squalor." The
country fears the city. It knows how little the average con-
gested district in a great city demands in ideals from its representatives. Perhaps it blinds itself to plausibility at home. The
sense that these two elements of American civilization were
opposing one another was clouded and inarticulate in many
minds but it had its part. It was clear to many of the city
dwellers. They were battling consciously in the big cities for a
man they knew to be "one of us." Even the "intelligentsia" of
New York knew it. Hadn't a man named Lewis written a
book named "Main Street" showing suburban littleness?

Wasn't Hoover a type to be worshipped by Rotary and Kiwanis Clubs, to show contempt for which is the dearest prerogative of our self-appointed intellectuals? For all they knew Hoover might enjoy reading Bunyan rather than James Joyce, among the Lowells exalt James Russell above Amy or prefer Shakespeare to Eugene O'Neill. Socially (in its deep sense) he was a middle-of-the-roader and that wouldn't do at all. Besides liquor was liquor and he was so naïve as to object to it. There was no queerer coalition in the history of elections than this of the struggling submerged and the consciously superior.

Perhaps I do not entirely discriminate between unpretentiously intelligent people and those who worship at the shrine of their own fancied and self-discovered brilliance. Smith had many supporters among the former. Some went to him on the ground that the American interference with little Latin American nations was unsound and that, as no man is good enough to own another man, so no nation is great enough to rule another against its will. Others, anxious to promote harmony among the elements in the nation, thought it unwise to defeat a Catholic. Certain social reformers were enraptured by his social program in New York State. Another group which included the Editor of the *Atlantic Monthly,* thought the cities entitled to their turn. Certain eminent lawyers believed the fact that Smith, if elected, would have the opportunity of putting the undeniably eminent Judge Cardozo on the Supreme Bench, took precedence of all else. A Harvard professor, after the election, made the singularly enlivening explanation that it had been "better fun" to lose with Smith than to win with Hoover. As I have heard that gentleman pronounce himself a "wringing wet" I assume that his reasons might have been more succinctly stated. Above all, Smith, whatever his educational foundation, has a natural genius for political administration and has been honorably successful in it. To this the thoughtful Hoover partizans replied that their man's administrative abilities were equally well established, that they were not set in a frame of constant political endeavor, and that without belittling Smith's undoubted achievements, Hoover's had been more far reaching and beneficent.

The claims of each element concerning the real ability of its candidate were practically unanswerable. But each candidate carried indelibly the stamp of his beginnings. Never in the history of elections in America did the voters so generally, if unconsciously, apply the natural standard found in the phrase "one of our own."

Hoover's supporters clung to him with unquestioned loyalty. For years the word Hoover had stood not alone for achievement, and great achievement at that, but for kindliness, humanitarianism and amiability. Perhaps Smith was a great man. They didn't know. But they did know about Hoover. Everybody did, everybody in the world. If the Republicans had named Lowden, Watson, or some man who, like Smith, had been playing politics for a quarter of a century, they would have put Smith in the other part of the scale and tested one by the other. But Hoover was Hoover. There was nobody like him. He hadn't made a political reputation, as most candidates. He had made a real and very great reputation before politics adopted him. He was a new kind of candidate and the kind they wanted. Smith, like an itinerant pedlar, might ring their front door bells, but they didn't care to examine the goods, which might be all right. They were satisfied with their own tradesman and if this chap put his foot over the doorsill, so he might argue, the housewife would call the dog. Hoover was a little too near perfection to be picturesque, but he appealed to Main Street, as we call it, that thoroughfare which runs through every town in America and (hush, don't tell) through every big city as well, though there its limits are not quite so clearly defined. If in doubt go to any John Golden play on Broadway.

As soon as the conventions were over the campaign was on. Secretary of the Interior Work resigned to take care of the Hoover campaign. He was not a great manager, but he made no spectacular blunders. The Democratic campaign was handicapped. In the first place the South went into early rebellion. Smith's wet letter was sent before the convention adjourned and was signal for immediate discussion. The campaign had not begun before it was evident that the Southern Democracy was split as never before. A conference was called to take counsel and out of it came a rebellion which was to prove unsuppressible. Those who are fanatical about temperance are apt to be fanatical about Protestantism and it was easy to wage a battle in the name of prohibition when another question was equally potent. That exceedingly smooth lady politician, Mrs. Mabel Willebrandt, realized this and made the most of it.

Smith appointed John J. Raskob, Chairman of the Finance Committee of General Motors, as Chairman of the Democratic National Committee. This was a huge mistake. To begin, Raskob was a Republican, a member of the Union League Club of Philadelphia, and his only affiliations with the Democratic party came out of his personal relations with Smith and his outspoken hatred for prohibition. Then he was a very prominent Catholic, a recipient of various Papal dignities. Of course this added fuel to the denominational fire.

Another curious blunder on Smith's part was his speech at Tammany Hall on the occasion of that Society's Fourth of July Celebration. With all its reeking history, with all the effort which was being made to convince people of a "new Tammany," Smith swallowed the old one, hook, bait and sinker and said that any organization which had lived as long as Tammany had "must be all right." Smith was accused of thinking during the campaign in "terms of votes." In defense he can point to his Tammany speech of July 4th.

Smith and his friends discovered a "whispering campaign." It is Smith's habit to bring into the light any secret charges against him that are vicious and untrue. It has always strengthened him, but in this instance it did him no good. He unearthed and ran down secret charges that he had been under the influence of liquor on certain public occasions. He disproved them handily but he stopped there and the omission of any broader statement concerning his personal habits hurt him quite as much as the unhorsing of his libelous opponents helped.

Both remarkable and interesting types of Americanism, both honorable examples of the elements they represent, Hoover and Smith probably could not understand each other. This did not affect Hoover in the least but it worried Smith. Smith is used to getting into a bitter argument with any antagonist, pressing him home with facts and ridicule. His success depends on finding an opening in his antagonist's armour. But Hoover did not make any such opening. Smith, in times past, had seized his opponents by the heels, turned them over, shaken them till their political teeth fell out and tossed them to one side, gasping and beaten men. But Hoover was ignorant of the rules of that game. While most statesmen had been serving apprenticeships as politicians, Hoover had been a builder in the world. He had never learned the game of politics and refused to play it even then, probably even unconscious of what was expected. He talked intelligently and well. But not having been used to politics, he did not think in terms of votes and had no taste for personalities. Now Smith has always, and very wisely, waited for his opponent to "start something." Then with the sympathy of the public on his side, he has turned aggressor and a terrible one, as William R. Hearst, Theodore Roosevelt the lesser, and Ogden Mills, know to their sorrow. But Hoover just went on talking and if he mentioned Smith at all it was in a way that he could not resent, as when he thanked a New York audience "in the home of my distinguished opponent." I doubt if Smith understands that "bird" who ran against him even now.

Undoubtedly Smith did talk and think in terms of votes. Why not? Did Roosevelt talk or think in any other way? Has Coolidge ever forgotten them? And how about Abraham Lincoln, that greatest of all combinations of acute politician and noble statesman? What was the famous question to Douglas, which he could only answer by taking one of two horns of a dilemma? It was a question asked to be answered so that Douglas would fail either for Senator or President. No, it is not wrong or unusual to think in terms of votes. But it is unlucky to be confronted by a candidate who has been so aloof from ordinary political training that he does not know how to look at things in that light. Hoover was so obviously sincere and so entirely different from the usual thing that the public was refreshed. Smith, the most pitiless political duelist of his time, simply could not fence with a stone wall.

Back and forth the candidates went over the country. Their trips were not made so that they spoke constantly. About a dozen speeches were enough. Each covered the issues as he understood them in his own individual way. The farm belt was visited, the Southern states were visited, the cities of the Middle West and the eastern seaboard. Far more than four years before, the radio played an important part. The visible spectators were a mere drop in the bucket compared to the audiences they were addressing. Though Hughes and Borah helped Hoover, and Robinson and some others did their best for Smith, the bulk of the interesting campaigning was done by the candidates, and a man who owned a radio had the opportunity to hear plenty of speeches by each of them. This was Smith's final handicap. The air and manner which had endeared him to his own people, the entire naturalness, informality and lack of cultural background, came out. He treated his nation-wide audience much as if they were a casual crowd at an alderman's rally. He wanted to emphasize points and did it in careless vernacular. He seemed not to know that anything of greater dignity was to be expected of a candidate for the presidency. No fair epitome of this election can be written without mentioning his appearance of glib inconsequentiality. It sat lightly on him, as, waving his hat, he was driven through throngs of admirers in the cities he visited. But the utter lack of elegance or symmetry of his language as his speeches unfolded made people wonder just how he would receive an ambassador if he were President. When he went south he stopped at the Lincoln cabin in Hodgenville in Kentucky. There he went to the souvenir booth and bought a corn cob pipe and immediately put it between his teeth, an innocent and unfortunate gesture for the time and place. And it was so all along. The motion-picture projector combined with the radio to give the public the "low down" as it is called on the candidates. Hoover survived it but there can be no doubt that it cost Smith many thousands of votes.

As the election approached the public eye was turned on the solid South, so called, and the Catholic states in New England. New York seemed not so sure even and its neighbor, New Jersey, showed tendencies which alarmed the Democrats. In Wisconsin, Senator Blaine had shifted to Smith and that was ominous for the Republicans. Norris, of the Grand Old Party, but always against it, was causing trouble in Nebraska. The anti-Smith crowd in Texas and Florida were making a lot of noise and the Virginians were out of step but the Republicans expected nothing but an increased vote in these states. North Carolina was different. It has the strongest Republican minority of any Southern state and Senator Furnifold Simmons, its Democratic leader, had bolted Smith.

If this state alone of the Southern group should go Republican it would be a great and heartening victory. In Oklahoma, Senator Owen, another Democratic leader, had bolted.

But straw ballots and betting all pointed the same way. Hoover was really known to be sure of election for a week before the poll. But Smith did not see it. No man could have been the recipient of such personal acclaim as he had seen and look beyond it. Raskob, being as new to political management as Hoover was to candidating, did not make any deduction for overstatements in reports made to him and issued claims that were positively ludicrous in their size.

And then election night! The Republicans were to learn that their most sanguine hopes had been far too conservative. The solid South was still solid, but how it had shrunk! Virginia and North Carolina had fallen away on the north, Florida on the south, and Texas on the southwest. In the other six states of the South the Republican vote had increased tremendously. Everything on the border had gone Republican and everything north of Mississippi and west of New England. There was not a single Democratic electoral vote in all that immense territory. Massachusetts and Rhode Island, which had never gone against the Republican party in an election when that party was not divided, now went for Smith. These states have the greatest proportion of Catholic vote in the country, but in Massachusetts at least the vote was so close (17,192 plurality) as to show that the state could have been carried for Hoover but for a small and determined body of Republican wets, ten thousand at the very least, who if they had stayed in their party, would have held the state Republican. The electoral vote was 444 for Hoover and 87 for Smith, one of the most overwhelming in history. The popular vote was 21,429,109 for Hoover and 15,005,497 for Smith, a majority of 6,423,612. It is said that this is not so overwhelming. It is pretty large for all that and more than most votes it represents the undeniable hardpan choice of the people, for so many of them never came to the polls before.

In all the campaign Smith never showed to better advantage than in defeat. He had been an able and unusual executive and it had availed him nothing. He has personally no understanding of religious political differences and has shown no predeliction for his "own kind" in appointments. He was to see thousands of his party abandon him on this issue, even though they concealed it—and not all of them did. It takes a pretty even tempered man, a clear-headed one and a patriotic one to make the speech he made over the radio after the election, pleading for good party government, a minority, not obstructive, but with a party program well thought out and adhered to with a real civic viewpoint. And then he asked us to forget campaign animosities. The irony of the campaign is that Al Smith delivered his finest and sweetest campaign speech after election. But it leaves him in our memory as indeed "the happy warrior."

As for Hoover, he went quickly about his business and on a trip to the nations south of us he sowed seeds the flowering of which is in the distance.

Before this book comes to the hands of its readers, Herbert Hoover will have stood before his countrymen and sworn to uphold the Constitution and the laws. He will find nothing in his oath relating to any party. Less perhaps than any of his predecessors since Washington, will he be inclined to include it by a mental amplification of that oath.

He will confront two elements calculated to make life uncomfortable for any warm-hearted man. One of these elements will be made up of those who, in behalf of his opponent, bitterly resent his election. The other will consist of those who voted for Hoover the magician and "judging each step as though the way were plain," will expect every action to be that of a superman. And Hoover, with all his ability, must humanly hew his way amid human difficulties. As always at inauguration, much is hidden below the horizon toward which the administration must march. From such a test only honest self-confidence and calm courage could fail to waver. And so the words spoken to every American boy, "You too may be President some day," are both an inspiration and a threat.

BIBLIOGRAPHY

Adams, Henry, *John Randolph* (American Statesman).
Andrews, E. Benjamin, *The United States in Our Own Time.*
Annin, Robert Edwards, *Woodrow Wilson, A Character Study.*
Barton, William E., *Life of Abraham Lincoln.*
Benton, Thomas H., *Thirty Years' View.*
Birney, William, *James G. Birney, His Life and Times.*
Bishop, Joseph Bucklin, *Presidential Nominations and Elections.*
Blaine, James G., *Twenty Years of Congress.*
Bowers, Claude G., *Party Battles of the Jackson Period.*
Bowtwell, George S., *Sixty Years of Public Affairs.*
Bradford, Gamaliel, *American Portraits.*
Charnwood, Lord, *Abraham Lincoln.*
Clark, Champ, *My Quarter Century of American Politics.*
Coleman, Edna M., *Seventy-Five Years of White House Gossip.*
Coolidge, Calvin, *Have Faith in Massachusetts.*
Coolidge, Louis A., *Ulysses S. Grant.*
Croly, Herbert, *Marcus Alonzo Hanna, His Life and Work.*
Crook, William H., *Through Five Administrations.*
Curtis, Francis, *The Republican Party, 1854-1904.*
Democratic Party, Proceedings of the various Democratic National
    Conventions.
Dunn, Arthur Wallace, *From Harrison to Harding.*
Gilder, Richard Watson, *Grover Cleveland, A Record of Friendship.*
Hamilton, Gail (pseud) Abigail Dodge, *Biography of James G. Blaine.*
Hapgood, Norman, and Moskowitz, Henry, *Up From the City Streets.*
Harvey, Peter, *Reminiscences and Anecdotes of Daniel Webster.*
Haworth, Paul Leland, *The Hayes-Tilden Disputed Election.*
Haworth, Paul Leland, *The United States in Our Own Times.*
Hendrick, Burton J., *Life and Letters of Walter H. Page.*
Hill, Frederic Trevor, *Decisive Battles of the Law.*
Hirst, F. W., *Life and Letters of Thomas Jefferson.*
Hoar, George F., *Autobiography of Seventy Years.*
House, Edward M., *Intimate Papers.*
Irwin, Will, *Herbert Hoover, A Reminiscent Biography.*
Johnson, Gerald W., *Andrew Jackson, An Epic in Homespun.*
Kohlsaat, H. H., *From McKinley to Harding.*
Kent, Frank, *The Democratic Party, A History.*

BIBLIOGRAPHY

Lane, Franklin K., *Letters, Personal and Political.*
Lathrop Thornton Kirkland, *William Henry Seward,* (American Statesmen).
Lingley, Charles Ramsdell, *Since the Civil War.*
Lodge, Henry Cabot, *Alexander Hamilton* (American Statesmen).
Lodge, Henry Cabot, *Daniel Webster* (American Statesman)
Lodge, Henry Cabot, *The Senate and the League of Nations.*
Long, J. C., *Bryan, The Great Commoner.*
McCall, Samuel W., *Life of Thomas B. Reed.*
McClure, Alexander K., *Our Presidents and How We Make Them.*
McElroy, Robert, *Grover Cleveland, The Man and the Statesman.*
McMaster, John Bach, *A History of the People of the United States.*
Meyers, William Starr, *The Republican Party, A History.*
Minnigerode, Meade, *Presidential Years.*
Minnigerode, Meade, and Wandell, S. H., *Aaron Burr.*
Morse, John T., Jr., *Abraham Lincoln* (American Statesmen).
Morse, John T., Jr., *John Adams* (American Statesmen).
Morse, John T., Jr., *John Quincy Adams* (American Statesmen).
Morse, John T., Jr., *Thomas Jefferson* (American Statesmen).
Nevins, Allan, *Fremont, The West's Greatest Adventurer.*
Nevins, Allan (Editor), *Diary of John Quincy Adams.*
Nevins, Allan (Editor), *Diary of Philip Hone.*
Nicolay, John C., and Hay, John, *Abraham Lincoln, A History.*
Nock, Albert Jay, *Jefferson.*
Oberholtzer, Ellis Paxon, *A History of the United States Since the Civil War.*
Olcott, Charles S., *Life of William McKinley.*
Peck, Charles H., *The Jacksonian Epoch.*
Peck, Harry Thurston, *Twenty Years of the Republic, 1885-1905.*
Republican Party, Proceedings of the various Republican National Conventions.
Rhodes, James Ford, *History of the United States, 1850-1877.*
Roosevelt, Theodore (President of the United States), *Autobiography.*
Schurz, Carl, *Henry Clay* (American Statesmen).
Schurz, Carl, *Reminiscences.*
Shepard, Edward M., *Martin Van Buren* (American Statesmen).
Sherman, John, *Recollections of Forty Years.*
Smith, Theodore Clark, *Life and Letters of James Abram Garfield.*
Smith, Mrs. Samuel Harrison, *First Forty Years of Washington Life.*
Stanwood, Edward, *History of Presidential Elections in the United States.*
Stanwood, Edward, *James G. Blaine* (American Statesmen).
Stoddard, Henry L., *As I Knew Them.*

BIBLIOGRAPHY

Sullivan, Mark, *Our Times*.

Sumner, William Graham, *Andrew Jackson* (American Statesmen).

Thayer, William Roscoe, *Life of John Hay*.

Thayer, William Roscoe, *Theodore Roosevelt*.

Tumulty, Joseph P., *Woodrow Wilson, As I Knew Him*.

Villard, Oswald Garrison, *John Brown, A Biography Fifty Years After*.

Washburn, Robert M., *"Calvin Coolidge, His First Biography."* First and A.B.C. editions.

Werner, M. R., *Tammany Hall*.

White, William Allen, *Calvin Coolidge, The Man Who Is President*.

Whiting, Edward Elwell, *President Coolidge, A Contemporary Estimate*.

Williams, C. R., *Life of Rutherford Birchard Hayes*.

Wilson, Woodrow, *A History of the American People*.

Wister, Owen, *Ulysses S. Grant*.

INDEX

303

INDEX

INDEX

INDEX

INDEX

INDEX